Herbert Maxwell

Post meridiana:

Afternoon essays

Herbert Maxwell

Post meridiana:
Afternoon essays

ISBN/EAN: 9783337809669

Printed in Europe, USA, Canada, Australia, Japan

Cover: Foto ©ninafisch / pixelio.de

More available books at **www.hansebooks.com**

Post Meridiana:

Afternoon Essays

BY

SIR HERBERT MAXWELL, Bart., M.P.

WILLIAM BLACKWOOD AND SONS
EDINBURGH AND LONDON
MDCCCXCV

Dedicated to

M. M.

who will be less ready than others to discern shortcomings in this volume, and has never withheld helpful sympathy in the schemes, hopes, disappointments, joys, and cares of more than a quarter of a century.

PREFACE.

WE do not commonly give much heed to our shadows; indeed, those people who are not so fatuous as to practise the art of fly-fishing may easily pass a whole summer without being conscious of the little area of gloom which each one carries about with him. Least of all is one likely to have it forced on his notice at high noon, when the sun is sailing bravely aloft and all the busy world is astir; or, otherwise, when the heat drives men and beasts to what shade may be had. And so it generally happens that the moment passes unobserved when the tell-tale companion begins to lengthen, bearing silent witness that the summit has been crossed, the orb of life has entered on its decline, and the night cometh when no man can work.

It is probable that since, a few years ago, I published a collection of 'Noontide Essays,' a change, imperceptible to myself, has come over the tenor of my thoughts and observations. If so, it will be traced in these 'Afternoon Essays,' which have appeared already in the 'Nineteenth Century' and 'Blackwood's Magazine,' and are now reprinted by the courteous permission of the editors.[1]

The night cometh.

It may be a long way off still, and the hours that lie before it may be the sweetest in the day. The evening breeze has none of the sharpness of morning, but, alas! it has parted with the dew. Each minute the wayfarer's shadow occupies more of the sunlit space around him. Shadows, too, from other objects begin to creep across his path; peradventure a sigh escapes him as he remembers how much of the morning's work remains for the afternoon.

Still, despite the growing shadows, his vision is clearer than when he set out; the early mists

---

[1] The paper on London trees appeared in the 'New Review.'

have drifted away, and much of the landscape that was vague or deceptive can now be understood. It is not very late yet, and, laying down his load, be it heavy or light, precious or of little value, he may rest awhile and muse on past and future.

It is out of these musings that 'Afternoon Essays' have been woven. Shallow enough some of them may seem; too trivial to tell, perhaps, seeing that the night cometh; yet not altogether idle, but such as may serve to beguile the journey of fellow-travellers, bound, like the author, through the night that lies on this side of the breaking of day.

HERBERT MAXWELL.

MONREITH, *September* 1895.

CONTENTS.

AFTERNOON ESSAYS.

CLOTHES.

THE further we travel from the origin of our species
the less concern does male humanity show to
enhance what share of beauty it may lay claim to, or
to screen the ugliness it is generally heir to, by grace
of garments. Among civilised and well-to-do men, gala
costume has no key-note now but respectability: at
weddings as at funerals, at garden-parties as in Parliament, costume is attuned to harmonise with the
hurtful cylinder of sable which the supineness of our
great-grandfathers allowed the hatters to impose on
them as a head-dress, and a hundred hopeless years
have but served to bind more tightly on our aching
brows. If the chimney - pot hat were comfortable
wear—were it sun-proof or rain-proof, or easily carried when not in use — our allegiance to it might
be monotonous, but at least it would be intelligible.
But, in plain sooth, it is intolerable in sunshine; it

A

is so sensitive of rain-drops that an umbrella must
be carried for its special shelter; and, when we travel,
it is as difficult to dispose of as a murdered corpse. It
cannot be concealed; the accursed thing will fit in
with no other portion of our raiment, and must be
provided with a special case of grotesque and im-
practicable shape. In wear or out of wear, we cannot forget its existence nor neglect to make provision
for its protection. Cephalalgic humanity has tried
every means to be quit of it, but in vain. The creature has not even a serious name, for no one, except
the fiend who frames it, knows it as a silk hat; school-
boys, with the contempt born of familiarity, call it a
"buster" or a "topper"; soldiers, scornfully, a "stove-
pipe"; civilians, realistically, a "chimney-pot." In
vain has bountiful Nature provided straw, and human
ingenuity fashioned felt: two more perfect substances
for head-covering could not have been devised; but,
perversely, littering our horses with the one, and roof-
ing our barns with the other, we thrust our thinking
organs into unyielding towers of pasteboard. In a
simpler age we should have made a god of It—prayed
to It, sung to It, bowed to It, propitiated It; but,
having adopted monotheism, we are outwardly consistent, and are content to insist on taking it to church
with us. The first inhabitant of Mars who visits the
Earth, and publishes a volume of travels on his return,
will probably describe how, in Western Europe, the
possession of a chimney-pot hat is held to be essential
to salvation.

There is, at present, no glimmer of hope of escape
from it. Even ridicule, most potent of solvents, runs
from it like rain from a duck's back, leaving it intact

in all its pompous, gloomy, perpendicular absurdity. Nay, the very derision with which it ought to be treated, is reserved for those who attempt to resist its tyranny. Witness the fate of Mr Keir Hardie (with whom in this, if in nothing else, we are in complete sympathy): did he not take his seat in the new House of Commons of 1892 wearing on his haughty brow an amorphous arrangement in toast - coloured tweed? which might, indeed, have been designed on more statesmanlike lines, and conceived to harmonise more closely with the Senate than with the rat-pit, but at all events indicated a brave man's effort to set at naught the frowns of fashion. But, alas for manly independence! all the recognition he obtained was a supercilious stare from other members, and a rebuke from the Speaker for venturing to the table of the House without uncovering. It was a gallant attempt, but it has failed; and the hard fact remains that the influence of a member of Parliament depends more upon what nature has put *in* his head than upon what he chooses to place *on* it.

Mr Keir Hardie's appearance on that memorable occasion, signalising his outset as a legislator by studied unconventionality of attire, irresistibly called to remembrance an observation of Teufelsdröckh, whose theory it was that the first purpose of vesture was not warmth or decency, but ornament. "Neither in tailoring nor in legislating," he declared, "does man proceed by mere Accident, but the hand is ever guided by the mysterious operations of the mind." The tweed cap, the flannel shirt, the reach-me-down suit of the Labour Leader were, then, not merely the every-day attire of the horny-handed one, too intent on his lofty purpose to bestow a thought upon how he should be clothed, but the vestments thoughtfully selected from a slop-shop round the corner, as those most becoming to the *flamen* of a robust democracy. If legislation is to proceed on the slipshod lines of the tailoring, then heaven help the statute-book!

Teufelsdröckh, by bracketing tailoring with law-making, has landed us straight in the House of Commons, which, in the matter of dress, is remarkably, even monotonously, conservative. If it were possible to repeople the benches with those who occupied them thirty years ago, it would be found that the fashions of 1862 were almost identical with those which prevail now. Younger men might detect minute differences of detail in the cut of trousers, the height of hats, or the fold of neckcloths, but the general effect would be the same. Mr Denison was Speaker then, and there is a legend that he was the last occupant of the Chair who took on himself to animadvert officially on the cut of a member's coat. It is said that he once gently but firmly remonstrated with the late Sir William Stirling Maxwell for appearing in a garment known, we believe, to the careless and worldly as a "shaver," but charged for in tailors' bills as a "lounging jacket." Now, if that be true history, it marks a change which might otherwise escape notice, interesting as denoting a "mysterious operation of the mind." For in the Parliament elected in the year of grace 1892 the "shaver" received its apotheosis.

In this wise. The first duty of a new House of Commons is to elect a Speaker, and the progress of the Speaker - elect from the position of a private member to that of the First Commoner in England is marked, according to immemorial usage, by nice gradations of attire. On the first day he appears in mufti—in the morning dress of a private gentleman—and takes his seat like any ordinary mortal. Speeches are delivered moving him into the Chair, to which he replies with suitable modesty, tinged with menace to evil-doers. The House then adjourns; when it re-assembles next day the Speaker takes the Chair, not in plain clothes, nor yet in full costume, but in an intermediate, fledgeling state of small-clothes, dress-coat, and bob-wig. The faithful Commons are summoned to the Lords, whither they proceed, headed by the Speaker, to receive the Royal assent to his election. The custom of late years—deeply, we think, to be regretted—has been for this to be delivered not by the monarch in person, but by a Royal Commission, consisting of the Lord Chancellor on the Woolsack, supported by three other peers. It is the opportunity for a remarkable sartorial display. The Commission sits motionless in a row, robed in scarlet and ermine, balancing three-cornered cocked-hats on their noble heads, and looking, for all the world, like a show of very rickety waxworks. The Speaker's election having been approved, he returns to the other House, passes to his private rooms, and presently reissues in all the panoply of full-bottomed wig and silk robe. The operation is complete, and its various stages have each been signalised by a change in costume. But on this occasion it was in the first stage of all that the Portent was manifested—when the Speaker-elect sat among his fellow-Commoners. Time will show what was foreshadowed by the phenomenon: it may have

presaged the shortness of the new Parliament, or
the looseness of its manners; but none will be found
to maintain that, in a ceremony rigidly accentuated
by prescribed changes of costume, it was a meaningless
accident that *the Speaker-elect wore a " shaver."*

Now it was all very well for Mr Arthur Peel (now
Viscount Peel) to play such pranks,—he is gifted with
a handsome head and lean and commanding figure;
but fancy recoils from speculating on the effect, supposing the choice of the House ever to fall upon one of
the fat kind with which the pastures of Westminster
abound. We name no names: we point no invidious
finger; but whether of Lilliputian proportions or on
the scale of Falstaff, there are plenty of members whom
it would have been simply impossible to promote to
honour thus scantily draped.

Benvenuto Cellini describes in his autobiography
how, having been summoned before the Florentine
Council of Eight to answer for his part in a brawl, he
was unfavourably received because he chose to appear
only in a short cloak, whereas his adversaries wore
mantles and robes. It was considered the mark of a
disreputable character if any one, except a sóldier,
went about the streets of Florence in daylight unless
in a mantle of becoming length; but that prejudice
we must consider finally put an end to by the sanction
given in his own person by the late Speaker to free-
and-easy costume.

Before leaving the House of Commons, we must
return once more to the irrepressible Hat; for it plays
a leading part in that assembly. Gentlemen to whom
it would never occur to wear hats in their own houses

sit glued to the benches for hours, closely covered. It may be said that they keep their hats on their heads because there is nowhere else to put them. But why bring them into the House at all? Although the Fatherland has not yet been persuaded to remunerate its representatives, it has, at least, been thoughtful to provide each of them with a peg, whereon hat and cloak may be suspended as naturally as in one's own hall. If it were the custom to convey umbrellas and clouded canes into the Chamber, one might discern and sympathise with the motive, because of the known altruism which inspires some people in regard to these movables; but one must be in the last stages of kleptomania before he is tempted to appropriate his colleague's headgear, especially in an assembly where the average quality of the article is so far below par.

There is indeed a certain symbolism, a mute intelligence, in the parliamentary Hat. For instance, if you should notice that an honourable member, whom you are accustomed to see going about as constantly and ceremoniously hatted as the artists represent Napoleon to have been in crossing the Alps, suddenly appears bareheaded in the lobbies, him you may know to have been appointed a Whip of the party to which he belongs. A hatted Whip would be an apparition as unfamiliar as an ordinary member in shirt-sleeves.

Again: the Hat derives constitutional importance from being the only article of attire referred to in the Standing Orders. Members are directed to uncover when they rise to address the House or to move from their places; but nobody is obliged to wear a hat unless he has a fancy to do so, and nobody requires to have command of one except in the presence of one

of two contingencies. The first is when, at a certain
stage of private business, the Royal assent has to be
intimated by a Privy Councillor, who does so by raising his hat. The other is of a still more exceptional
kind, when, some irregularity having taken place or a
point of order arisen, a member desires to address the
Chair in the interval between a division being called
and the tellers appointed. If he speaks at that time,
it is prescribed that he must do so without rising from
his seat and with his hat on. It was one of the
comical moments during the '80 Parliament, when Mr
Gladstone, having to take part in a discussion which
arose at this precise moment, and having left his hat
in his own room, borrowed one from a colleague on the
Treasury bench. It was many sizes too small for him,
and it required nice carriage on the part of the Prime
Minister to poise it on his head. Mysterious punc-
tilio! Yet how fondly the House clings to it! It
will suffer the very existence of the other House to be
menaced; with a light heart it will tamper with the
very tap-root of the Constitution; but no one has ever
been heard to utter a disrespectful word against the
awful dignity of this point in its own ritual. It is far
from our purpose to do so now. We know not in
what sacred episode of our history this custom may
have taken its rise, and we are disposed to treat
it with the unquestioning reverence due to the
Inscrutable.

But seeing how exceptional is the contingency above
described, and seeing how greatly it would contribute
to the comfort of members, without, surely, detracting
from their picturesque aspect, if they took to leaving
their hats on the pegs provided in the cloak-room,

might not provision be made for its occurrence by hanging a public Hat in some place of easy access within the House, say behind the Speaker's chair? or let it even be laid on the table with the Mace at the commencement of each sitting. It is strange that this was not thought of in the good days of sinecures. The parliamentary Groom of the Hat might have defended his privilege and salary with far more reason than the Hereditary Grand Falconer or the Comptroller of the Pipe.

It must be owned that if members ceased to carry their hats into the House, one of the few sure sources of honest mirth would disappear from the debates. A member would no longer be able to emphasise an impassioned peroration, or illumine a halting one, by sitting down on his own hat. Nor would it be possible for any one to emulate the feat of Mr Willis, Q.C., who, standing immediately behind the Treasury bench, did thrice in the course of one speech knock the hat of one of his leaders over his right honourable nose.

And now let us dismiss the Hat from consideration (would that it could be as easily dismissed from wear!) with a passing speculation as to the tenacity with which, in its present form, it has fixed itself in our scheme of costume. This probably has its origin in the jealousy felt by those under middle height towards others of more commanding stature. The desire to level humanity down to one standard has undoubtedly given rise to many of our fashions. A small man may *look* no bigger with a tall hat on, but he *feels* so. A hat which adds 4 inches to the height of each of two men—one, A, being 5 feet high, the other, B, being 6 feet high—reduces the advantage possessed by B. For although he will still be 12 inches taller than A, A will no longer be shorter than B by one-fifth of his (A's) own height, for 64 inches is to 76 as 16 to 19, whereas 60 inches is to 72 only as 15 to 18. £999 is much nearer £1000 than £9 is to £10, though between each pair there is the same difference of 20s. So it looks as if in this matter of hats the small men are the chief culprits.

The same jealousy of superior physical advantage has brought about many of our ugliest fashions. Sculptors and painters sigh with vain regret for the small-clothes of eighteenth-century Macaronis, and the trunk-hose of the Elizabethans; but so long as some men continue to be born with spindle or crooked shanks and doubtful ankles, so long will well-turned limbs be doomed to the obscurity of trousers. The excuse that trousers are more convenient and comfortable than breeches and hose is groundless and insincere. Wherein lies the convenience and comfort of a chimney-pot hat? Yet we have clung to it for a hundred years. The real reason is that, inasmuch as indifferent legs are in the majority, it has been resolved that all alike shall be entombed in shapeless tubes of cloth.

It was on the eighth anniversary of Waterloo that the British infantry first appeared in trousers,—an order from the Horse Guards in 1823 having directed that blue-grey cloth trousers and half-boots were to be worn instead of breeches, leggings, and shoes. The boots were certainly an improvement on shoes, but it is equally certain that marching is much harder work in trousers than in breeches. Herein the cause of artistic clothing received a serious blow; for there are always plenty of young men affecting a military model, who, when the army was forbidden to wear breeches, were not slow to follow that example.

See in what a dilemma our poor portrait-painters find themselves. Our clothes are now so ugly that they have to resort to all sorts of device to palliate their evil cut, and play pranks with light and shade to relieve their tiresome colourlessness. Perhaps the most successful treatment is that adopted by Mr Whistler in his portrait of Carlyle, in which the canvas is kept to a low and limited tone—a kind of gloaming, with no sparkle of bright light or vivid colour—and the cloaked figure looms like a ghost-like reflection of the departed sage. It is a masterly piece of work, yet a gallery filled with such shadows of humanity would be oppressive; one would long for the flashing glance, the gleaming metal, the flush of rich colour in which the Venetian masters rejoiced.

As a rule, when a man is to be painted, his clothes must be dealt with too. Attempts are sometimes made, rarely with success, to avoid this necessity. The late Mr Johnston of Straiton, who collected a large gallery of pictures, stood for his portrait as S. Sebastian, in the nude, with arrows sticking in various tender parts of his body. One clear objection to that device is that, inasmuch as English gentlemen are not in the practice of appearing in public without their clothes, they are not easily recognised in that unfamiliar state. To be satisfactory, a portrait ought to represent the subject thereof as he is best known. Moreover, most of us would shrink from exposing

simulacra of our acalypt forms to be dusted daily by
the diligence of our own housemaids. There would
be something uncomfortable if the head of a sedate
household had to take his place, clad in his native
home-spun or ceremonial broadcloth, to read family
prayers, under a picture showing him as he might
have been surprised in the act of leaving his tub an
hour before. The fact is, few artists in this climate
succeed in painting the nude: it almost invariably
gives an impression of the undressed. It is most
difficult to avoid this effect, for to paint the human
body faithfully some one must undress and sit to the
artist. The skin usually clothed upon is of a different
colour and texture to that on which the sun shines,
the wind blows, and the rain beats; a man's back
and arms are as different from his neck and hands as
a blanched stalk of celery is from the leaves. The
painter has to supply from his imagination the warm
tones to which the upper surfaces of shoulders and
limbs would be tanned by habitual exposure, and
usually fails to do so. Etty's groups of undraped
figures convey an unpleasant suggestion of live bait;
and, leaving out of account the beautiful confectionery
prepared each year by the President of the Royal
Academy, and skilful abstractions like Mr Hacker's
" Syrinx " in the Exhibition of 1891, there has been
in the annual show at Burlington House only one
picture during the last three or four years which
dwells in the memory as a thoroughly satisfactory
rendering of the nude figure, yielding at once a poetic
ideal and conscious interpretation of warm palpitating
flesh and blood. This was Miss Henrietta Rae's " La
Cigale," also in the Exhibition of 1891. On the

whole, therefore, for these and other reasons too obvious to specify, it cannot be urged that the British statesman, capitalist, squire, author, or other notability, should sit for his portrait otherwise than fully clothed.

Sculptors enjoy more freedom in this respect than painters, the absence of colour helping to conceal the difference between what is nude and what is merely naked. But even they are heavily handicapped in their art by the brutality of modern garb. Consider the *sic sedebat* statue of Francis Bacon by Sir Thomas Meautys in the church of St Michael at St Albans. The sculptor has rendered the great philosopher's "full portraiture in the posture of studying," reclining in his elbow-chair, hatted and cloaked; every detail of dress is given down to the rosettes covering the shoe-ties, yet everything pleases; all harmonises with the feeling of restful contemplation. The hand that has undertaken an equally faithful likeness of Darwin in the Natural History Museum at South Kensington had not the material from which to prepare so beautiful a memorial. The very boots may be heard to creak—"See how vulgar the human foot can be made to appear!"

Whence comes it that we men have lost all sense of grace in our habiliments? Of course it is otherwise with women — some reflections upon their clothing may be entered on presently. How comes it that, to quote a high authority, the surest test of a well-dressed man is that, after parting with him, one should be unable to remember the colour or material of any particular article of his raiment? Penelope took just

pride in weaving for Ulysses a purple cloak with a
hunting scene in gold thread.   Ought one to be
ashamed of the pleasure derived from reading the
luscious details of the clothes supplied to Jehan le
Bon, King of France, to solace him withal during his
captivity at the Savoy in London ? or may one share
in imagination his agreeable feelings in putting on
for the first time, as he did on Easter Day 1358, a
suit of marbled violet velvet, trimmed with miniver;
or again at Whitsunday in the same year when he
wore a new doublet of rosy scarlet, lined with blue
taffeta ?   Has Goldsmith forfeited any share of our
esteem because of the delight he expressed in his
bloom-coloured coat ?   The Diary of Samuel Pepys
would not be half so readable if it wanted the affec-
tionate mention of the writer's " close-bodied, light-
coloured cloth coat, with a gold edgeing in each seam,
that was the lace of my wife's best pettycoat that she
had when I married her ;" his " black cloth suit, with
white lynings under all, as the fashion is to wear, to
appear under the breeches ;" his " velvet coat and cap,
the first that ever I had ;" or his " new coloured silk
suit, and coat trimmed with gold buttons, and gold
broad lace round my hands, very rich and fine."   It
does not, perhaps, much impress the reader with the
greatness of the diarist's mind to be told how, when he
went to church, " I found that my coming in a perri-
wigg did not prove so strange as I was afraid it would,
for I thought that all the church would presently have
cast their eyes all upon me ;" and he brings into relief
his prudence at the expense of his loyalty when he writes,
" Hearing that the Queene grows worse again, I sent
to stop the making of my velvet cloak, till I see

whether she lives or dies." But these details add to
the lifelike interest of the journal, whereas description
of nineteenth-century tailoring would be simply intolerable.

We smile in our superior way at Samuel Pepys's
little vanities, and affect to be as unconscious as the
lilies of the field what we are arrayed in; but it is
a shallow imposture. In reality, we take as much
thought and pains how to be inconspicuous and as
little different from our fellows as, in chivalrous times,
knights did to make their coat-armour distinctive.
Most men like to wear well-cut clothes: no one cares
to go about in things that look as if they had been
made by the village carpenter. Trifling differences,
which can be indulged without attracting inconvenient attention, are very dearly prized.

One of the most guileless and cultivated men I
have ever known betrayed some of this pardonable
affectation. He lived almost constantly on his estate
in the north, and certainly was far from extravagant
in the matter of tailors' bills. He declared that
during a quarter of a century he had only bought a
single pair of white kid gloves, one of which he wore
at his own, the other at his daughter's wedding. But
he was the reverse of untidy in his person, and invariably dressed for dinner, even when quite alone, and
always buttoned his dress-coat across his chest. During one of his rare visits to London, Stultz, who was
then at the top of his profession, and, for aught I
know, may be so still, was called on to make him a
new dress-coat, which was duly executed, and the
garment sent home. A few days later my old friend
reappeared at Stultz's, bringing his dress-coat.

"Look here," he said, "this coat is not the thing at all; it must have been made for some other man."

"Indeed, Sir William," replied Mr Stultz, "that is surprising; we have always succeeded satisfactorily with your orders. Some slight alteration in the figure, perhaps. We don't grow any younger, Sir William, eh! Let us try it on." Which being done, "It appears a perfect fit, Sir William," continued the artist, standing back to admire his own handiwork; "your figure does not seem to have changed in the least."

"But it won't button, man," rejoined the customer, tugging at the lapels.

"No, Sir William; it is not intended to do so. Dress-coats are invariably worn open."

"But I like mine to button across."

"Most unusual, Sir William," sighed Mr Stultz; "in fact, I may say it is *never* done."

"But I tell you I always wear my coat buttoned in the evening, and I don't care two straws what other people do."

"Oh, Sir William! if it is a CHARACTERISTIC, that is another matter"—and the cutter being sent for, the necessary alterations were planned on the instant.

The name of Stultz recalls an incident in my own early days, illustrating how, in spite of apparent disregard, the slightest departure from the prescribed cut brings ridicule upon the innovator. Every one who has been at Eton has realised the gravity of "going into tails." The round jacket, falling collar, and black tie are discarded for a cut-away coat, stick-ups, and a white choker. Well, the day had arrived when I was to go into tails, and repairing to Mr Stultz, I desired to be supplied with a coat.

"What sort of coat, sir?" inquired the dignified gentleman in the front room.

"Oh, one with tails," I said, nonchalantly.

"A frock-coat, I presume, sir."

"Yes," I replied, profoundly ignorant of the terms of sartorial art; and a frock-coat was made and duly sent down to my tutor's. Oh, the shock on unpacking it to find it was not the correct article! Oh, the heartless laughter of the other fellows and the merciless chaff that had to be endured! Oh, the sickness of hope deferred till the right vestment could be made! So wide is the chasm in etiquette between a coat with one row of buttons and another with two.

In like degree, as graceful shapes have ceased to be sought for in designing men's garments, beauty of colour has also been rejected, and a preference shown for black, white, or neutral tints. In no article of clothing is this more rigidly prescribed than in leg-covering; and this is the more remarkable because the word " breeches " is supposed to be derived through the Roman form *braccæ*, from the Celtic *breac*, which means variegated, of many colours. This marked preference for sombre hues arises, in part, from the same desire to neutralise the effect of physical superiority which has spoiled the shape of modern clothes.

It is part of the same plan which, as is well known to ethnographers, takes the form of tooth-breaking among primitive people in different parts of the world. Just as an influential Batoka of East Africa, or a Penong of Burmah, whose teeth happened to be defective, felt happier when he had persuaded other young men of his tribe to deface their faultless ivory, so a European grandee, of bilious or dyspeptic habit, would look with prejudice on one whose clear complexion and ruddy cheeks gained brilliancy by contrast with pale-blue satin or carnation silk: he might at least have the sense to eschew such combinations in his own attire, and, by showing preference for sombre tints, tend, in virtue of his position and influence, to set the fashion flowing that way; for, as Quinctilian observes, *quidquid principes faciunt, præcipere videntur.*

But another motive probably contributed to the discouragement of bright hues — namely, the difficulty of making up one's mind amid competing dyes. Montaigne declares he would not be bothered about it, and never wore anything except black or white. He lived in age of polychrome clothing (*François accoustumez à nous bigarrer*, as he observes), and a mind so full of activity as his might well be impatient of the problem of colour arising every time he ordered a suit of clothes. But he can hardly have foreseen the lamentable effect upon the aspect of society brought about by universal compliance with his practice. Viewed at a little distance, a crowd of men, whether on a race-course, on the streets, in an assembly, or elsewhere, looks as cheerful as a flock of rooks without their gloss, or a meeting of chimney-sweeps without their usefulness. And there are plenty of vacant minds which might be profitably applied to a revival of beauty in dress. We prate much more about beauty now than men did when there was far more beauty about. Sir Francis Dashwood used to say that Lord Shrewsbury's Providence was an old, angry man in a blue cloak; future students of the history of the nineteenth century will picture to them-

selves the notables of that age as animated pillars of
soot.

It is difficult to decide whether the gradual sup-
pression of magnificence in male attire and the development of feminine finery among civilised races is
more interesting to the zoologist, the anthropologist,
or the moral philosopher.

To the first of these it is a perplexing departure
from the scheme of nature, where it is a rule that any
marked difference between the sexes confers greater
splendour upon the male. The peacock and peahen,
the lion and lioness, the stag and the hind, are common examples of a principle which, among the higher
animals, finds its only exception among certain fal-
cons. But the scheme of sexual colouring embraces
living creatures very low in the scale of animated
nature. Even the pretty blue butterflies which dance
about the thyme cushions on the downs are all males.
The females are dingy little creatures with wings of
sooty brown.

The anthropologist will find a departure from the
primitive custom in the practice of the Fiji islanders,
whose women are decoratively tattooed, but not the
men. On the other hand, among a neighbouring
people, the Tongans, it is the men who are tattooed
and not the women. Moreover, the Fijians, who consider themselves much superior to the Tongans, have
invented a legend to account for this anomaly. It is
said that long ago a messenger was sent from Tonga
to Fiji to obtain information about the correct fashions
among people of social standing. Swinging merrily
along on his return journey, he kept repeating aloud
the precept he had committed to memory, so as to be

sure to deliver his message correctly. " Tattoo the women, but not the men ; tattoo the women, but not the men ; tattoo the—DAMN !"—he had struck his bare shin against a stump in the grass. After some minutes' halt to rub the bruised limb, he resumed the route, but the rhythm of his chant was broken, for by the time he arrived at Tonga, he had it—" Tattoo the men, but not the women." And ever since, the Tongese braves have been beautifully ornamented; but the ladies are allowed to remain as Nature planned them.

As for our moral philosopher, his opinion does not count for much in matters of dress, or its substitute— tattooing. He probably wears a shocking bad hat, with marks of ancient rain-drops, which, like those on the Corncockle flags in the New Red Sandstone, having once been allowed to dry, are practically in- delible. His umbrella is robust enough to shelter three abreast, but, honest man, he had left it in the stand at the British Museum, or his mind was too busy with a complicated train of thought to allow him to put it up at the right moment. His theory of feminine dress finds no favour with the wife of his bosom or his daughters; they bewilder him by the mutability of their fashions, for no sooner has he found a parallel in dress-improvers to the worship of Venus Callipyge, than, lo! they have melted away, and an unaccountable protuberance appears somewhere else. He prepares unanswerable arguments against the cruelty of adorning hats with feathers and the bodies of little birds, but, before he can produce them, ribbons and flowers are all the mode.

Perhaps women devote themselves to the details of

millinery all the more because we men have allotted to them more than a fair share of the dull things of this life. We have left them comparatively little on which they can occupy themselves agreeably. They have books, of course, but books only serve as a whet to active employment. The daily round of household duties, the weekly discharge of bills, the tedious routine of morning calls, visitation of the sick—everything, in short, that bores a man is cast upon his wife; no wonder if her thoughts attach themselves to matters of toilet, which we despise as being beneath our dignity. And thereby we, who are the oppressors, derive unmerited advantage, for we are free to feast our eyes on the pretty things in which the fair sex go pranked.

Not that our enjoyment is without alloy. Feminine costume is subject to the most sudden and excruciating variations. No sooner have we learnt to delight in a simple, becoming fashion, than instantly the Evil One, whose dwelling-place is in Paris, contrives some mock deformity, and every woman of spirit hastens to adopt it. There is nothing in the human frame more pleasing to the eye than the sweet lines of a woman's shoulder; yet this is precisely the part which, during the last year or two, the malice of *modistes* has concealed with every ingenuity of structure. Vertical humps have been placed there, contrived so as to make the chest look as narrow, the shoulders as high, and the neck as short as possible.[1]

Now, is it impossible to test the strength of this evil spell? Those who have analysed and intelligently contemplated beauty, know how humbling it is to have

[1] Written in 1892.

to confess that women who do not conform in some degree to the fashion, have a self-conscious, and therefore ridiculous, appearance. Yet there is nothing more certain than this, that all this restless craving for change is inspired and sustained by those whose interest it is to supply new clothes. In classical times, the part of their dress on which women spent most money and care was the *peplum* or shawl. In this there was great variety; new and elaborate designs were continually being imported from Tyre and Sidon, and their artistic merit was so great that the poets delighted in describing them. A collection of shawls often formed an important part of a citizen's wealth, or of the treasures of a temple. Imagine a nineteenth-century paterfamilias storing up the worn clothes of his womankind! How pleasing it would be to exhume a crinoline of thirty years ago, or a ponderous bonnet, decked with plumes, of the early Victorian age! The zone—$\zeta\omega\nu\eta$ $\pi\alpha\rho\theta\epsilon\nu\iota\kappa\eta$—has a whole anthology of its own in the Greek and Latin writers; but even the graceful fancy of Mr Andrew Lang is not equal to weaving tender sentiment into anything so fugitive as the waistbands of our daughters. Homer's description of Helen's trailing *peplum* was full of pleasing allusion for people of fashion many centuries after it was written, for the mode was seen to be good, and people had the sense to stick to it; but who would be equal to the task of framing in living verse the costume worn by a fair one at a modern dinner or garden party? Even Byron shrank instinctively from the attempt, and nearly three hundred and fifty stanzas of 'Don Juan' must be perused before any detailed allusion is made to the dress of one of the many fair women who bear parts in that romance. And then it is the Greek Haidée whose attire is touched upon, because it, too, is Greek.[1] Modern popular lyrics, it is true, derive local colour from allusion to costume, but their sentiment cannot be said to gain in depth or refinement thereby.

> " As I walked down Piccadilly
> A charming girl I met ;
> Her name it was Jemima, and .
> Her hair was in a net."

Ah, the pity of it! Paris fashions have killed national costume, and the modes endure not so many days as they used to last decades.

The serious part of this is, that the immense cost of women's dress leaves nothing of value behind it. Sables are positively the only purchase that can be looked on as a safe investment. The most thoughtful selection and design of other materials is sure to be soon stultified by the imperious caprice of Monsieur Worth. By no means can the sorrowful folly of this thraldom be brought home to one more forcibly than by a visit to the cases in the British Museum, containing the little funebral figures from the tombs of Tanagra. The exquisite grace of raiment, the delicate hair-dressing, varied to suit each different cast of features, the care with which beauty of form is accentuated instead of being wrapped up or distorted—all convince one of the cruelty of the modern system which robs our eyes of legitimate delight. How would it be with us were it the custom to lay in the tombs of our departed ones little statuettes, representing them

---

[1] Don Juan, canto ii. 121.

in their best clothes? Should we not shrink from the criticism of posterity? It must be confessed that women would stand this ordeal better than men: still, a modern ball-dress, with corsage cutting horizontally across the bust, is a terrible violation of the natural lines of the figure, especially when, by means of long stays, the cincture is thrust away down where no sculptor would dream of placing it. Then, in the name of common honesty, whence comes the mock delicacy of forbidding the form of a woman's legs to be seen? Are they more suggestive of unlawful thoughts than arms and shoulders? Shall Diana be accounted less than chaste because her statue in the Vatican shows her with tunic girt well above her bare knees? The Spartan virgins were not the less reverently regarded because the graceful *chiton*, being open on one side to allow freedom of movement, flew open as they walked, and got them the name of φαινομηρίδες — thigh-displaying. It is utterly unjust that, because some women have indifferent legs, all should be compelled to wear long skirts on all occasions. Is it desired to see which is most becoming?—compare an Ayrshire dairymaid in workaday attire of short pleated petticoat and the linen jacket called a bedgown, snooded hair, woollen hose, and serviceable shoes, with the same girl figged out on Sunday with a fly-away bonnet on her head, a travesty of Paris fashions on her back, trailing skirts, and high-heeled Balmorals. Of the two, the first is not only the more pleasing, but infinitely the more modest in appearance.

Marie Bashkirtseff, in composing the most self-conscious journal ever penned, was in the habit of subjecting her own actions and those of others to frank analysis. She came to the conclusion that the sentiment of physical modesty was one arising from a sense of one's own imperfection; that if one could be quite conscious of perfect proportion and beauty, there would cease to be any motive or impulse to conceal the body and limbs. Perhaps it is as well that misgivings on this point are pretty universal; but, seeing that it is fixed by an utterly arbitrary rule what portions of the body may be displayed and what may be concealed, it may be permitted to enter a protest against the tyranny which forbids one young lady to let her ankles be seen because another one finds it expedient to conceal hers.

One longs for redemption from the barbarities of feminine fashions. One sighs to exchange the long wasp-like waists and tight-lacing for the simple, easy gowns of our grandmothers—to replace the girdle where the Grecian zone was bound, just clear of the ribs. But one has an uneasy foreboding that the simplicity of classical toilets might be interfered with by the diabolical devices of milliners. At the close of last century, before small waists came, in the inscrutable movement of the female mind, to be counted a beauty, there was an atrocious fashion of wearing pads below the girdle, so that the drapery should fall in unbroken sweep from the bosom to the ground. Many were the shafts aimed by ribald writers against this extraordinary device; many the unjust imputations to which it gave rise,—

> " Some say nature's rights 'tis invading
>   This sham swelling garb to put on :
> For how, with these false bills of lading,
>   Can ships by their rigging be known ? "

It passed away, and the last ninety years have seen the beginning and end of many other modes more unsightly and not less absurd. Is it hoping too much that, seeing how fast the fashions fly, all the ludicrous, hideous, and hurtful ones will, in the fulness of time, have been discarded, and a return be made to the only faultless model the world has ever seen? It was designed by the race whose genius led them by the straight avenue to consummate art, in dim - sighted attempts to reach which goal we have floundered into the ditches on either side. There is a modest little volume by Mr Moyr Smith, 'Ancient Greek Female Costume' (London, 1882), which well illustrates what wearing apparel might and ought to be. The *chiton* or tunic in various forms, whether made to fasten with clasps, as in the Doric fashion, or without them in the Ionic (which the women of Athens were made to adopt after they had killed with their buckles the only one of their countrymen who returned from the expedition to Ægina); the flowing *peplum* for indoors or fine weather, to be exchanged for the woollen *chlamys* or *himation* for outdoor wear; the broidered girdle; the *cothurnus* or laced boot, leaving the toes exposed, for rough walking or wet weather, and sandals of various patterns for town or house wear,—these were the chief items in the one perfect costume that women have ever been content to wear; the only one that should guide us in much-needed dress-reform.

GAMES.

THE world is growing old, and there be those who would have us believe that with its youth it has lost all the graces of the morning, and, with the gravity of old age, acquired also its selfishness. Precise analogy is assumed to exist between man and mankind, as if each generation brought the race nearer to decrepitude, as each lustrum does the individual. But a broader and, as we hold, a truer view, shows mankind as a whole to be as full of vigour as it ever was in any past age, with equal impulse towards and capacity for achievement in learning, in commerce, in literature and the arts, in philanthropy, and all other avenues of enterprise, and with opportunities vastly multiplied and safe-guarded by the blessings of civilisation.

Nor, if love of amusement may be considered one of the characteristics of youth, is there any sign of approaching senility; for the ingenuity in providing pastimes, and the ardour with which they are followed, have never in any former age been exceeded.

Cato tried to persuade his soldiers in the Lybian desert that

     " Serpens, sitis, ardor, arenæ,
   Dulcia virtuti "—

snakes, thirst, burning heat, and sandy wastes are the delights of brave men; and the modern sportsman finds in such incidents only the becoming counterpoise to his enjoyment.

The moralist may be concerned because at this particular epoch there is, all over the globe, a larger proportion of leisured folk—idlers, if you will—than was ever to be reckoned with before; but the political economist sees nothing deplorable in this: on the contrary, it is the direct result of the wealth developed by ages of patient industry finding its way into the hands of those who, under less fortunate circumstances, would have had to earn a livelihood out of the wants of their fellow-creatures. But the moralist and economist alike are concerned in the means which people adopt to spend the leisure made abundant by wealth.

We spout loftily of the dignity of toil, especially when we want to get the toilers on our own side; but very, very few of us care to undertake hard work—really hard, sustained work—except from necessity, either immediate and material or deferred and spiritual. The fact is, labour is hateful to us; none of us, unless we were compelled, would work except by fits and starts, in spells of agreeable length, to be left off as soon as head or limbs were weary. The motive requisite to really hard sustained work, if not one of life and death, or the choice between pauperism and independence, must at least be one between comfortable and needy circumstances. If the ploughman could do without his hire, think you that he would harness his team, day after day, in all moods of weather, to toil "from the rising of the morning till the stars appear"? We have the authority of one of his own craft, Robert Burns, for the sentiment—

> "Then up wi' my ploughman lad,
>   And hey my merry ploughman !
> Of a' the trades that I do ken,
>   Commend me to the ploughman."

But it is certain that there are many bitter days in the year when he would never stir from his fireside unless the alternative were starvation.

Certain philanthropists, it is true, do good and hard work without compulsion; but not many sustain it incessantly during six days in the week or three hundred days in the year. They can fix their own hour for rising, and, rightly enough, take relaxation at their own time, with comfortable conscience, and without apprehension. Theirs need be no life of drudgery; there is no penalty on intermission from their labours, for they are free from the strain of competition in the struggle for existence. It is humiliating, perhaps, but let no one doubt the truth of it, that all thorough work is done for hire. Amateurs are not in it.

In art, for example, if a young man sets himself to learn painting, the moment he has mastered the intense complexity of the craft he ceases to be an amateur, and becomes an artist; but the labour is so great that no one has resolution to acquire this

standing unless he has to make a living by it. Facility
—a turn for drawing—won't do: if it is not a hindrance, it is a snare.

In the summer of 1892 the owner of a large London
house filled it with the works of an accomplished
amateur, now no more, and threw open the exhibition
to the public. It was, perhaps, the best, both in
quality and quantity, that has ever been afforded of
unprofessional painting. The works collected were
those of a lady who had possessed resolution to apply
her leisure hours regularly to one favourite occupation
—who had been gifted with perception of colour and
instinct for composition in an extraordinary degree,
and, in addition, had a remarkable poetic insight.
Some of the sketches—that, for instance, of a young
King of Spain—were exquisite examples of pure and
harmonious colouring; others suggested a deep and
tender vein of thought, like the composition in two
panels of "Hope and Memory," in which Hope is
represented standing, brush in hand, her palette set
with brilliant colours, before an empty canvas on the
easel, and Memory droops with averted head, gazing
at the indistinct forms limned long ago. Another
study, named "Chivalry!" had been conceived in the
bitter irony which is the motive of some of Luke
Fildes's compositions. A stalwart Northumbrian
foreman stands leaning on his staff, overlooking the
work of a crowded group of girls and women, who,
crouching in the drills, are laboriously weeding a
field of turnips. But, with the single exception of
one careful study of a turkey-cock, there was not a
piece in the rooms which approached the degree of a
picture; ideas, suggestion, pleasant colour abounded,

but the *technique*, essential to completion, was wanting. Visitors were indulgent in criticism, liberal in admiration, for they knew that they were viewing the work of an amateur; but the standard of judgment was, though unconsciously, very different from what would have been applied to the labours of a professional painter. The conclusion to which a thoughtful critic was irresistibly drawn was, that had these faculties been thoroughly trained, the amateur might have become an artist to rival the great Venetian masters.

So hard it is for a rich man to enter into the kingdom of Art.

Sir Francis Grant, the late President of the Royal Academy, was a gifted amateur till, at the age of thirty, having spent his patrimony, he was face to face with necessity. He then buckled to, painted for hire, and rose to the highest post in his profession; but, as a painter, he never recovered the years lost to technical discipline. He owed his election as President, not to his standing as a painter, but to appreciation of his social qualities.

In literature, few if any remarkable works have been achieved unless under pressure of eleemosynary circumstance, except in the department of science; but this exception is a very important one. Scientific treatise is not, as a rule, of high literary aim: that Plato, Aristotle, and Francis Bacon expressed themselves in passages of great beauty, was owing to their fine faculties finding expression, almost accidentally, in the discussion of technical themes. Their object, however, was not literary, but scientific. But although Bacon, in realising his ideal of a life of "leisure without loitering," was far from undergoing daily prolonged and obligatory toil, the fact that his work has proved of permanent service to the advancement of learning must be admitted as evidence that, even where no necessity for toil exists, the desire of knowledge sometimes suffices as the motive of sustained exertion.

Incalculably the greater number of those who find themselves under no necessity for effort to keep the wolf from the door, are content to spend their days in loitering.

> "Haud equidem invideo, miror magis;"

to some temperaments it seems the harshest destiny to lead life without a precisely defined object—without some occupation which makes a man impatient of lying abed of a morning — without some stimulus, hardly less potent than love, and infinitely more enduring. Howbeit, there are tens of thousands of well-to-do folk to whom, morally, it seems to be of as little importance to themselves as it is to the rest of the world whether they ever leave their beds at all. Economically, of course, it would be a loss to the cobblers, as persons interested in the consumption of shoe-leather, if these idlers never came abroad; in fact, the best retail customers in many trades consist mainly of loiterers, and with this consideration philosophers must console themselves for the lamentable prospect of a large class living only to live, without ever taking thought how to ripen, or ever stiffening a sinew to reap, the fruits of time.

But all men feel the necessity of beguiling the hours; the veriest sloth will soon fall out of his senses if he does nothing but count the ticks of the clock; so man has invented for his solace an infinite variety of deliberate pastimes—artificial work of head or hand —which lull his perception of the slipping sands as effectually as productive labour does that of the artisan. The energy which has been cited above to show that there are no signs of decrepitude or senility in the world—society—mankind as a mass—is nowhere more manifest than in the elaborate and costly preparations for amusement—for sheer pastime—which ensues as soon as people get respite from the task of bread-winning. A notable and somewhat unsatisfactory feature in this mimicry of work is that the professional is coming more and more to the front, to the discouragement of the amateur. To excel in billiards, in cricket, in golf, tennis, or any of the myriad games played with balls of various size and material, more time must be filched from serious business than can by any means be afforded by those who have to earn a living. To become proficient in the spot-stroke postulates an apprenticeship at least as severe and as prolonged as that of any skilled handicraft; and the extraordinary perfection attained by those classed as "gentlemen" cricketers, as distinguished from "players," implies that for them it is the business of life, and not mere relaxation. The tendency of all games, in this age of wealth and leisure, is to turn players into athletes, and in these, as in serious work, "amateur" is synonymous with "immature."

Yet games are of such excellent use in themselves, not only as recreation from strain but as safety-valves for the dangerous or mischievous forces in human nature, diverting the thoughts from unhealthy tend-

encies and chastening the frame unto symmetry and
grace, that it were a pity if room were not kept for
people who can never aspire to professional proficiency.
They are potent safeguards against two of the most
deplorable deformities to which human nature is liable
—dulness in the hard-worked, and vanity in the idle;
each of which brings many a man and woman into a
tragic degree of ridicule. Some young people are so
constituted as to feel no inclination to games, but very
much the reverse: their minds are of such fibre as to
retain elasticity without having recourse to systematic
diversion. That they are not characters of small capacity which exhibit this trait may be shown by quoting two well-known instances of men highly distinguished in widely different careers. The Duke of
Wellington could never be induced, when at school, to
throw any spirit into the sports of other boys; he preferred wandering about alone to the engrossing occupation of football or cricket. Rousseau consumed days
and nights of close study in an attempt to master the
game of chess; but, though he persevered in repeated
endeavours, they all came to nothing, for as often as he
sat down to a game, all that he had learnt went out of
his head. But such instances are exceptional, and in
most characters hard work, unrelieved by competitive
games, is apt to produce " grooviness," and superfluous
leisure stupidity. It is difficult to imagine a young
woman fond of lawn-tennis falling a prey to the morbid self-consciousness which consumed the Comtesse
de Senecterre, whom Tallemant des Réaux describes as
a beautiful but very foolish woman. One of her fancies
was to have pillows of every size in her bed—even for
her thumbs—for she prided herself on her beautiful

hands, and slept with them open, to keep the joints small.[1] Athletes, it is true, are peculiarly prone to vanity, but the form that vice assumes in them is that of the pride of life, by many degrees more pardonable than the deliberate self-love of indolence.

The games of primitive races are chiefly confined to children—the business of life among uncivilised people being so hazardous and difficult that they can spare no energy for amusement. Even their boys and girls, with plenty of time on their hands, only find diversion in mimicry of adult occupations. The men of Australian tribes rely upon capture to obtain their wives, and so the lads, armed with miniature boomerangs and spears, play at carrying off the lasses. Just as there is no more popular toy in our nurseries than a box of bricks, so the Esquimaux children construct little huts of snow—the recognised building material in that community.[2] Often the game or toy, thus devised in imitation of the serious affairs of life, outlives the practice in which it originated. Thus bows and arrows continue to be favourite playthings, not only with children, but with grown persons—witness the archery clubs which still flourish in some parts of England.

Jousting and tilting, though they survived the invention of artillery, seem finally to have passed out of vogue: the last attempt to revive them was the magnificent tournament at Eglinton Castle, more than fifty years ago. But the chivalrous spirit which inspired and regulated these knightly sports has not died out: it is of the essence of modern games; for nothing is held so despicable, or brings a man into such irretriev-

---

[1] Les Histoirettes de Tallemant des Réaux. Paris, 1834.
[2] Primitive Culture, by E. B. Tylor, i. 72.

able disgrace, as cheating. If there were nothing good in games besides this honourable understanding, without which they could not be carried on, that alone would earn for them the approval of the moral philosopher. The methods of politics, of the Stock Exchange, of the betting ring, even the ordinary transactions of buying and selling, of borrowing and lending, present queer aspects under the moral microscope: men of honour permit themselves to do things of a complexion they would shrink from in horror at cards or billiards. All this is part of the labyrinthine ethics which so puzzled Alfred de Musset :—

> " Philosophes de nos jours, je vous arrête ici ;
>   O graves demi-dieux, expliquez-moi ceci,
>   On ne volerait pas, à coup sur, un obole
>   À son voisin ; pourtant, quand on peut, on lui vole
>   Sa femme."

Leaving this never-ending conundrum to be solved by each one according to his conscience, it is satisfactory, seeing how universal is the devotion of civilised man to games, to observe that their success depends on the existence of a sensitive code of honour among the players, and that it has always been so from the earliest times. The sacred games of Olympia were instituted nearly seven centuries before Christ; and an oath, confirmed by sacrifice, was imposed on the athletes before they entered the lists, binding them to play fair, and take no fraudulent advantage over the other competitors.

Reference to these national festivals of ancient Greece calls to mind their extraordinary duration. There is no modern parallel to them in that respect. We reckon our Derby, our University boat-race, our

Eton and Harrow cricket-match, to be venerable institutions, but they are truly ephemeral observances compared with, say, the Isthmian Games, which, founded about B.C. 560, still constituted, three centuries and a half later, such an important anniversary that Flamininus selected it as the occasion for proclaiming the liberty of Greece in B.C. 196, and, two centuries and a half later still, Nero chose it as the most suitable opportunity for renewing the proclamation in A.D. 67. Such permanence puts to shame the life of a dynasty; and there is certainly no important event in our sporting world which derives its origin from the year 1300.

But there is another remarkable feature about these gatherings—namely, the unchanging character of the performance enacted at them. Assuming the era of Homer to have been five centuries earlier than the inauguration of the Isthmian Games, that is, about B.C. 1000, the sports which he enumerates as taking place at the funeral of Patroclus were identical, not only with those of the Olympian, Nemean, and Isthmian celebrations, but strangely similar to a programme of the present day. Chariot and foot races, boxing, wrestling, putting the stone, are counterparts of competitive exercises of the nineteenth century.[1]

Mr Francis Storr has traced the decadence of public athletic competition from the palmy days of Olympia and Pythia, through the spectacular performances in the Roman circus and amphitheatre, to its latest degradation in the Spanish bull-fight. In the popularity of the last named amusement, said to have been the invention of Julius Cæsar, may be recognised the ignoble delight of the populace of Southern Europe in

[1] Iliad, xxiii.

the shedding of blood, to which the Roman emperors were at so much pains to pander. To gratify this guilty lust, nine thousand beasts were done to death at the opening of the Colosseum, and ten thousand at the celebration of Trajan's victory in Dacia. The steam of carnage was as essential to the proper enjoyment of a holiday by the rulers of the world as it is held to be to the right enthronement of a King of Dahomey; and the pool of human blood across which that black potentate is periodically ferried does not imply more gigantic cruelty than what was involved in the artificial sea-fights prepared with elaborate cost in ancient Rome. In these, prisoners of war or criminals were marshalled in opposing fleets, and forced to mortal combat, till one side or other was exterminated. Claudius broke the record by one such *naumachia* on Lake Fucinus, where not less than 100 ships and 19,000 combatants took part. There is little enough to be recorded to the renown of the weakling emperor Honorius, yet it was an edict of his (probably dictated by his powerful Minister and father-in-law, Stilicho) which finally put an end to these inhuman festivals.

But all these celebrations, from the noble sports of Olympia down to the gladiatorial contests of Rome, partook more of the nature of spectacular entertainment than of games. They were performed, primarily, for the delectation of vast audiences, not, as football, cricket, and golf among ourselves, for the amusement of the players themselves. The fervid inclination of the British people to games of skill or chance has occupied the attention of Parliament from very early times. In 1477, an Act (17 Edward IV. c. 3) made the players of certain games, including "hand in, hand out," which is supposed to have been the primitive form of cricket, liable to two years' imprisonment, and their implements to be burnt. The genius of Dr Grace would, probably, in those days have led to lifelong languishing in the Tower. In a preamble of portentous length to an Act for the "maintenance of Artillary debarring unlawful games" (33 Henry VIII. c. 9), it is set forth that "many subtyll inventative and crafty persons have founde and dayly fynd many and sondry new and crafty games and plaies, as logating in the fieldes, slyde thrift, otherwise called shove grote," &c.; and that warlike exercises had fallen into disuse, owing to these allurements to idleness. "Dyvers bowyers and fletchers," runs the dolorous plaint, "gone and inhabyt themselves in Scotland and other places out of this realme, there workyng and teachyng their science to the puissance of the same, to the great comfort of estraungers and detriment of this realme." Therefore it is enacted "that no maner of artificer or craftesman of any handycraft or occupacion, husbandeman, apprentice, labourer, seruant at husbandry, journeyman or seruant of artificer, maryners, fyshermen, watermen, or any seruing man . . . plaie at the tables, tenys, dyce, cardes, boules, closhe, coytyng, logatyng, or any other unlawfulle game."

Here was class legislation with a vengeance! But the gentry also were put under some restraint in this matter of games, for it was further enacted that "no maner of person shall at any tyme plaie at any boule or boules in open places out of his gardeyn or orcharde." This Act remained on our statute-books until 1846, when so much of it as applied to mere games of skill was repealed by 8 & 9 Victoria, c. 109.

But if this was the policy in Merrie England, a comparatively rich and a powerful country, the lieges of Scotland, a poor and hardly beset realm, were not likely to fare more liberally. Accordingly, the statute-books teem with Acts directed against golf and foot-ball as "vnprofitable sports for the common gude of the Realme." Members of Parliament, called on to subscribe to innumerable football clubs in their constituencies, may cast wistful retrospect towards the policy of James I. of Scotland, whose Parliament passed an Act couched in the following terms of commendable brevity: "Item: it is statut and ordainit that na man play at the futball."

In 1457 it was enacted "that wapenschawingis be halden and that the fute-ball and golf be utterly cryit down and nocht usit," because they interfered with warlike exercises, and it was desired that young folk should "buske thame to be archeres fra they be twelff yeares of elde." James IV., however, a monarch of fervent piety, who died a soldier's death at Flodden, was a keen golfer, as is shown by his Lord Treasurer's accounts, and this in spite of an Act of his own Parliament which ordered that "in na place of the realme there be usit futeball, golfe, or uther sik un-profitabill sportis."

The distinction between games of skill and games of chance is one that can hardly be rigidly drawn. Chess, and its inferior derivative draughts, are perhaps the only intellectual recreations in which accident or luck has no part. In the former, the sole point decided by chance is the right of making the first move in the

first of a series of games; but even that is said to be
of no advantage to either player, for it was Staunton's
opinion that every game of chess must end in a draw,
supposing neither player to make a mistake.   But
infallibility in chess almost implies omniscience, for it
has been calculated that the first eight moves (four by
each player) admit of 72,000 variations.   Such an
appalling consideration justifies Robert Burton in
hesitating to recommend the game as a remedy for
melancholy :—

It is a game too troublesome for some men's brains, too
full of anxiety, all out as bad as study; besides, it is a
testy cholerick game, and very offensive to him that loseth
the mate.   William the Conqueror, in his younger yeares,
playing at chesse with the Prince of France, losing a mate,
knocked the chesse-board about his pate, which was a cause
afterwards of much enmity between them.

Another awful example of the risks to be encountered by those who play chess with adversaries of
uncertain temper is recorded in the ' Annals of the
Four Masters.'   Two kings of Irish provinces began
a game on the best of terms, but he who got the worst
of it seized one of the rooks and flung it with such
force at his royal opponent that it entered the brain
and killed him on the spot.

Of the high antiquity of chess there can be no
doubt, and in a diplomatic correspondence which took
place between the Roman Emperor Nicephorus and
the celebrated Harun-al-Raschid there is some evidence that it was so universal as a pastime in the
East as to lend its technical terms to ordinary illustration.   The Arabian historian, Abulfeda, has preserved the letters.   Nicephorus reminds Harun, whom

he addresses respectfully as "Sovereign of the Arabs," that the Empress Irene is dead, and claims repayment of the tribute which Harun unjustly exacted from her.

She looked upon you as a *rukh*, and on herself as a mere pawn, therefore she submitted to pay you a tribute more than the double of which she ought to have exacted from you. . . . If you hesitate, the sword shall settle our accounts.

Harun's diplomacy was of the heroic kind, and he replied :—

In the name of God, the merciful and gracious: from Harun, Commander of the Faithful, to the Roman dog Nicephorus. I have read thine epistle, thou son of an infidel mother. My answer to it thou shalt see, not hear.

He followed this epistle by invasion of the Roman province, and soon brought Nicephorus to adopt altered views on the question.

A pretty fable exists somewhere illustrating the absorbing fascination of this game. A certain monarch, observing that his subjects had become so addicted to chess that they were withdrawn from public and private duties, issued an edict prohibiting play, except under a scale graduated according to age. Children and youths were restricted to an hour's play daily; grown men and women were allowed a little longer, until in old age all limitation was removed. Then arose murmurs and lamentation throughout the land; a young man sighed, not for his mistress, but for his next birthday, when he might claim an extension of chess-time; a maiden studied her mirror, not to exult in the bloom of her cheeks or the lustre of her eyes, but craving for the advent of the first wrinkle, the first grey hair, harbingers of fuller surrender to the ruling passion. The hearts of men and women grew lighter in proportion as their eyes became dim and their tresses thin. "Ah, happy old age! beautiful decrepitude!" they prayed, "come to us quickly. Thou mayest be toothless, hairless, bloodless, but thou art the sole deliverer from the uneasy bondage of youth—from the harsh restraints that hold us from the only noble exercise of mind."

The perfection to which chess may be carried almost implies its imperfection as an amusement. Chess giants like Mr Blackburn and the late Herr Zukertort act as warnings rather than ideals to ordinary people in search of amusement. The latter gentleman once undertook to carry on eighteen games simultaneously, without looking at the boards. The performance did not end very satisfactorily, for after more than two days' play the mental acrobat surrendered the contest. But the fact of having carried it so far implied a bewildering feat of cerebration; for if the first four moves on either side, in a single game, admit of 72,000 variations, the first four in eighteen games make the appalling total of one million two hundred and ninety-six thousand possible combinations. Mr Blackburn is unrivalled as a blindfold player, and he has actually succeeded in winning the majority of twelve simultaneous games without the assistance of sight. The possible variations in the first four moves of these, number eight hundred and sixty-four thousand. Performances such as these leave on the mind the exhausting impression of infinity: it is too much of a good thing. One can scarcely imagine how a brain, called on to steer through such vast and barren complexities, can have any faculties in reserve for useful ratiocination.

In the other great intellectual pastime, whist, chance of course bears an important part, and it is probably to this that it owes its chief fascination. A confident player may console himself for any error he may have committed by the hope that the fall of the cards in subsequent deals may restore his advantage. On the other hand, to whist must be allotted a lower purely intellectual standing than to chess, because to arouse the full attention of the players, it seems necessary to play for money; whereas the votaries of chess are usually quite content to play for love.

Howbeit, this is not a sure test to the intrinsic virtue of a game. No one will be disposed to question the eminence of cricket among outdoor games, and stakes are almost unheard of in connection with matches in these days. But formerly large sums were played for. One thousand guineas, it seems, were the ordinary stakes in county matches at the close of last century. Taking up the 'Sporting Magazine' for 1793, one may read how twenty-two of Middlesex win that sum from eleven of England at Lord's on 26th August in that year, and in the return match on 9th September win another cool thousand; and Surrey, in the same year, twice won a thousand guineas from the eleven of Hants. Surrey also played All England, and Essex played Herts, on the same terms: altogether a good deal of money must have changed hands between the wickets of Lord's when George III. was king.

But those were the heroic days of play. It was in that year that, as the same magazine records, Mr Br—gh—n lost £15,000 at billiards in a single night to Mr L—s—n B—ck—d ; and at White's Club the Prince of Wales lost eleven thousand guineas to a gentleman at the same game. It would be amusing to see Peall and Roberts set to play a match for the championship on one of the tables whereon such mighty issues were decided—tables with wooden beds and stuffed horsehair cushions.

The prodigious passion for golf developed in England within the last few years may in part be owing to the extent to which in that pastime chance tempers skill. The finest drive may be reft of its reward by a hazard ; a rabbit-scrape the size of a teacup may, by receiving the ball of his opponent, give an inferior player the chance of winning the hole ; and, to one of the multitude of duffers at this royal game, the ecstasy of seeing his adversary struggling with difficulties is almost as perfect as successfully negotiating them himself. There is no game of skill which lures the devotee with such delusive hopes as golf. You shall see one whose waist - belt circles the mellow growth of fifty years addressing himself to the ball with as much solicitude as the neophyte of twenty summers. He is as precise in pointing his toes in the prescribed direction, in swinging slowly back, in revolving on his proper axis, in observing all the rest of the seventeen maxims with which he has been taught to charge his aching memory each time he intends to strike the ball, as he was a quarter of a century ago ; yet the result is not much more effective to-day than it was when he began. He is as prone as ever to slice, draw, heel, horn, force, or top; but from time to time he *does* strike the ball fair, and it flies far and sure: the resulting sensation is so exquisite that the recollection of it carries the player proudly through all the inevitable subsequent disasters of the day. Nay, sometimes for a whole day, or even for two or three days in succession, his coquettish mistress will be all sweetness; he hardly misses a single tee-shot, and his approaches come off with masterly precision. He smiles as he reflects on bygone disappointment: after all it is a simple matter; once acquire the knack of keeping your eye on the ball, don't force for long drives, and there you are, you know. He whispers to himself—

> "One crowded hour of glorious life
> Is worth an age without a name."

On the morrow he feels as fit as ever, with the same limbs and harmony of joints, the same keen eye, his favourite clubs, even the identical dress he wore in his triumph yesterday. He steps out jauntily, disguising his impatience to begin the match, and adorned with the modesty that meetly veils just confidence. Marry! what mysterious influence is abroad? Gone is the easy poise at the tee; gone, the noiseless swing and the indescribable elastic "rap" of a rightly smitten ball; gone, the cunning wrist-jerk of the iron, wherewith to "lay it dead." From some inscrutable cause everything is as it should not be; do what he may, the muscles of his arms *will* grow rigid as he raises the club to the swing: it makes a discordant *swoosh* through the air, like the rod of an unskilful salmon-fisher, the ball describes a complicated parabola to the right of the true direction, lands clear, but, taking the "side" communicated by the slice, bounds sharply still further astray, and buries itself in irremediable grief. The spell endures throughout the day, and in the level light of evening he wends sorrowfully home, murmuring—

> "Who then to frail mortality shall trust,
> But limns the water, or but writes in dust."

In an age of faith a phenomenon like this would have been set down to witchcraft; the victim would have been entitled to the aid of justice to rid him of the glamour: many an old woman has been grilled at the stake for inflicting sufferings not more poignant than those he has endured. But we are a coldly sceptical generation: scientific method, it is true, forbids that any mystery should be finally pronounced insoluble; but there are some problems which, it is admitted, cannot be explained in the present state of our knowledge, and among these must be placed the sinister influences affecting the game of golf.

In spite of the anguish which lies in wait for all but players of the first class, few who have once fairly taken to golf have ever been known to give it up. The instinct of pursuit and the sense of attainment are both stimulated; prowess may be so nicely adjusted by allowance of strokes that men of far different degrees of proficiency can play an exciting game together, and improvement in the art is promptly signified by an increase in the player's handicap. It is, moreover, a game for all ages, in which the hale veteran of threescore and ten may hold his own with a university youth.

But, above all, the pleasantest feature about it is that it is all innings: there are no long hours of leather-hunting while the enemy is punishing the bowling. These are the qualities that hold its votaries enthralled; these the merits that produce such touching examples of perseverance as that said to have been shown by a certain municipal dignitary who, emerging from the Maiden at Sandwich, sat down to eat his luncheon, having played "seventy-two more," and resumed work with the niblick when he had refreshed himself.

It is a long descent from games which exercise mind or body to those of pure chance, yet these have as firm a hold upon human inclination as if they possessed merit in themselves. No more piteous impression can be made on a thoughtful mind than that left by a visit to the tables at Monte Carlo. Hour after hour, day after day, year after year, the same crowds gather round them, blind to the beauty of sapphire sea and glorious sunshine, content to swelter and scramble and wrangle—for what? Well, they are under thrall of one of two motives—two deplorable motives; one, the lowest, the other, the saddest, that can be conceived. For the first is avarice—of all lust the most obscene, of all passion the most disastrous. Valour, self-devotion, truth, humanity, may (so complex is human nature) coexist with much that is evil in a character; but avarice taints the whole being: unlike other desires, it is never satisfied, it is never at rest; nothing sweet can flow from the source which it has polluted. Let there be no mistake or palliation about this: avarice is the primary lure to the Casino. Take away the gold, and who would be so childish as to play for counters or sweetmeats?

The other and subsidiary motive which collects a crowd round the tables is the desire of idle men to rid themselves of that most precious possession—time; which, once it is gone, can never be recalled; the loss of which is ever the cause of fruitless regret.

Sero sapiunt Phryges—knowledge comes, but wisdom tarries, as was said long ago; but here even knowledge seems to be set at contempt. Crowds of educated people, with ready access to all the stores of knowledge laid up through the laborious ages for present use, affirm the contemptible creed of luck. Never was there a god so false, never one before whom so many bowed the knee in profound and ignorant faith. It would be lost labour to combat the belief—almost universal and wholly ineradicable among gamblers—in an inscrutable influence upon human occasion, capable of being offended or propitiated. It differs in no respect from idolatry; for civilised, well-educated people behave just as the pagan does in regard to the Great Spirit, the souls of his ancestors, or the deified powers of Nature. It is, in fact, a kind of lusorial animism. "Don't disappoint your luck!"—the gambler's cardinal precept—implies the same dread of offending a powerful being, impatient of slight, as still moves the inhabitants of Tinnevelly, in Indo-China, to lay brandy and cheroots on the grave of a certain British officer whom they hated and feared on account of his tyrannical rule over them, believing that his spirit can only be kept from mischief by being plied with the same little luxuries he loved when alive. "The Lord thy God is a jealous Lord" is dogma not peculiar to Jewish worship: it is the idea uppermost in all religion. Perhaps it may seem only by forced analogy that the gambler's infatuation can be compared to the superstitious awe of primitive belief, but one needs not to go back a long way in our own history to realise that they can be traced to a common source. In 1619, Thomas Gataker, a Puritan minister, published his essay on the "Nature and Use of Lots," in which, while arguing against it, he states the common belief to be as follows:—

Lots may not be used but with great reverence, because the disposition of them cometh immediately from God. . . . . The nature of a Lot, which is affirmed to bee a worke of God's speciall and immediate providence, a sacred oracle, a divine judgment or sentence: the light use of it therefore to be an abuse of God's name: and so a sinne against the Third Commandement.—(P. 91.)

Jeremy Taylor, while approving of games of chance played without stakes, for pure amusement, held that a pecuniary motive entering into such pastimes was enough to bring down divine, or at least demoniac, intervention:—

I have heard from them that have skill of such things, there are such strange chances, such promoting of a hand by fancy and little arts of geomancy, such constant winning on one side, such unreasonable losses on the other, and these strange contingencies produce such horrible effects, that it is not improbable that God hath permitted the conduct of such games of chance to the devil, who will order them so where he can do most mischief; but without the instrumentality of money he could do nothing at all.[1]

____

[1] Jeremy Taylor's Works, xiv. 337.

How deeply rooted in men's minds the belief in divine interposition in such matters has been from early times, is shown by recourse having been had to lots in the first momentous act performed by the primitive Christian Church—namely, the election of an apostle. Human direction was relied on so far as to reduce the number of candidates to two, the qualifications of whom were so evenly balanced that the decision between them was left to pure chance, to control which, as was believed, supernatural interference might be looked for.[1]

Even to one accustomed to balanced method of thought, there may be a lurking difficulty in believing that, in tossing up a half-crown, the odds each separate time are exactly even whether it comes down heads or tails. Suppose "heads" to have turned up five times in succession, the chances remain precisely the same on its so turning up the sixth time, and are not in the least degree affected by the fact that the odds originally stood heavily against its turning up six times running. There are but two sides to half-a-crown, and it must be exactly even betting, each time the coin is thrown up, which side falls uppermost.

But in going through a well-shuffled pack of cards, the odds are, of course, infinitely affected by the fact that there are only fifty-two cards: if, in the first twenty-six, fourteen black cards have turned up against twelve red, the odds of course become slightly in favour of red turning up in the last twenty-six, but are liable at any moment to be reversed by a succession of red cards turning up, and so leaving a preponderance of black in the residuum. But such

[1] Acts i. 26.

is the glow of success—of gratified greed—felt by one
who, by backing his luck, has landed a large stake;
so keen is the envy felt by others at the success of a
plucky player, that the result is attributed to a supernatural influence upon the laws of gravity, affecting
the fall of the dice, or specially interfering with the
series of cards. It is forgotten that disappointment
and ruin have overtaken thousands who have adopted
means precisely similar to those of the successful
gambler; attention is concentrated upon the immediate
and peculiar instance in the chapter of accidents. To
argue against the potency of luck with those who believe in it, is as hopeless as it would have been to do
so against the efficiency of libations poured to the sun
by the ancient Peruvians. They could point to the
disappearance of the liquid, a process which the educated man would account for by evaporation, but
which the pious devotee regarded as the acceptance
of the sacrifice.

Admitting the object of games of skill and games
of chance to be the same—the withdrawal of the
mind either from the tedium of idleness, or, by the
substitution of minor predicaments, from the pressure
or apprehension of calamity—it is evident that the
former class effect that purpose by the exercise of
commendable qualities of mind or body, or both; but
that the latter do so by developing ignoble faculties.
Good games are more than merely frivolous and trivial
methods of killing time, they deserve serious consideration. The tendency has hitherto been to let them
become the prerogative of the well-to-do; but, at a
time when attention has been forcibly directed to the
question of shortening the hours of labour, it may be

of advantage to remember that thoughtful men in all ages have put in a claim for a counterpoise to toil on behalf of those who live by the sweat of their brows. There is a sentence in Sir Thomas More's 'Utopia,' which reads like a paraphrase of some of the evidence given before the Royal Commission on Labour:—

As no man should be idle, so let none be compelled to work till night-fall like a beast of burthen; for the life of our labouring folk is but bitter slavery.

On which Robert Burton passes the following comment:—

If one half-day in a week were allowed to our household servants for their merry meetings, by their hard masters, or in a year some feasts, like those Roman saturnals, I think they would labour harder all the rest of their time, and both parties be better pleased.

But we are a serious people—a fact lately emphasised by the London County Council in forbidding the performance of dance-music on Sundays by the bands in the Parks.

SPEECH.

A RTICULATE speech has sometimes been arrogantly claimed as the monopoly of man; for that restless and supercilious mammal is constantly casting about for some distinctive attribute to serve as a bridgeless gulf between himself and his fellow *viviparæ*, whom he contemptuously classes as beasts. Clothing, laughing, thinking, counting—to each and all of these he has had to surrender his exclusive claim, and perhaps the only feat in which he has as yet discovered no rivals is the production and use of fire.

Speech, indeed, could never, except on slenderest grounds, be claimed as the peculiar property of the human species. One has only to go afield some mild December noon, and watch the proceedings of a flight of rooks, to be led to the firm conclusion that the sounds he hears are part of conversation, at least as intelligible and intelligent as the confusion of tongues arising at a fashionable lady's reception. It is true that an Englishman, standing close on the skirts of some such entertainment in London, will hear snatches of conversation and disjointed words which he can understand; but let him pause and listen on the stairs outside, and the human chatter has no more significance to him than the cackle of a poultry-yard. He recognises the cry of the human animal, just as he might pronounce the other to be the cry of cocks and hens, of ducks and geese; but as for conveying anything to his understanding, it is *vox et prœterea nihil.*

Still less suggestion would the sounds emitted by an evening party in London convey to the mind of a South Sea Islander. His intelligence and experience would certify to him that these men and women were not uttering syllables without meaning; but 'even separate sentences, in which every vowel and consonant might be distinguished, would fail to touch his understanding, and would mean as little to him as the sentence in quick guttural Gaelic, spoken by the stalker to his gillie in a Highland forest, conveys to the Southern sportsman. But in order to realise how little difference there is between the phonetic value of the human voice and that of the calls of some of the lower animals, one has only to listen to some of the common street cries. In London, for instance, " Strāū-brĭz—fў'—strāū-brĭz ! " "Mĕ-ō-ō-ō ! " (Milk-ho!) " Clŏ'-clŏ', clŏ'-clŏ ! " and in Edinburgh " Caller ha-adiz ! Caller oo ! " are sounds as monotonous and not more articulate than many of the cries of beast and bird. It is said, by the by, that no animal except man can sound consonants; that a dog says " wow-wow ! " not, classically, " bow-wow ! " a rook " yaw-yaw," not " caw-caw ! " a peacock, not, as the consensus of nations affirms, "pay-ō!" but "hay-ō!" and so on; but that point remains to be decided by the nicer application of the phonometer.

To return, then, to one of the most convenient examples that may be had of the deliberate behaviour of wild animals—that of a flight of rooks settled on a grass-field. Look at that sedate individual (as like a Fellow of the Society of Antiquaries as a biped in black feathers can be to a biped in broadcloth) busy turning over the stones with his strong beak, and with head aslant, scrutinising the exposed surface for worm or grub. Finding nothing, "Caw!" says he, and flies off to another part of the field. Now if that sound means nothing, why does the bird make it? Almost certainly it expresses something, either in the way of information to his companions or of expletive to relieve his own feelings, just as a disappointed man (not, *bien entendu*, a Fellow of the Society of Antiquaries, but an ordinary mortal) is prone, under similar circumstances, to pronounce a profane monosyllable. Here is another holding forth to a detachment of the flight, which sits motionless and silent, with hunched shoulders. His speech seems to our gross faculties only monotonous repetition of the same sound, but is probably well understood by his hearers as exhortation, advice, narrative, or speculation. Meanwhile, observe the flirtation going on between yon ardent couple in a corner of the field. In this community the garb of male and female is identical; but the male—an accomplished wooer—is easily to be distinguished by bowings and clumsy struttings, and behaviour as awkward and comical as that of any human lover. Shall we be told that the low guttural notes exchanged between the pair have no reference to the coming nesting season, and are not a language charged with all the unreason of passion and the flattery of mutual preference? All the immeasurable variety of vocabulary, from the lion's roar to the field-mouse's squeak — from the hiss of an angry goose to the song of the soaring lark, constitutes more than mere sound; it is language, and who will be so bold as to say that human ears may not be capable of being trained to interpret it? At present, though we can distinguish the dominant notes of pain, terror, anger, love, persuasion, and content in the cries of those animals with which we are most familiar, our faculties are not of sufficient delicacy to detect in them the fine modulations of sound which constitute speech. The area cat of a modern city perhaps purrs in the very same tone in which its predecessor, embalmed as a mummy four thousand years ago, in the reign of Thothmes III., expressed its happiness; but it would be rash to assume that study and the application of delicate instruments may not some day explain feline phrases as clearly as patient comparison produced the clue to Egyptian hieroglyphics. The squeak of a bat is in so high a note that it lies beyond the hearing range of some persons. If this sound, which is audible to most people, eludes the sense of others, it is impossible to estimate how much there is in the common cries of animals, of which our auditory sense gives us no notice. Professor Garnier has devoted some years to the study of the language of apes. By means of the phonograph he claims to have proved that they laugh aloud; and that careful comparison of human and simian voices preserved in this instrument fails to show any difference between them except compass, pitch, and flexion.

But, it may be argued, if the cries of beasts and birds are an intelligible, though imperfect, language, how comes it that a parrot may be taught to utter words of which it cannot possibly understand the meaning? The explanation of this may be, that just as children, and even grown persons, often imitate the natural cries of wild animals, without, of course, understanding any meaning these may be supposed to have, so, in their turn, certain animals may be induced to imitate human vocables; and just as a certain sound or group of sounds becomes, by frequent repetition, associated in our minds with fixed ideas, so a parrot, repeating given phrases, comes to unite them with fixed ideas, though not the same ideas as we associate with these phrases. When the English lady, explaining to the French hotel-keeper certain arrangements necessary for her comfort, startled him by saying, "Je dors toujours avec deux matelots," she failed to convey to his mind the image which would have been perfectly expressed by "sur deux matelas." So the parrot which says "Three cheers for the Queen!" may associate the phrase with the idea of food, or head-scratching, or the unsatisfactory nature of our climate. In love, anger, or fear, he expresses himself in his native screams, which are wholly unintelligible to us; equally unintelligible to us are the ideas he intends to convey by means of words which have come to signify to him something quite different from that which we understand by them. Nay, instances are not wanting wherein, owing to a confusion between two vocables of similar sound, we derive a totally wrong impression from expressions in our own language. An instance of this occurs in Isaiah viii. 19, "Seek unto . . . wizards which *peep* and mutter." Almost every modern reader receives from "peep" the idea of spying; but in reality it means to chirp, to make a small sound like a chicken, and is used in that sense in widely different families of language.

There is, however, an intrinsic significance in syllables besides the meaning associated with them by familiarity. No more arbitrary arrangement of vowels and consonants could be imagined than Lewis Carroll's celebrated lines—

> " 'Twas brillig, and the slithy toves
>   Did gyre and gimble in the wabe ;
> All mimsy were the borogroves,
>   And the mome raths outgabe ;"

yet was there never written anything that conjured up more effectually the sensation of a drowsy summer noon. There are, too, delicate shades of expression in the stanza—

> " ' And hast thou slain the Jabberwock ?
>   Come to my arms, my beamish boy !
> O frabjous day ! calloo, callay !'
>   He chortled in his joy."

The interjection "calloo, callay !" conveys an idea of grateful and peaceful content that could never have found utterance in the recognised "hooray!" and as for "chortle," it is a verb to live in our language having less of selfishness than "chuckle," and more of tender pride than "cheer." There is nothing puerile in this incomparable nonsense-writer; and

to test his superiority over every other that has
tried his hand at this apparently simple exercise,
it is only necessary to compare with it such gib-
berish as that of Taylor, the Water Poet—

"Hough gruntough wough Thomough Coriatough, Adcough
    robunquogh
Warawogh bogh Comitogh sogh wogh termonatogrogh,
Callimogh gogh whobogh Ragamogh demagorgogh palemogh;"

and so on through a lot of dreary rubbish. Or again—

" Nortumblum callimunipquash omystoliton quashte burashte
Scribuke woshtay solusbay perambulatashte ;
Grekay sous Turkay Paphay zums Jerusalushte,
Neptus esht Ealors Interrimoy diz dolorushte."

So far as can be seen, it is pretty safe to assume
that the vocal sounds of animals constitute speech
in the sense in which it has been so well defined
by Mr E. Tylor—namely, " the expression of ideas by
articulate sounds habitually allotted to them." We
have adopted and imitated some of them, attaching
to them ideas other than those conceived by the
animals that produce the sounds. The cock has
coined for himself a name in almost every country
where he is known, from British *chanticleer* to Malay
kălaruk and Spanish *quiquiriqui;* the crow was known
in Sanskrit as *kăka,* just as to this day he is *kăh-kăh*
in British Columbia. The association of sound with
an idea (which is the basis of all language) is very
clearly exemplified in such bird-names as cuckoo,
peewit, chiff-chaff, &c. While we thus coolly appropriate, for our own purposes and to express our own
ideas, words borrowed from the language of beast
and bird, we are inclined to deny that they have the

faculty of communicating thought and observation among themselves.

Meanwhile, however, before learning to become eavesdroppers on beast and bird, men and women may profitably consider what progress they have made in developing the means of oral communication with which nature has endowed them, and extending language beyond its primitive emotional and interjectional stages. It seems almost as if some races had been so absorbed in carrying on the laborious work of civilisation that the niceties of conversation had fallen into neglect. Our own language, for example, is lamentably slipshod in construction and harsh in sound compared with that of ancient Greece. Again, in the speech of so highly developed a people as the Celts, there is no equivalent to "yes"; thus it happens that you shall never hear an Irish waiter pronounce the shibboleth "yessir" of his English *confrère*, for he invariably expresses an affirmative by some such phrase as, "I shall, sir!" "It is, sir!" Yet among some uncivilised tribes not only is there a word expressing "yes," but it assumes a different form according to the sex or age of the speaker. Thus among the Abipones of South America, as Dobrizhoffer informs us, for "yes" the men say *héé*, the women say *háá*, and the old men give a grunt. This is a refinement which we Aryans have decided, perhaps rightly, to be unnecessary; for though our "*ay!*" and "*nay!*" carry no more information now than the Sanskrit *hi* and *na* did many thousands of years ago, they are quite sufficient for all practical purposes. But the Abipones might feel as much embarrassed by the use of our sexless affirmative and negative syllables as we should do in attempting to express our meaning in the language of the Grebo tribes of West Africa, in which the use of personal pronouns is dispensed with, and gesture is employed to show whether a verb is in the first, second, or third person.

"Let your communication be Yea, yea, and Nay, nay!" It is remarkable that in many parts of the world, though very distant from each other, peculiarities of the affirmative and negative have been seized on as a device for naming different tribes or nations. Thus in Australia the tribes known as Gureang, Kamilaroi, Kogai, Wolaroi, Wailwun, Wira-theroi, take their names from the words they use for "no," *gure, kamil, ko, wol, wail*, and *wira;* while the tribe of Pikambul are called from *pika*, their word for "yes." In Brazil the Cocatapuya are literally the "no men" (from *coca*, no; *tapuya*, man); and nearer home, as is well known, the distinction arose in the middle ages between the districts of Langue-d'oc and Langue-d'oil: the former being Southern France, where the people expressed the affirmative by *oc*, that is, the Latin *hoc;* and the latter, Northern France, where they said *oïl—i.e., hoc illud*—afterwards softened to *oui.*

Gender, except as a bare and logical expression of sex, has been completely dispensed with in English speech, not without detriment to its poetic qualities; but in Anglo-Saxon even inanimate objects were classed as masculine, feminine, or neuter. The principle is obscure which ruled that *ache* and *tear* should be reckoned masculine, but *bliss* and *care* feminine; *death* and *ghost* masculine, but *thought* and *deed* feminine. We acknowledge the fitness of classing *arm* and *will* as masculine, and *heart* and *tongue* as feminine, but why should *eye* be neuter rather than *arm?* And to place *wife, child,* and *maiden* in the neuter gender was an uncomplimentary suggestion that they were to be reckoned among a man's chattels. The sole survival of this system in modern literary English is that *ship* is accounted feminine, though, oddly enough, in Anglo-Saxon it was of the neuter gender. In our language there is possibly still a trace of the refinement of primitive speech, which varied an interjection according to the sex of the speaker; for, just as among the Algonquin Indians the men express surprise by exclaiming *tiau!* and the women *nyau!* so an English butler will be apt to say *lor!* and the lady's-maid *la!*

Music and the drama apart, the highest purpose to which human speech can be applied is oratory, to regulate which the rules of rhetoric, called by Aristotle the art of persuasion, were formulated in very early times. Considering how great has been the development of the platform recently as an engine of government, and how many persons are daily engaged in the attempt to warn, exhort, excite, amuse, instruct, wheedle, or otherwise influence their hearers, a corresponding advance in the style and finish of oratory might have been looked for; but tens of thousands of exasperated listeners in all parts of the kingdom could testify to the intolerable deficiency in eloquence shown by most public speakers.

More than 2300 years have gone by since the principles of rhetoric were first laid down. In 466 B.C., the rule of Thrasybulus, despot of Syracuse, was brought to a sudden close by insurrection: his over-

throw was the signal for hundreds of people, ousted
from their possessions by him or his predecessors, and
driven into exile, to flock back to their native country.
In order to regain their property, it became necessary
for them to prove their claims before the judges, each
acting as his own counsel. Probably the result was
about as edifying as if a number of Conservative candidates, none of whom had ever spoken in public
before, were suddenly to be required to expound their
political faith before an audience. Flesh and blood
could not be expected to endure for long the infliction
of such torments, and the necessity for some recognised code of rules in forensic oratory became urgent.
One Corax came timely to the rescue, and we are
filled with admiration by the completeness of the
scheme which he produced. Modern artists, so far
from attempting to emulate or surpass, are content if
they approach the excellence of Greek sculpture:
even so we might sigh for more general knowledge
and observance of the rules of Corax on the part of
our public speakers. Though modified in a slight
degree by Isocrates and Aristotle, the arrangement
by Corax remains as valid to this day as when it was
first promulgated. The division of a discourse into
proem or exordium, narrative, arguments, and epi-
logue or peroration, satisfies our sense of order, has
never been improved on, and is as essential to modern
oratory as it was convenient to the pleaders of Syracuse. Unhappily, these masterly principles no longer
form the subject of instruction in schools, and the
consequence is a lamentable waste of two of God's
most precious gifts to man—time and speech. It is
difficult to overrate the influence over his fellows

which right instruction and practice in oratory gives to a young man, and as difficult to estimate the amount of enjoyment which these put it in his power to confer, for there are few intellectual pleasures keener than that of listening to a good speaker. Language, tone, gesture, expression—how rare is it to see these made the most of, even when the sentiments are unexceptionable! Often a speech which reads well in the morning papers has been marred in its effect upon the audience by awkward attitude—the speaker, perhaps, clinging to the Treasury-box with crouched shoulders and bent knees, as if he was afraid of sinking in deep mire—or, *summum nefas!* standing with his hands thrust in his breeches-pockets.

In the 'Souvenirs de Mme. Récamier' there is a pleasant description of a scene which took place during her exile at Lyons in 1813. Almost every cultivated or fashionable individual who passed through that city was sure to be attracted to her house. Talma, the tragedian, happened to be giving some representations in the Grand Théâtre, and was dining with Mme. Récamier, when the Bishop of Troyes (better known as Abbé of Boulogne) was announced. This celebrated preacher, though devoted to literature and familiar with the works of the great play-wrights, had never seen a play performed: after dinner, Talma was persuaded to recite, to the intense gratification of the Abbé, parts from his principal *rôles*. In return Talma begged the ecclesiastic to repeat some passages from his sermons. When he had done so—"It is splendid, monseigneur, as far as *this*," exclaimed Talma, touching the chest of the preacher, "but the lower part of your body is deplorable. Clearly you have never bestowed a thought upon your legs."

It is certainly a serious counterpoise to the privileges we enjoy under a popular form of government that so much speech-making has to be endured. By how much might the burden be lightened if speakers would consent to be rightly instructed in the art of addressing their fellows. In the course of a recent debate in the House of Commons on the subject of the system of reporting, sundry members uttered complaints that it was far from perfect, and that they had often been reported incorrectly. "But," observed Mr Labouchere in his speech, "we want a great deal more than mere accuracy: we want reporters who will put the remarks of honourable members into decent English, for there are certainly not more than half-a-dozen gentlemen in the House who can be relied on to handle nominatives and verbs with precision." There is not much exaggeration in this, but ungrammatical expression is one of the least of the evils which have to be endured. What legislators chiefly require is to be drilled out of tiresome tricks of attitude, the repetition of threadbare phrases, and tautology. The last defect is very insidious, because by repeating different words with the same meaning, the speaker gains time to reflect on his next sentence. No other excuse can be offered for the constant use by an excellent and right honourable gentleman, now occupying high rank in the House of Commons, of the expression—"How and in what manner?" a pleonasm as egregious as that so dear to journalists—"a young baby." A common form of tautology in parliamentary debates is that employed by members who begin their speech, "Mr Speaker, sir"!—a puerile inelegancy enough to mar the finest exordium.

Metaphor and simile, puissant weapons in the armoury of a skilled debater, produce disastrous effects in the hands of the inexpert. Certain figures, originally of force and freshness, cause a bleak sense of depression from the frequency of their employment by halting speakers; and one who desires to engage the understanding of an audience ought, at whatever sacrifice, to take a pledge of total abstinence from such outworn phrases as "the thin end of the wedge," "oil on the troubled waters," &c. Sometimes, it must be confessed, the audience derives unexpected and lasting enjoyment from the delightful incongruity of figurative discourse. The pages of Hansard bear, or, at least, ought to bear on record, the poetic flights of the late Sir Patrick O'Brien, who became the very darling of postprandial debate. Those who were fortunate enough to be present on the evening when he was denouncing the course taken by one of his colleagues in the representation of Ireland, will remember the rich brogue in which he referred to him as "the young sea-serpent from County Clare," and how he was promptly called to order by the Speaker for using the expression. "Very well, Mr Speaker," he rejoined, "I bow to your ruling, of course, and beg leave to withdraw the sea-serpent." Not less difficult, and even more painful, was the operation described during the session of 1891 by an honourable member, who, though representing an Irish county, is not of Irish birth. He was vehemently opposing a bill introduced by the Irish Secretary. "The right honourable gentleman," he said, "is trying

to thrust this bill down our throats behind our
backs ! ”

Aristotle, whose treatise on rhetoric remains the
most elaborate and scientific hitherto published,
showed no tolerance for the use of wrong or re-
dundant words. Excellence of diction should be, in
his judgment, the chief object of a speaker. But,
although·he held the skilful modulation of the voice
to be of high importance, he does not so much as
mention gesture or facial expression, on each of which
Cicero and Quinctilian rightly insisted as essential
to effective oratory: “ For,” said the former, “ action ·
is as it were the speech of the body, and ought therefore the more to accord with that of the soul.” Aristotle was the first to explain why compact and
systematic speech holds the attention fixed, while a
loose running style is intolerable. He gives as a reason
that listeners like to know where they are in a discourse : they weary of sentence strung to sentence
with no indication of a necessary end ; but a speech
well ordered, according to the recognised rules of
oratory, pleases because it is within prescribed limits ;
—“ for,” says the philosopher with a twinkle in his
eye, “ all men wish to descry the end.” It does not
follow from this that they desire the end to be near,
for men have listened rapt for hours to Mr Gladstone,
who, it is said, was the only Chancellor of the Exchequer
who ever thrilled the House with a Budget speech.
He was a rare master of phrase ; but even his oratory
would have failed in its spell, but for the accompany-
ing gesture and expression, by which Aristotle set so
little store. His power of investing dry and complicated financial details with absorbing interest was akin

to that of Eastern story-tellers, who, as travellers say, are able to hold their listeners enthralled, even though these may not understand a word of the language.

But in truth the British Parliament is the place of all others where the chief vices of oratory may most conveniently be studied; neither is there any hope of improvement till somebody convinces us of the lesson which Isocrates taught the Greeks, and, later, Hermagoras taught the Romans, that oratory is to be acquired, not by birth or by knack, but by special study.

It *was* a special study in this country up to, say, the end of the seventeenth century. Steele made lamentation in 1712 that Oxford and Cambridge had "grown dumb in the study of eloquence." All through the middle ages, grammar, logic, and rhetoric constituted the undergraduate's *trivium*, and we are suffering heavily by reason of its alteration. For what chance is there that a young country gentleman aspiring to enter Parliament, to whom, in discharge of our duty as good citizens, it becomes our duty to listen, shall have invented for himself that harmony—that fitting together of parts which makes speech endurable—the art essential to eloquence? Perhaps his highest feat in oratory hitherto has been to stammer out thanks for the toast of his own health at his coming of age, or to repeat to the company at an agricultural society dinner the time-honoured and unblushing paradox that " the interest of landlord and tenant are identical." It is possible that, with an eye to a political career, he has practised debate in the Oxford Union; a course which, while divesting him of one of the chief graces of youth—modesty—has failed to confer the habit of disciplined speech, and has set him fairly on the way to become one of the bores of the House; but, generally, even that slight training is neglected, and Mascarelle's axiom is acted on—*les gens de qualité savent tout sans avoir jamais appris.*

Our Parliament, then—our House of Speech—is filled with speakers who, for the most part, have never learnt their trade; and the result, from the point of view of art, is about as edifying as if the walls of Burlington House were to be hung with the works of those who had never learnt painting, or a choir for St Paul's were to be drawn at random from the crowd at Sandown races. It is true that a proportion of practised speakers do enter Parliament in the persons of barristers and solicitors; but, strange to say, it is a matter of common knowledge that it is not to these that the House listens most patiently, nor by these that it is wont to be moved from indifference. Those members who have made themselves some reputation for eloquence have succeeded because natural aptitude and steadiness of nerve have enabled them to scramble into something like a style. This, aided by a commanding figure, an agreeable countenance, or (rarest of all gifts to dwellers in the British climate) a pleasant voice, have had far more to do with the positions attained by some men than have their statesmanlike qualities. Many a mute, inglorious member, or, if not altogether mute, then inglorious, because no one can be got to listen to him, may be conscious of administrative powers which, had he been instructed in the art of eloquence, might have brought him into the first rank; but having neglected that in the days when his vocal chords were elastic, and before he had contracted evil tricks in speaking, all that is left for him now is to cultivate the Art of Sitting Down, not, as too often happens, on his own hat.

Encouragement is not wanting to induce a man to undergo the pains of instruction and practice in public speaking. No reward is so immediately, so spontaneously, so gratefully given as the popularity accorded to a successful orator. Every lofty or lively thought which comes to him is sure of its liberal meed of sympathy—witness the readiness with which a good-natured audience will show approval of sadly shallow sentiments and thin pleasantry. I was much struck with this characteristic on an occasion when I was present at a meeting of an honourable member with his constituents. There were five or six hundred people in the room, and it must be confessed that the affection they undoubtedly felt for their representative, a gallant soldier, was sorely exercised by the dreariness of his discourse. He had been speaking for twenty minutes or so: not a sparkle of wit nor even a happy expression had been suffered to relieve the monotony of his speech, and the audience sat respectfully but hopelessly mute. Presently, the speaker, in referring to the late Mr Forster, then Chief Secretary to the Lord Lieutenant of Ireland, observed " that the right honourable gentleman seemed to him to be a round man in a square hole." There was nothing particularly luminous in this remark; had it been made in the course of conversation it would have excited no attention, still less merriment. But the despairing assembly caught at the straw: the metaphor seemed to remind them that there did exist somewhere the quality of humour; like one man they fell a-laughing, and continued so for a considerable time.

If this, then, be the reception accorded to such an indifferent performer as my friend, how much greater will be the reward of any youth who, possessing the faculty of clear, consecutive thought, either lights by happy accident on the means of expressing himself vividly, or will be at the pains to learn how to do so effectively!

Cicero held that the chief secret of effective speech lay in the right choice of words, which satisfies the hearer's natural sense of what is right. But after all, more essential than order, more immediately effective than gesture, expression, or choice of language, is vivacity; and Aristotle laid great stress upon this quality. It is one that cannot be acquired; the fact that it must be inborn is precisely what enables so many Irishmen to carry themselves so well in debate. But the most conspicuous instance in recent years which occurs to memory of the touch of genius lifting the most unpromising subject out of hopeless dulness was not that of an Irishman, but an Englishman. It was a hot afternoon in July; the House of Commons had met, as usual on Wednesdays, at twelve o'clock, an hour which in itself predisposes the chamber to dolorous and dilatory discussion. Sir Edward Watkin's bill for reducing England to the insecurity of any Continental nation, by making a submarine tunnel to France, was under consideration, and, after a business-like reply from the President of the Board of Trade, the debate had degenerated into the dreary, amateurish trickle of a Wednesday sitting. About four o'clock, Lord Randolph Churchill sauntered into the House and took his seat at the corner of the bench behind the Ministers, which he used to occupy after his resignation in 1866. It seemed as if he was hardly aware what subject was under discussion; no one knew that he took any interest in it, still less did any one know to which side of the question he inclined. It was not long, however, before he rose to address the House. Members crowded in, curious to know which side he would take. They were soon enlightened. In brisk trenchant language, Lord Randolph at once declared himself an uncompromising opponent of the scheme, and proceeded to swamp with pitiless ridicule the arguments by which it had been supported. Sir Edward Watkin had endeavoured to allay the nervousness of his opponents by showing that the tunnel could be flooded on the first note of alarm by an electric apparatus under control of the War Office. None who listened to Lord Randolph that afternoon can forget the humour with which he sketched a Cabinet Council, sitting round a white button and debating — first, should the button be pressed at all; second, at what moment it should be pressed; lastly, by whom it should be pressed—by the Prime Minister, the Secretary for War, or the Commander-in-Chief. The House shook with hearty laughter; the debate had been raised by the hand of the master from the slough of dulness in which it had wallowed for hours, and the defeat of the bill was secure. The effect on the minds of men of such an incident is not transitory. They are lastingly grateful to a speaker capable of taking up a subject, dealing with it unhesitatingly and without ambiguity, and illumining his arguments with the play of wit. Half the effect of this speech lay in the apparent absence of effort. Whatever might have been the real facts, the appearance was that the ex-Minister had strolled down to look in upon the debate, had suddenly become impressed with its importance, hastily informed himself of the arguments used in his absence in support of it, and resolved on the spur of the moment to overthrow them.

The fame of a skilful retort is very enduring; but the pleasure people take in recalling it is in proportion to its good-nature. When Sheridan, in replying to a speech made by Dundas, declared that " the right honourable gentleman was indebted to his memory for his jests, and to his imagination for his facts," he achieved a consummate oratorical feat; for he infused into a delicate adjustment of ordinary vocables just that suspicion of humour which disposes men to laugh at another, and is far more damaging to an opponent's arguments than more ponderous invective.

But if the level of political oratory be low among us, not less barren is the prospect revealed by that part of the Church of England's system which constitutes every priest, irrespective of his natural gifts, a preacher, and makes preaching of equal importance to worship, or more so. There have been times, of course, in the Church's history — times of active mission work or of urgent doctrinal controversy— when much preaching has been indispensable; and, of course, in these days there is as much need as ever of moral precept and spiritual warning. But it is not difficult to estimate whether these are conveyed best by oratory in the pulpit or by personal admonition. Every one acquainted with the conduct of popular elections will agree that the candidate who is willing to undertake the irksome task of personally canvassing voters, steals a vast advantage over a rival who relies on his public speeches, however excellent these may be. We may agree with Selden's conclusion, though demurring to the justice of his sneer, when he says: "Preaching, for the most part, is the glory of the preacher, to show himself a fine man. Catechising would do much better." Paul, preaching in Troas, was carried, not by vanity, but by the magnitude and novelty of his subject, into such inordinate length, that poor Eutychus fell from the third loft, and was taken up dead. But if the apostle might have pled the novelty of the Gospel as an excuse for prolixity, that excuse no longer exists: to repeat the glad tidings over and over again, in archaic, and too often indifferent phraseology, is to weaken what ought to be a vivid impression. Granted that there remains as much to be said on the ethical grounds of religion as, in an earlier age, there was on the dogmatic, religious literature, as a channel of instruction, is a thousand-fold more abundant. Jeremy Taylor's judgment is of more weight than ever: "If I may freely declare my opinion, I think it were not amiss if the liberty of making sermons were something more restrained than it is; and that such persons only were intrusted with the liberty for whom the Church may make herself responsive."

On the other hand, comparing the average quality of sermons delivered in our churches with the price we are not ashamed to offer for them, it must be confessed the public have no right to complain. Suppose a course of six lectures is to be delivered by some competent specialist on a prescribed branch of natural science, it is not likely that less than £35 apiece would be stipulated for. If we are sincere in our profession that spiritual science is of infinitely greater importance than natural science, how comes it that we are not ashamed to remunerate our clergy, taking an average from an archbishop to a poor curate, at the rate of about £5 a sermon, without taking account of their other ministerial and pastoral duties? There is surely little room for complaint about the quality of the article so poorly paid for. We are in this matter as cynical and less business-like than the congregations of Thibet, whose priests employ mechanical means of devotion, and, at stated hours, set in motion the praying-machine, which offers the same prayer over and over again—"O Lord! the jewel in the lotus."

To require of imperfect men that each of them should preach fifty-two sermons of thirty minutes each in the course of the year has proved to be an exaction beyond what there is means efficiently to fulfil. Protestant hearers allow themselves great liberty in commenting upon the result, and grumble freely if the preacher exceeds his stipulated time; nevertheless, whatever they may permit themselves to say, some may be scandalised at the expression of this criticism in print. But it is best to be frank, and to admit that there is need and room for improvement.

Some obvious defects may easily be mentioned, and, one would think, almost as easily avoided. In the first place, the attempt so commonly made by preachers to read from a manuscript without the appearance of reading, renders impossible all the assistance derived from gesture or attitude. It would seem as if one having an important message to deliver, or desiring to convince his hearers of some vital truth, could express in intelligible words the idea or image that ought to be clearly present in his mind. The most that he required, one would say, would be a few notes of consecutive heads. If the idea is not well defined in his own thoughts, he has no business to waste people's time by trying to elucidate it. It does not follow because such preaching is called extemporary, that it is so in the strictest sense of the word— that it is uttered without preparation as careful as when every word is read aloud from manuscript. But it is termed extemporary preaching, and it is said that most of the clergy find it difficult to deliver a sermon unless it is lying on the desk before them. Well, then, let it be read without any ambiguity. Why should a man affect to be delivering a sermon — a speech — when, in fact, he is reading a lecture, and spoiling the lecture by trying to make it look like a speech? That turning of the leaves, that surreptitious gaze at the page, alternating with mechanical glances at the congregation, divest the performance of all interest or dignity, and a political or theatrical audience subjected to such treatment would very soon make their impatience known. One thing or the other—let the lecture be read, for there are few things more impressive than good reading ; or let the sermon be preached, and so give the congregation the feeling that they are listening to the preacher's genuine convictions. The middle course, which is almost universal, is always uninteresting, and sometimes disastrous. I listened not long ago to a sermon delivered in this way. The sentiments expressed were lofty, the language was adequate, and the narrative well connected; but the effect of the whole was marred by the ridiculous affectation of the preacher that he was independent of his manuscript. And then, at the close, came the disaster. The subject had been the life-work of the Saviour, and what happened would have been impossible if the clergyman had either been reading aloud or speaking the thoughts in his brain. He was doing neither: his attention was occupied in trying to recollect how he had written each sentence, the beginning of which he suffered his eye to catch, and became riveted on the form of words rather than on their meaning; hence it came to pass that he brought what ought to have been an impressive peroration to a close by the startling announcement that our Lord had spent His life "raising the devils and casting out the dead." A slip like this is indelible; it remains in the memory when all the lesson sought to be conveyed has melted into oblivion.

Another inveterate defect in preaching addressed to European listeners is the wearisome and excessive use of metaphor. Pointed illustration is useful, and always grateful to intelligent minds; but preachers would find a much readier road to the sense of Western and Northern people by discarding metaphor altogether. There are no greater transgressors in this respect than Presbyterian divines, and they repeat the same strained phrase none the less persistently because their Church discourages the use of set forms and ritual. One of these I know, who prays, Sabbath after Sabbath, for the special protection of " this loved corner of Thy vineyard." Probably not one in a hundred of his congregation have ever seen a vineyard, or have the faintest notion what it is like ; words that conveyed a distinct image to the attention of Eastern disciples, fall on listless ears when addressed to the dwellers in a rural Scottish upland; and it is clear that by using them the pastor weakens the appeal to the understanding of his people. If he chose to have resort to metaphor in alluding to his parish, he would touch his hearers much more closely by following the example of the preachers of old, who chose illustrations from everyday life, and would refer to it as the loved corner of a corn-field or a potato-garden.

Of course this fashion had its origin in the language of the inspired writings, which were addressed to Orientals accustomed to, and delighting in, florid imagery ; but to adopt this vocabulary in order to quicken the apprehension of people of a totally different mental fibre, is to dissociate religion from the incidents of everyday life, and, at the same time, to detract, by familiarity, from the force of Scriptural expression. Bible phrases, like every other form of literature, become threadbare by frequent and inappropriate application. It may be objected that faith is a thing apart, and is not to be affected by a fastidious intellect. That is too large and too grave a matter for discussion here ; but one thing at all events is clear, that sermons (and it is the manner and form of sermons that is under consideration) are professedly intended to establish faith by means of the intellect, and that they are defective in such measure as they discourage or fail to engage it. No one in this generation has spoken from a pulpit with such effect upon masses of people as the late Mr Spurgeon, and one secret of his success lay in this, that he knew how to release moral instruction from the tedious figurative language with which it has become the fashion to load it, and to convey it in practical, though often homely, speech. Euripides, it is said, did the same for dramatic poetry, and at once found the direct way to the hearts of Athenian play-goers.

But to descend from these high levels of speech, how do we employ our natural organs in everyday conversation? It is supposed that language had its origin in emotional and imitative sounds, which in course of time grew more and more articulate, till they became the exact expression of ideas allotted to them. But that association of separate sounds with definite ideas had to be assisted by gesture to a degree which we should find highly inconvenient now. Gesture still forms an important part in the intercourse of the lower races of men. "To this prominent condition of gesture," writes Mr Tylor, "as a means of expression among rude tribes, and to the development of pantomime in public show and private intercourse among such peoples as the Neapolitans of our own day, the most extreme contrast may be found in England, where, whether for good or ill, suggestive pantomime is now reduced to so small a compass in social talk, and even in public oratory." Yet a quiet bystander may derive much amusement from the amount of pantomime in a conversation, even when it is carried on by persons of our own phlegmatic nation. I was sitting opposite some English people one day at a *table-d'hôte* in the

Engadine. A lady was describing in an animated way a disturbance she had lately witnessed in a Spanish town: she finished up by telling how the troops had been called out and charged the people, "and their bayonets were quite sharp, you know," and saying this she seized a table-fork and tapped the points with her finger, as if to emphasise the sharpness. Here was a distinct trace of primitive gesture-language.

"Go up to my room and bring me a square box you will find on the dressing-table," and perhaps the speaker describes with his fingers an aërial square, indicating approximately the size of the box. It requires less effort to do this than to say, "a rectangular box about six inches by eight," and all languages show a tendency to save effort. Thus in modern English we say *bone, home, foam,* where our Anglo-Saxon progenitors said *bán, hám, fám* (as the Lowland Scots still do), because the broad vowel *o* requires less muscular effort to pronounce than the narrow *á,* so we have gradually slid into the easier sound.

An interesting illustration of the extent to which information may still be conveyed by gesture was given lately in London in the performance of " L'Enfant prodigue," by a Parisian company of *Pierrots.* Not a word was spoken from beginning to end of the piece yet the audience were able to follow every incident in an intricate drama by watching the action of the players. The piece occupied about two hours, and the interest of the spectators never flagged; but their general experience at the close was one of great fatigue, owing to the constant strain upon the attention required to follow the thread of the story. Civilised races, therefore, have more and more discarded gesture and developed language as a means of intercourse, because of the effort called for by the former from both parties to a conversation.

We have been a literary nation long enough, it might be thought, to have devised symbols for every sound that we have occasion to use. But that is not so: like the Zulus, we sound a lateral " click " with our tongue, but it is not represented in our alphabet; like them, we almost invariably sound it, from some unknown cause, on the left side of the tongue; though, unlike them, we do not let it enter into the construction of vocables. We have no symbols to represent the sound of a sigh, a kiss, a chirp, a groan, though characters expressive of these would be of great service to novelists; but on the other hand we have three distinct characters—*f*, *ff*, and *ph*—expressing exactly the same sound.

Then how imperfect and arbitrary we are in the use of those symbols which we possess: *th* is all we can do to express the initial sound of *thing* and *thine*, though a Welsh writer can show the difference by making the former an aspirated *t*, the latter an aspirated *d;* yet in this respect we are better off than the French, who cannot employ the aspirated dental at all. Englishmen are inclined to wonder why the Chinese, with all their ancient civilisation, have no symbol for the consonant *r*, and are apt to forget that, except at the beginning of a syllable, that letter has become in their own language a mute redundancy. The following sentence, for example, might be perfectly well expressed in Chinese characters: "Sour barts are more alarming than certain earls," [1] for, in colloquial English, not one of these seven *r*'s would be trilled.

When the Portuguese first explored Brazil they made great fun of the natives of that country, because they had in their alphabet no *f*, *r*, or *l;* a people, the invaders declared, without *fé*, *ley*, or *rey*—without faith, law, or king. The Mohawks, again, have no labials, and vowed it was absurd when the missionaries tried to teach them to pronounce *p* and *b;* "for who," said they, "can speak with his mouth shut?" [2]

Some nations show a deficiency more serious than merely the absence of vowel and consonant signs employed by others; they are lacking in words to express ideas inseparable from the existence of human society. It is difficult to say how it comes that the Algonquin tribe of Indians have no word for "love," seeing that they are not inferior to others in amorous understanding and practice. Other tribes, again, have no word to express the virtue of kindness or charity, which is the more remarkable, because that this virtue is of the essence of human nature is implied by our use of the terms "humane" and "humanity." The Esquimaux have no terms of affection or endearment, but on the other hand, there is not a curse in their language, nor any expression of ill-will. *Kujana !*—"it must be "—equivalent to the Moslem *kismet !*—is the ejaculation with which these gentle fatalists encounter the many calamities and hardships inseparable from their lot.

---

[1] Purists may object to the use of "bart" as an English word, but, at worst, it is only premature. The order of baronets will some day come to be known as "barts" as universally as cabriolets are now spoken of as "cabs," the motive of contraction being the same in both cases, namely, the avoidance of effort.

[2] Primitive Culture, by E. Tylor, i. 171.

Moravian missionaries have made Christians of most of them—not without special difficulty, however, arising, not from their natures, but from the poverty of their vocabulary. For, having never seen sheep or lambs, they have no words for these animals, nor for seed-time and harvest, gold and silver, so Scriptural metaphors convey no meaning to them. Readers who form their estimate of a typical French household from the perusal of French novels, may come to the conclusion that the French can get on very well without any single term equivalent to our "home"; but those practically acquainted with the people know very well that the *idea* is as present with them as it is with ourselves, and can only wonder that it has never found convenient expression in their affluent language.

The impression left on the mind by an examination of the various forms of oral communication in use by men is that all are more or less imperfect; that Athenian Greek is the nearest approach to consummate speech that has ever been devised, and that every living language is capable of improvement by cultivation. The pleasure imparted by a good, crisp, correct speaker —whether in conversation or in a public part—is so distinct, that pains should be taken to make his occurrence more frequent. In Great Britain, the effect of a moist changeable climate must always have a disastrous tendency on the tone of voice, for the vocal chords— resembling two films of india-rubber brought over the edges of a tube, so as to leave a narrow open space between their edges—can rarely preserve that resonance which gives such exquisite *timbre* to the voices of Italians or Spaniards; but at least we may avoid the

gross errors of diction which so commonly offend the
ear, even in educated society; we may check such an
ugly blunder as is almost universal in talking of "*those*
sort of *things*" instead of "that sort of thing"; and we
should at all cost overcome that mischievous shame
which makes us use common or ugly words instead of
the clear direct expressions of our native tongue.

ORNAMENT.

DE gustibus—of course, yet there is no subject which people dispute so fiercely, or on which they dogmatise more confidently, than questions of taste. Mr Hamerton, in his essay on the "Death of Friendship,"[1] dwells on the bitterness caused by difference of opinion; and, putting theology or religion first, and politics second, he assigns the third place to divergence in critical doctrines in art as a source of estrangement.

This is natural enough, considering how essential sympathy is in the enjoyment of the beautiful. No mind so finely trained, or naturally of such sensitive fibre as to be stirred by a lovely picture, a cathedral aisle, or a Grecian frieze, but straightway longs for the concert of another mind in beholding it. Such a nature is impatient of solitude in presence of grand scenery or in hearing noble music, and the man will not rest till he has shared his delight with those with whom he is accustomed to hold communion. A

[1] Human Intercourse, 105.

French writer — was it Sainte Beuve ? — pronounced conversation a sacred thing, the real communion of saints. If conversation is tarnished at its source by disagreement on matters keenly affecting sensibility, right communion cannot ensue : discussion degenerates into argument, and no sweetness can ever flow from that.

It is, if possible, less useful to argue on matters of taste than on any other subject. If your ear is so fully educated as to receive the highest pleasure from Wagner's music, you may despair of convincing your friend who is satisfied by the airs in the *Barbiere.* To put an extreme case. If your friendship has no other basis of sympathy than in music, it will cease, that is all. And Mr Ruskin may discourse with the voice of men and of angels on the eternal supremacy of Venetian Gothic over Grecian architecture, yet never move the judgment of him who has once embraced the perfection of the Parthenon. Even the echoes of that consummate strain of human accomplishment, wakened in the Italian Renaissance, and feebly reverberating through our streets and squares to this day, will ever touch some men more nearly than the full chord of the Doge's Palace or Giotto's Tower. Style is dead with us now, but we possess the galleries of the ages to wander through, and each one lingers round the beauty which touches him most closely. Many remain insensible, and therefore indifferent : so much the more reasonable for those who do care for the adornment of our land to take thought for the means employed to carry it out.

Ornament is created when the surface of structural

forms is made to receive lines of calculated symmetry, which may either simply mark it off into rhythmical proportion, enclose flat or relieved spaces, or, by arabesque, or geometrical design, or adaptation of natural forms, carry the eye agreeably over tracts which, without the aid of decoration, would give an unpleasant feeling of barrenness or austerity. Colour may be introduced, but is not essential to the purpose. Ornament is to architecture and furniture what variations are in music or an *obbligato* accompaniment to a melody. Perhaps by a juster analogy it may be said that ornament is to form what music is to sound. We perceive sound by means of atmospheric waves beating on the ear-drum, and exciting the auditory nerves. These sound-waves, when caused by the concussion or friction of two or more bodies, by the sudden liberation of electric fluid or of confined gases, are created with a rapidity not exceeding 25 to 30 in each second of time, or about 15 times as many in a minute as the wing-strokes of a flying heron; and the sensation on the ear is that of ordinary noise, such as a peal of thunder or the postman's knock. But sound caused by vibration, either of a strained string or of metal, is not only the result of infinitely more numerous waves produced in a second, but also of waves varying greatly in shape. Sound of this kind is known as tone, which is the basis of music. In Helmholtz's scale the lowest musical note is C in the contra octave $C_{,}$—$B_{,}$, produced by 33 vibrations or sound-waves per second; the highest is B in the fourth marked octave C''''——B'''', produced by 3960 vibrations or sound-waves per second. Between these two extremes, comprising seven octaves, is contained all the music of which human senses are susceptible. Difference in *timbre* or quality of tone is caused by difference in the form of the sound-waves created by different instruments.

But the perception of tone or musical notes depends upon a much more complicated and delicate structure than that which in the human ear receives the impression of ordinary sound or noise. In the deepest and most secret recess of the auditory chamber is situated the coil of the cochlea, containing an instrument of the utmost delicacy, called, after its discoverer, the fibres of Corti. These bow-shaped fibres exceed 3000 in number, arranged somewhat after the fashion of the interior of a piano; and just as the layers of rods and cones in the retina of the eye, vibrating responsively to the various coloured rays composing white light, convey to our perception the sense of colour, so these fibres of Corti, vibrating responsively to tone and its various notes, convey to our perception the sense of music. The reader most likely knows all this already, and is wondering what on earth it has got to do with the subject of this paper. Well—this much, that the faculty of perceiving beauty in ornament seems to be seated in some compartment of an organ or department of the intelligence not yet identified more precisely than that of the faculty of memory. That it is innate seems to be shown by the early preference which children exhibit for some forms over others, quite independently of association with external ideas. Most children will be found to have favourites among the characters of the alphabet, and agree in preferring H, R, and S to G, P, and T. M is esteemed more highly than N, and D than B. Something indefinable in the form of certain capitals touches their æsthetic sense more favourably than that of others. Grown persons feel the same indefinable preference for certain groups of letters over others, but there is a remarkable difference in the sensitiveness of various races to this delicate kind of beauty. The Teutonic peoples are far behind others in this respect. Most of us feel that the name "Thomas" is harsh and unmusical: in abbreviating it we accentuate its disagreeable quality by preserving the first and homelier syllable; but the Italians intuitively dwell on the second and softer half, and their endearing equivalents to our "Tom" and "Tommy" are "Masaccio" and "Masolino." Just as in some races the faculty of apprehending and producing music is more highly developed than in others, so the faculty of enjoying and creating ornament is variously manifested. But whereas scientists, who can minutely describe the physiological action of sound, are baffled in tracing perception of fitness and proportion of ornament among the known functions of any organ, that quality is usually referred to as artistic instinct.

That this connection of harmony in sound, or music, and harmony in form, or ornament, is not merely a fanciful illustration, may be proved by a simple experiment. Place a drum on or beside a piano, and sprinkle some fine sand on the parchment. Then let chords or a simple short air be played on the piano; the sand will be seen to move into symmetrical forms under the influence of the sound-waves.

Again, an interesting series of experiments has lately been conducted showing the effect of sound-waves upon sensitive films of gelatine spread upon glass. Musical tones cause the gelatine to assume elaborate and beautiful forms, varying according to the *timbre* of the instrument or voice, and showing the intimate relation of sound and form.

More recent signs are not wanting that we are on the threshold of discovery reaching into domains hitherto the exclusive possession of poets and dreamers. The forces which affect our sensation through the avenues of hearing and sight are often figuratively spoken of as if they were subject to identical laws; the interchange of terms between the arts of painting and music is habitual, but, hitherto, could not be defended on the ground of scientific accuracy. We recognise the happiness of the well-known analogy traced by a blind man between scarlet and the sound of a trumpet, because those who can both see and hear accept the aptness of comparison between the two forces which powerfully affect, one the optic, the other the auditory, nerves. But scarlet is not the exact analogue of a trumpet-blast. The sensation of colour is imparted to the brain by means of vibratory waves communicated to the all-pervading medium, ether; that of sound by similar waves communicated to the denser medium, atmosphere. If the analogy between scarlet and a trumpet-blast were a true one, each should affect the sensorium by means of vibration of a rapidity similar in proportion to that caused by other colours and tones. But that is not so. The pitch of a tone increases with the number of vibrations in a given time; the tone of a trumpet is high, because it causes relatively rapid sound-waves. But the vibrations caused by a ray of red light are few compared with those caused by other rays, for the vibrations arising from the red end of the spectrum amount only to about 456 billions in a second, whereas those from the violet end amount to about 667 billions. So the blind man was only vaguely successful in comparing a lively sound with a vivid colour.

The agency of colour and sound-sensation has, of course, been explained long ago; but it is only within the last few years that the researches of Professor Balmer have established a veritable analogy between the laws governing light and sound. In order to understand his method, it is necessary to bear in mind the difference between mere noise and a tone or musical note. Noise is simple; tone is compound. When a tone is sounded, its harmonics also become audible—that is, corresponding tones are called into being by the creation of the fundamental tone. When C is struck on a piano a trained ear perceives in the note the C an octave higher. The relation of harmonics is perfectly well understood; and, taking C as the fundamental tone, the first seven harmonics may be thus expressed in notes :—

Thus the known harmonics of any given note may be listened for with certainty by the musician.

Professor Balmer has applied an analogous system to the investigation of the spectral lines yielded by incandescent matter, and has found "that the exact number of vibrations which produce each of these lines increases in the same succession as the number of vibrations in sound harmonics: the growth of the numbers can be expressed by a simple formula, analogous to that used for sound." Incandescent hydrogen yields to the spectroscope a spectrum of four bright lines in the visible solar spectrum—that is, within the span of decomposed light forming the colours of the rainbow. Besides these four Mr Huggins has discovered ten more, beyond the violet end of the spectrum, and these fourteen lines, composing the known spectrum of hydrogen, were arranged by Professor Balmer to correspond with the harmonics of a note of music. This enabled him to search further, and by means of his scale he has been successful in identifying five additional lines placed exactly where the application of his formula caused him to look for them; so that the spectrum of hydrogen, originally defined as consisting of four bright lines, is now recognised as yielding no fewer than nineteen.

It is evident then that, inasmuch as ornament depends for its effect on forms and colours so disposed as to reflect rays which shall reach the eye in harmonious succession or coincidence, we have to deal with a subject as susceptible of, and dependent on, rules based on innate properties as we have in music. The eye is an organ of a sensitiveness not less exquisite than that of the ear. But the ear — even the untrained ear — is intolerant of discord. How comes it, then, that men can endure vicious ornament with more indifference than they do discordant music? Not only so, but they are willing to pay heavily for ornament, ignorant of its merit, regardless of the limits within which it contributes to the beauty of the objects to which it is applied, or of how far repetition is endurable. Mere indifference to ornament would be intelligible; deliberately to refrain from or prohibit it might, under conceivable circumstances, be meritorious or prudent; there would, at all events, be consistency in either course. But what gives the matter importance is that, will we or nil we, ornament is forced upon us: it is the subject of enormous public and private expenditure; in addition to which Parliament annually votes a vast sum of money to the instruction of those who are to produce it. Hence the subject is one surely worthy of some consideration.

It so happens that these thoughts are being committed to paper during a railway journey, and as this sentence is being penned (or—with stricter accuracy—pencilled), the train draws up at a wayside station in Scotland. Near at hand is a villa of considerable size approaching completion. The design is pleasing and suitable to the climate; the material is admirable stone, and no doubt the workmanship is excellent; for it is a common mistake to suppose that medieval masons were better handicraftsmen than are to be found now. If the architect be competent and the specifications liberal, no fear but our masons will do their part worthily. But this unfinished villa yields an instance of misapplied and therefore vulgar decoration. There is no detail more characteristic of Scottish architecture of the sixteenth and seventeenth centuries than the "crowstep"—a simple device whereby the long slopes of a high narrow gable are broken into a stepped outline. It is thoroughly effective, and changes what would be a forbidding feature into a pleasing one. But in this modern adaptation of a venerable style, the architect has applied crowsteps to the gables of all the dormer-windows, showing a complete misapprehension of the intelligent purpose of the earlier builders, which was to relieve a long inclined line, without irritating repetition in dormer gables, which are themselves a relief to monotony of roof, and are seldom or never so treated in old examples.

But misapplication of material in ornament is as common as that of design; and an instance is at hand in the first-class compartment of the carriage in which I am travelling. It is the property of the Midland Railway Company, and is as luxuriously appointed as one is accustomed to expect when travelling on their system. Blue cloth cushions contrast agreeably with fittings of bird's-eye maple: there are no tiresome advertisements of soap that you don't want, or cocoa that you don't like, or cherry - brandy that you are better without; only convenient notices of the company's hotels along the route, and other information which it concerns the traveller to know. Nevertheless there are two little details, not apparently of much moment, yet bearing on the question of the right application of ornament. The number of the carriage is painted in gilt numerals on the mahogany lining of the door, and the ceiling of pretty white wood is picked out with gilt beading, amounting, according to a rough and rapid calculation, to some 122 lineal feet. Now the numerals would be just as legible if painted in white or colours; and 122 feet of gilt moulding at, say, 2d. a foot, cost 20s. 4d. The number of the carriage is 214. Supposing the company has no more than 214 carriages with two first-class compartments in each (a calculation far short of the real amount), that is, twice 214 = 428 times 20s. 4d. = £435, 2s. 8d. spent on gilt beading. An appreciable sum, even out of the resources of a great company, but unworthy of comment, were it not part of a system which is debauching and deadening the public taste. The ceiling would be better without these gilt lines, of which the most obvious effect is to attach an air of sham to the honest brass fittings below. Not a single additional passenger is attracted to these carriages by means of the gilding, which is part of a silly and needless fashion, rendering the eye insensible to the perception of beauty.

Gold—not yellow, but the hue of the precious metal—yields the most satisfying colour-sensation of which the human retina is capable. It behoves the designer to employ it most sparingly, save where an effect of utmost splendour is aimed at. Unhappily, many people with no right to splendour desire to be splendid; everybody, seeing that society has become impatient of sumptuary laws, has a legal right to be as gorgeous as he can. Every hackney-driver on his cab, every publican on his premises, every publisher on the miserable cloth covers of his Christmas books, may vie with his neighbour and rival in the cheap and lavish use of what is the ideal of costliness and rarity, in the fictitious display of what used to be the emblem of truth—pure gold.

The evil resulting from this is twofold. Gold has

alike ceased to be used by the designer, or regarded by the beholder with any reverence; for, taking excessive advantage of that property which makes it possible to spread it in infinitesimally thin layers, it is used to impart merit to faulty design and spurious value to cheap material. It is not a single jackdaw, but every contemptible or obscene bird that flaunts itself in peacock's plumes. Gold is flared on our aching orbs from every direction, till we lose perception of its quality, thereby sacrificing the most exquisite of chromatic perceptions. Like the people of old Tyre, we "heap up silver as the dust, and fine gold as the mire of the streets."

Ormolu (the gods be praised!) has passed temporarily out of vogue: do not our hearts grow heavy at the remembrance of wedding presents in the style of five-and-twenty years ago; and what guarantee have we against a return to the barbarous custom of loading harmless bridal couples with candlesticks in ormolu, paper-knives in ormolu, *étuis*, writing-cases, clocks, photograph-frames in ormolu? None, it is to be feared, in the taste of the public; the only hope lies in the forbearance of manufacturers. Two monuments of supremely imbecile conception survive to this day amid the wreck of those gifts which served to accentuate a marriage in which (alas! how many years ago) it was my privilege to bear one of the two leading parts. They seem ugly enough now to have been caskets of envy, hatred, malice, and all uncharitableness; yet they were then of the latest and most ingenious design, and formed the outward and visible signs of hearty goodwill and affection. One of them represents a rustic gate, which will not stand upright as any satisfactory gate ought to do, but reclines at an angle, supported from behind by an ormolu prop. You open it, and behold — a photograph. Why a photograph? Why not, just as appropriately, penny stamps, luggage-labels, or diachylon plaster? Had the designer been required to explain the fitness and merit of his conception, seeing that there is no innate beauty in an ill-made and decrepit gate, he could but have pointed out how cunningly it had been plated with gold.

The other ornament consists of a group formed of three Lilliputian croquet-mallets, supporting a Brobdingnagian ball, which, on being opened, displays an ink-pot. Again, it has been sought to exalt the amazing puerility of this design by electro-plating. Not less successfully might you pour champagne of the finest growth over the throats of African savages, in order to improve their manners. The chances are that after the draught their savagery would force itself on your cultured susceptibility with aggravated intensity.

And yet—O Pallas Athene! and yet—O fellow-creatures of the Etruscan goldsmiths and of Benvenuto Cellini! at the time these articles were constructed there had been, in this land of ours, during more than the span of a generation—for upwards of thirty years —schools of design supported by grants of public money. Nor is there yet much sign of improvement, though now the sum annually voted exceeds £500,000 a-year.

Why is it that, after ages of culture, and with easy access to thousands of examples of the subtle handicraft and brain-work of earlier peoples, we can only produce in one generation objects that earn derision in the next. Long before the Christian era Etruscan jewellers devised a cunning method of granulating the surface of gold. Modern craftsmen recognised the value of it as enhancing the quality of gold ornaments, but were hopelessly baffled in attempts to imitate it. But the secret still lingered among the gold workers of the Abruzzi, from whom, not many years ago, Signor Castellani succeeded in extracting it, and the mystery was solved. And how has it been applied? In the exact and servile imitation of objects designed thousands of years ago, the beauty of which our workmen fail to rival and rightly despair of excelling.

We gaze, not unmoved, as we affirm, on Michel Angelo's monuments of the Medici in the Sagrestia Nuova of S. Lorenzo at Florence: what demon then drove us to smear with tawdry gilding the statue of the good prince whom all the nation wished to honour? If Englishmen, as they aver, are capable of being conscious of the dark enigma propounded by the bowed head and shadowed face of that Duke of Urbino, how can they tolerate the bedizened effigy of Albert in Hyde Park? Let none of us hereafter be caught smiling at the Mikado of Japan, who, in his fervour for Western institutions, caused the metal plaques of empty sardine-tins to be collected and affixed as ornaments to the shakos of his bodyguard.

In no decorative craft is the use of gilding more scrupulously restricted than in heraldry; unhappily, none has come more fully under the doom—*corruptio optimi pessima.* Governed by rules of extraordinary rigidity, its emblems formed a system of chivalrous

hieroglyph, charged, even for unlettered understand-
ings, with historical and ethnical information. Confusion has fallen upon its code; few eyes can now
trace its hidden meaning; the precision of its phraseology is jeered at as tiresome jargon, and suspicion
attaches to the most illustrious scutcheons, because of
the impunity with which they may be filched by
ignoble persons. Still that might be condoned from
an æsthetic point of view, but worse has come to pass.
The masterly abstractions of living forms devised by
the early heraldic painters have suffered from a diffused
smattering of zoology, and they have been corrupted
by a clumsy naturalism into badly drawn lions, stags,
and eagles—spiritless caricatures of menagerie specimens. To increase the realism, shading has been introduced, whereby the pure gem-like tinctures and
firmly limned outlines, characteristic of heraldic drawing, have been smirched and blurred. Sir Walter
Scott had not a faultless taste in decoration—far from
it; witness the plaster-casts of carvings in Melrose
Abbey, which, painted in imitation of oak, serve as
cornices to the rooms in Abbotsford: but how justly
incensed he would have been at the ornament which a
witless binder has been allowed to stamp on the covers
of the latest edition of the ' Waverley Novels ' (*curâ*
Mr Andrew Lang)! A podgy lion, with nerveless,
pusillanimous tail, jigs it on a golden field. *This* the
Scottish lion which erewhile kept the English leopards
at bay? Why, it would not give the least enterprising
field-mouse one moment's apprehension. And where
is the double tressure counter-flowered—crowning
grace of the national shield?—the tressure which to
have the privilege to bear was counted a meet reward

for the most precious service to king and country. Oh for one hour of

"Sir David Lindesay of the Mount,
Lord Lion King-at-Arms,"

so he might read this varlet a lesson on the reverence due to knightly things!

But, lavish and indiscriminate as is the use of gilding among us, there is still room for thankfulness, inasmuch as its use has not yet been sanctioned in dress. Smart ladies of the Roman decadence aped the hetairæ of the East in gilding their breasts, but modern nymphs find their swains so susceptible that they have not found it necessary to have recourse to this allurement. False jewellery, also, is forbidden among people with any pretension to culture; moreover, perverse and backward as our standard in decorative costume may be, we have, so far, refrained from applying gilding to our Sunday hats, and "golden slippers" constitute a poetic ideal reserved for a different state of society.

There is another class of objects in which ornament has been the subject of admirable restraint. Gilding is never used now in the decoration of private carriages. It is difficult to assign any reason for this, for it was otherwise of old, as is testified by the archaic ornamentation of royal and other carriages of State; but so it is, that however gaudily a lady's drawing-room may be fitted, and however offensive to right taste may be every detail of her house, from the bedroom wall-papers to the dining-room chandelier, her brougham will be a model of rich sobriety. The coach-painter's art is no debased one; he relies on deep, pure tones, relieved by prescribed lines of lighter hue, and

half an hour may be vêry pleasurably spent in studying the panels of carriages in the Park.

The tradition of the craft has been taken up by
railway companies; the departures from it noted above
are exceptional to their general custom. With the
introduction of American cars a less chaste style has
been brought in; but these are rather rolling houses
than carriages, and the use of inlaid wood and bright
metal fittings is not inappropriate. It is interesting
to note the association with the old road coaches maintained in the distinctive colours still in use on the
main lines of railway. The London and North-Western
Company paint their panels claret and white, the
Great Western chocolate and white; the Midland has
inherited lake, the London and South-Western apricot;
while the Great Northern, probably from motives of
economy, have broken with tradition, discarded paint
altogether, and rely on plain varnish.

Is gilding, then, to be absolutely prohibited by strict
canons of taste? Is it never permitted to indulge the
eye with the feeling of gold, except in objects made of
the solid metal? Are we not to rest satisfied till Mr
Ruskin's aspiration is literally carried into effect, that
all shall be gold that glitters, or, rather, that nothing
shall glitter that is not gold? By no means. Have
you a casket of jewels or a cabinet of papers more
precious than the mass? then let the key thereof
be distinguished from common keys by gilding. Let
gold flash from the gates of your palaces, from the
domes of your temples. Let the delicate tooling on
bookbindings of costly leather be as veins of living
gold; it shall survive into a better day when cloth bind-

ings shall have gone to that limbo which is their only just destiny. To lavish gold in order to make common things conspicuous is like the shedding of gentle blood in a tavern brawl; but it is right art to display the precious metal in the form its peculiar properties enable the workman to give it—in leaf or dust.

It is especially adapted for use on picture-frames, both on account of optical effect and because a good picture is something precious and rare. It is no exceptional thing for a painted canvas to be sold for far more than its weight in guineas. But we have become so familiar with the application of gold to picture-frames as to have overlooked certain changes in their character brought about of recent years—changes which are not for the better. So soon as a picture leaves the easel and is placed on a wall, some device becomes necessary to separate it from the surroundings or from neighbouring pictures. Perhaps none is so effective as that of fitting it into a panel or other defined wall-space; but this, of course, is only possible when the wall is fashioned for the picture or the picture specially painted for its position on the wall, neither of which conditions it is usually convenient to provide in domestic architecture. So the canvas is generally fitted into a wooden frame, to be suspended from the cornice. But the natural tints of wood are not vivid enough to isolate the enclosed space from confusion with drapery or wall-surface: nor will it do to paint it a strong tint which would clash with or react on the artist's colouring. It was very early discovered that a gold surface, though its hue is yellow, owing to its peculiar lustre, does not possess in a perceptible degree the blue or violet reaction of yellow. The most delicate tints may be laid close beside it: the only effect is to enhance their proper quality. Moreover, gold clashes with no colour: it is distinct from any pigment employed in painting, and *ought to be* distinct from anything employed in the decoration of a wall on which paintings are hung. Alas that it should be necessary to comment on the execrable practice of introducing streaks and splashes of gilding into the design of wall-papers![1]

Therefore the use of gilding on picture-frames is intelligent and commendable. But the design of the frame should be kept scrupulously within its proper function. A frame may be heavy; the picture within will be so much the more completely severed from external interference. It may be carved, but only with the intention of letting the light penetrate interstices, and so be less obtrusive than if reflected from a flat metallic surface. But the design of the frame must have no significance of its own to compete with that which it encloses. The moment the beholder remarks on the beauty of a frame, rely upon it, something is out of place.

This principle was deliberately set at nought by the modern Pre-Raphaelites. Holman Hunt, the late D. G. Rossetti, and others, thought out their frames as carefully as they did the subjects represented inside them. In his picture of the "Finding in the Temple," Mr Hunt introduced an edging of ivory between the gilding and the canvas, although it is well known that oil-painting suffers in effect from a white margin.

---

[1] This is written with due remembrance of Mr Alma Tadema's gold room; but the difference between his deliberate scheme and the house-decorator's aim at display is perfectly apparent.

His object was to convey the impression that the whole exhibit, canvas and frame together, was something of extraordinary merit and preciousness; but the means were unworthy of such an accomplished painter, for it is by the picture, not by the frame, that an artist's work shall be esteemed.

The fashion set by this school of painters may be traced in the self-conscious arrogance of certain frames displayed in the Royal Academy Exhibition each year. Wrong, wrong, wrong! and the Council would do well to consider whether it is their object to encourage the exhibition of paintings or upholstery, and, if both, whether they had not better assign separate rooms for the purpose. The excuse is offered that certain pictures are of a decorative character and intention. Then their proper place is not in a frame but on a wall or ceiling. They ought not to be suffered in any but the simplest temporary frames for convenience of exhibition.

One of these artists, the late Mr D. G. Rossetti, who was also an author, must be held responsible for setting the unsound example of expending time and thought in designing covers for his own books: not *binding*, mark you! but covers of common cloth; not designs to be wrought on enduring leather by patient skill of cunning craftsmen, but to be mechanically stamped with a pattern, which, however meritorious in original conception, must infallibly become wearisome when repeated by the thousand and dishonoured by union with cheap and perishable material. If the shepherds hold so loosely to right principles, what wonder if the flock go astray!

On the whole, considering the present condition of

architectural decoration, the man possessed of sensitive taste is rather to be condoled with than envied. Our lot is cast in an intellectual atmosphere the very reverse of that described by Mr Symonds as pervading Italy during the fifteenth and sixteenth centuries. In that age, "from the Pope in St Peter's chair to the clerks in a Florentine, counting-house, every Italian was a judge of art. . . . During that period of prodigious activity the entire nation seemed to be endowed with an instinct for the beautiful, and with the capacity of producing it in every conceivable form."[1] In our age and in our nation the demand for ornament is as ceaseless, the supply as profuse, as it was during the full tide of the Renaissance ; but discretion in its application, genius in design, and understanding of its spirit, seem to be asleep or dead.

To few manufacturers has indifference to the art of building lent such an impetus as to that of wall-papers. Like a parasitic growth, they have spread through our houses, increasing in luxuriousness with the increase of decay, obliterating every other form of mural decoration, and substituting cheap cleanliness for sagacious adaptation and delineation of structure. Wall-papers were little used in Europe before the eighteenth century, though they had been long before that applied to house decoration by the Chinese. Those that were first manufactured in the West were adaptations of design from Italian brocades, and at first they were used in an unobjectionable manner, just as hangings of the costlier material were employed—namely, to fill spaces between obvious structural lines—and, so applied, no objection could be made to their use

[1] Renaissance in Italy : The Fine Arts.

On the contrary, the invention brought it within the means of almost every householder to fill blank wall-spaces with agreeable tracery and harmonious colour. But the cornice, frieze, and dado remained intact: coigns were protected with moulding or plaster-work, and the inmate might feel that he was living in a built room and not in a bandbox. But gradually the wall features disappeared ; paper crept over everything except window and door openings, even into the very angles of the walls, and it is nothing uncommon now on entering a saloon of considerable pretension and proportions to find the walls closely covered with paper from floor to ceiling, save a narrow skirting-board to protect the plaster from the housemaid's broom and a cornice reduced to a meagre moulding. Credit has been claimed on behalf of our house-decorators for the greater refinement recently achieved in the designs of wall-papers. It is not so much the design that has been at fault as the use of wall-papers. Keep these in their proper place, and the design is of less moment than the colour. The fact is, too much importance attached to design is calculated to tempt the designer to prove how clever he is and how much he knows of the orders of art. There is an insuffer-able degree of self - consciousness in most of the art papers produced, and people have to be reminded that wall *space* is not the thing to be emphasised by orna-ment, but wall *structure*. With most of these am-bitious wall-papers a paper dado and paper frieze is supplied. Can anything be more puerile ? What sense is there in pasting a block-printed paper frieze round a room already furnished with a frieze of its own ? Yet this is no uncommon arrangement.

Taste is nothing if not fastidious; but the fickleness of fancy, brought about by absence or ignorance of principle in ornament, is a wholly different and lower influence. There is nothing in art more remarkable than the steadfastness with which sound style was adhered to throughout the vast period of Egyptian civilisation. The method of that wonderful people in producing mural decoration is shown by some unfinished designs discovered in the ruins of Thebes. The space intended to receive ornament was marked off with red chalk into small squares. Then with a brush the artist limned the outlines of his design, preserving a just proportion between the surface to be sunk and that to be in relief. Afterwards the plain surface was chiselled away, leaving the ornamental figures countersunk, the utmost effect being obtained by the least possible amount of relief. The figures were afterwards brilliantly coloured, and sometimes the ground also received a coat of paint. Consistent reserve forbade that temptation to realism which ever besets the workman with perfect command over his tools and material. In the figures employed individuality is kept sternly subordinate to masterly unity of effect.

This method of design endured with little change for nearly five thousand years. Compare with steadfastness such as that the feebleness of purpose in our modern school of design. For the nonce, we are impatient of the objects which gratified the sense of ornament in the early years of the present reign. We get rid, at almost any cost, of the heavy mahogany sideboards, the chairs with gouty legs, and the polished rosewood tables, bequeathed by our fathers. None of our native styles will serve except Old English, Queen Anne, or Chippendale; and with foreign styles we are easily satisfied about workmanship provided the design is Louis XIV. or XV. But who shall say that, in a dozen years hence, people will not be as eager to "pick up" examples of early Victorian work as they are now to exhume articles long since relegated to the housekeeper's room or the servants' hall? There is an example of this unaccountable caprice in the reaction lately manifested in favour of cut glass. Very few years ago nothing would please but glass blown to the utmost thinness, either plain or engraved with ornamental designs. But now we have returned to the heavy faceted decanters and goblets which we were brought up to despise. Which is the stricter taste? Undoubtedly that which we have just discarded; for the special quality of glass, which can be rivalled in no other material, is its transparency and capacity for being blown into exceeding lightness. When cut into facets, the former quality is impaired; the latter is not displayed, and the object depends for beauty on its brilliancy, in which it competes at a disadvantage with rock-crystal. The virtue of an art consists not less in bringing out the highest quality of material than in revealing the mind of the artist.

The same consistency of purpose which characterised Egyptian decorative art distinguished the work of Grecian designers. If the frieze of the Parthenon be carefully examined, it will be found how resolutely the figures of men and horses are kept subject to the dominant motive of ornament. It is not merely a collection of statues or a sculptured narrative. That the sculptor had the power of realism, who can doubt in the presence of masterpieces of Greek statuary? But he possessed the higher power of subordinating parts to the whole,—that power which, it has been suggested above, is the result of a faculty, as yet undefined, corresponding to the faculty of music. The frieze was instinctively recognised by Greek architects as the proper place for ornament; the name it bore with them—ζωοφόρος, *zophorus*, the subject of life—marked it out as the field for display of living pageantry; artistic instinct forbade that it should be so used irrespectively of the general architectural effect. So in that perfect symphony of form, the Parthenon frieze, though each limb and fold of drapery is true, everything is made to serve the general harmony, like chords in processional music. One who has devoted much attention to the study of Greek art lately remarked on the relation maintained in this masterpiece of mural sculpture between the relieved figures and the ground-space: each piece of relief is balanced by an empty space of the same extent, though, of course, different in shape, so that could the *relievo* be compared with the *basso* in the whole design, they would be found to correspond in extent.

There is something pathetic in the pains we take to be ornamental. We spare no expense—we lavish ornament in a degree that no race, except the Moors, have exceeded, and yet it won't come right. The principal public building erected in England during this century is in a style exclusively the property of the southern half of this island. Westminster Palace, constructed in the Tudor style, a form of debased Gothic, which is the only contribution ever made by English architects to the art of design, is covered—

every foot of it—with mural ornament. Imagine it to be in ruins; imagine a party of antiquaries excavating it two thousand years hence, and compare their reward with that which crowns the labours of exploration in the ruins of Thebes, of Athens, of Rome. How wearisome it would be to exhume tens of thousands of stone panels, all carved to exactly the same pattern; hundreds of yards of black-letter inscription of pious and loyal ejaculation, repeated with the persistence of Moslem texts on the porticos of the Alhambra.

Yet there is room for hope. The first step towards amendment is to know that one is wrong. Mr Ruskin has prevailed by his insistence on the paramount necessity of truth to make people dislike graining in imitation of marble or wood, a mode of surface decoration almost universal when he published the 'Seven Lamps of Architecture,' and peculiarly vicious because of the suspicion it entails on genuine material. It is satisfactory that it is hardly to be seen now in better-class buildings, plain painting or staining having been generally substituted. A little more patience—a little more perseverance—on the part of teachers and critics, and other corrupt tastes may disappear. The most hopeful sign is that it is rather deadness than corruption of taste that has to be combated. There is no reason to despair of a high national school of design by reason that we are of Teutonic race. Nations from time to time awake to artistic perception and performance; and, after a while, die to it. The gift of ornament may be latent among us, as it was among the Latin race till, in the thirteenth century, it was born to mighty life in Niccola Pisano.

Besides, there is a strong current of Celtic blood in

our veins, and no race ever excelled the early achievement of that race in exquisite workmanship and intellectual quality of decoration. It was all the more
remarkable because, in this country at least, it took
precedence among them of architecture, generally the
first of the arts to rise from the level of barbarism.
Ornament has died among the Celts as it has died
among the Greeks and the Italians; is it incompatible
with the ruling passions of this age—science and
commerce ?

Though the Teutonic genius has never yet excelled
in ornament, which, with some notable exceptions, has
generally received from the hands of workmen of Ger-
manic race a harsh, uncouth, or jejune character, yet
the Northern people could build in a masterly fashion
unknown to medieval Italy. Not until Bramante and
Michel Angelo designed, and Vignola and Palladio
studied, among the ruins of Roman splendour, and
stirred the dry bones of the dismembered empire, was
there anything to compare in grandeur with the
cathedrals of Germany, France, and England. The
decoration of Salisbury Cathedral pales into triviality,
it is true, before the splendours of Siena and Orvieto;
but the structures of these Italian examples are almost
contemptible compared with the splendid unity of the
English architect's achievement. Lofty gables were
reared, not to sustain the flattened roof, which lay far
below and quite independent of them, but to form
frontispieces for the display of precious material and
intricate design, as in the churches of Crema and
Orvieto. The fabric of the building served but as
scaffolding for the display of gorgeous ornament,
which, in Northern Gothic, was only suffered to ripple

round capitals and cluster sparingly on the western façade. Even now we can build. It is true that Westminster Palace has none of the reposeful grace of Somerset House or Greenwich Hospital, but it is a master-work of its particular style; and after evil and overdone ornamentation have combined with a wretched site to impair the effect to the utmost, there remains with it that merit which Italian builders neither strove for nor obtained — the majesty of unity.

To one European race only has it ever been given to unite the gifts of noble building and perfect ornament. Were it not for Greek art and the monuments it has bequeathed, it had been held impossible to excel at once in structure and decoration. But who shall say, with that example before him, that the like shall never be again? Stupidity and ignorance are more easily overcome than vicious habits. The vigour of Italian Renaissance was owing to the fostering policy of the rulers of the people, which led the rivulets of wakening art, feeble at the source, into channels conducting them to the full-flowing river of national art. The London County Council has, in domestic affairs, functions almost identical with the Italian Republics. In power it is scarcely inferior to the Commonwealth of Florence; in funds it vastly exceeds it. Its members have decreed a spirited policy in public works; may they raise up another Arnolfo del Cambio for their architect. Then may be witnessed again that which came to pass in the fruitful season of Italian Hellenism—while the artist spread his colour on the wet plaster, the goldsmith fingered his wax model, or the sculptor struck his clay into forms of immortal beauty, the reflex action of the brain gave birth to sonnet and ode; for Orcagna and Giotto, Lionardo and Michel Angelo were all accomplished poets, as if the artist spirit in them would not suffer such beautiful material as their native speech to go to waste.

'Tis a pretty dream, though one that may perchance disturb the slumbers of ratepayers. When the Florentines determined to complete the bronze gates of their Baptistery, they invited the sculptors of Italy to submit competitive designs. The umpires awarded the prize to Lorenzo di Cino Ghiberti, who was 49 years accomplishing the work, and received for it during that time 30,798 golden florins—a formidable figure if rendered in the modern equivalent of currency, and somewhat dwarfing the salary of £700 a-year which, it is said, the County Council has fixed on as adequate remuneration for their chief architect and master of the works!

BORES.

ONE of Montaigne's chief charms as an essayist consists in the levity with which he handles serious subjects, and the gravity he applies to light ones. But Montaigne wrote for a limited circle of friends; it would clearly be to set at defiance all the ordinary rules of prudence were one to ape his manner and discourse lightly before the general public about that of which we all move in dread. One may speak frivolously of the influenza, for it comes and goes according to inscrutable physical conditions, not likely to be affected by any irresponsible observations; or of the crack of doom, about which nothing is known, and everybody cherishes the hope that it is a long way off. But Bores are of us and in our midst; do we not stand in peril of them every hour? Nay, who shall say that he is free from the risk of himself developing some of their most terrible attributes? It is meet, then, in submitting to analysis the subject which gives this paper its title, to apply to it only such dispassionate and penetrating consideration as is due to a weighty matter.

Bores, then, pervade every habitable, or at least every civilised, part of the globe; penetrate every layer of society; threaten the integrity of every system of human intercourse. Though intensely gregarious, they abhor each other's company, and cling to association with their natural prey—ordinary men and women. It is believed, therefore, that the Bore might be extinguished, either by isolation or by forced association with his own kind, for he cannot exist, even through a single winter like the bear, by sucking his own paws; but neither experiment has yet been tried, for he is equipped with unerring instinct, whereby he is ever able to elude the most crafty devices for his destruction.

Among all the men of violence who have figured on this world's stage, none has openly avowed the purpose of carrying war against the Bores. Ezzolino da Romano, Vicar of Ferdinand II. in Northern Italy, exceeded all other tyrants, and Alexander III. all other popes, in the sickening cruelty with which each pursued his purpose—the secular ruffian aiming at selfish aggrandisement, the ecclesiastic animated by avarice, lust, and narrow nepotism; but neither they nor any of their competitors in the obscene calendar of crime have ever been suspected of the virtuous purpose of exterminating Bores.

Yet in casting about for some palliation or intelligible motive for the monstrous offences against humanity perpetrated by the medieval rulers of Church and State in Italy, it may be possible to detect, in reading between the lines of edicts condemning men

and women to unspeakable tortures, some purpose,
sedulously veiled, not unworthy of our sympathy. It
may be that the family of princes whom Ezzolino
walled up in their country-house in Lombardy and
left to perish of famine may have been of the generation of Bores, for—publish it not in the streets of
Askelon—the blood of that race *has* been known to
run in royal veins. It is even more plausible to con-
ceive that when Paulus II. threw certain members
of the Roman Academy — Platonists — into prison
and tortured them to death upon the rack, he was
impelled to do so, not by blind jealousy of erudition, but because he was goaded to distraction by
their interminable talk, and was ridding society of
creatures who were making life a grievous burden.
If this were so, then, seeing that these despotic and,
in other respects, fearless rulers were fain to conceal
their real purpose, and, rather than incur the vengeance of a terrible race, accept the infamy of the
sordid and vicious motives usually attributed to them,
so much the more reason for a humble critic, clinging to his peaceful obscurity, to frame no phrase
which, by its apparent levity, may bring him into
closer relations with the powerful family which is the
subject of his observations. To treat this subject with
less than its proper gravity might involve him in
trammels from which he probably would never escape.
He would afford an excuse for every Bore within speaking or writing range to concentrate attention upon him,
in order to prove how incompetent he was to deal with
one of the most important phenomena of civilisation.

For the Bore has no place in primitive stages of
society. What times men go with their lives in their

hands, and it is matter of concern how each day's dinner is to be come by, they are disposed to welcome any companion from whom violence need not be apprehended. Job endured his friends through many long chapters before he ventured to hint he could stand them no longer. It is so difficult to be "not at home" when living in a tent; in fact, Achilles is the only person of any note who seems to have managed it effectively. The Athenians gave evidence of pre-cocious culture, when, bored by interminable praise of Aristides, they sent him to Coventry, and brought the lectures of Socrates to a close by a timely dose of hemlock. But those were extreme and isolated cases; in our own country there were few signs of coming evil till wealth began to abound and foreign campaigns took the place of civil war, with result of much re-dundant leisure. It was probably in the reign of Queen Anne that Englishmen first became conscious of the presence of Bores. Pope sounded the first note of alarm in the 'Dunciad':—

> "Still her old empire to restore she tries,
> For, born a goddess, Dulness never dies."

The British essayists of the eighteenth century have suffered not at all from want of posthumous appreci-ation: it may be whispered, indeed, that their pro-ductions are not of a uniform degree of effulgence, and that, remarkable as that school of literature undoubt-edly is, it owes much of its renown to having marked a new departure in our country, in the wake of nations earlier in culture and freer in fancy. To be perfectly candid, Addison, Johnson, even dear old disreputable lively Steele, wrote a great deal of unmitigated twaddle, wholly unworthy of the immortality for which it has been embalmed. Nevertheless one is often refreshed, in voyaging through the mellow print of last century, by papers written for that day but bearing upon all times, poignantly expressed and full of the clear spirit of philosophy. Of such are Swift's 'Hints towards an Essay on Conversation.' Swift does not often lead his readers on lofty levels: most of his work is tainted with mordant cynicism or rank with gratuitous grossness, less palatable than open immorality; but there is fruitful thought garnered in this short essay, and one enjoys it as much as the experienced gourmet who, discouraged by the monotony of a dry, sinewy fowl, picks out those sapid morsels in the loins, aptly named *les-sots-les-laissent*. No mature person can peruse these hints without gaining a clearer view of the machinery of human intercourse and the impediments to its easy working. Perhaps one closes the book sighing, "Ah! had I but seen all this when I was younger, how many blunders I might have avoided!"

Swift does not weary his readers with abstruse doctrines or complicated propositions: what he has on his mind is expressed in plain, temperate sentences, and it is no more than might have been uttered by any one of us. But it is all so true, so direct, so far-reaching, that it ought to be printed as an appendix to the rules of every club in London. He tells us that he was moved to write his thoughts on conversation "by mere indignation to reflect that so useful and innocent a pleasure, so fitted for every period and condition of life, and so much in all men's power, should be so neglected and abused."

He goes on to analyse some of the ways in which people succeed in wearying each other in conversation. So far his task is a simple one. Any one has but to reflect on his own experience and put it in plain words in order to show up his fellow-men as clearly as Swift has done. When the new Law Courts were about to be opened the judges assembled in conclave to prepare an address to the Sovereign. The draft submitted to them began with the words, " Conscious as we are of our own infirmities." The question arose whether this was not just a trifle too abject; upon which Sir Charles Bowen asked, " Would it not be more true to say, Conscious as we are of the infirmities of others ? " It is not recorded that the suggestion was adopted; yet how right it was! Motes in the eyes of others are so plainly visible that every one is impatient for their removal. It is so easy to recognise how good a thing is articulate speech; how flexible, how subtle, how obedient it *ought* to be — how cramped, muffled, ambiguous, it usually is. All this, and much more, we are in as good a position as Swift was to observe and deplore; but smaller men than he would be apt to make the unintelligent mistake of imagining that matters were better *dans le temps.* He knew men better than that: he knew that the defects of one age are the defects of all. How often and how unfavourably we compare the vapid, listless chatter of the club smoking-room—its stale scandal and nerveless comment upon passing events—with the limpid stream that played through Wills' Coffee-house! It is useful to listen to Swift's description of it whereby he ruthlessly dispels the golden atmosphere with which our fancy invests that chosen resort of the wits :—

The worst conversation I ever remember to have heard in my life was that at Wills' Coffee-house, where the wits (as they were called) used formerly to assemble—that is to say, five or six men who had writ plays or had share in a miscellany came thither and entertained one another with their trifling composures, in so important an air as if they had been the noblest efforts of human nature, or that the fate of kingdoms depended on them.

Here indeed is unwelcome disillusion, and were this, and other passages like it, all, one might throw the book aside and comfort oneself with the thought that some day, perhaps, our own little coteries, albeit dingy and tepid enough in the present, may acquire in virtue of distance a respectable warmth and lustre of their own. But what distinguishes this essay above all those of its period is that its author has struck out in a single bright, sharply cut sentence a profile of the malignant principle at the root of the evil. Through a score of pages he dwells on the nature of the disease; in a short paragraph he lays bare its source and prescribes the sure remedy. Here it is:—

Of such mighty importance every man is to himself, and ready to think he is so to others, without once making the easy and obvious reflection that *his affairs can have no more weight with other men than theirs can have with him,* and how little that is he is sensible enough.

There is here none of Swift's disagreeable cynicism. He has infused this sentence with the concentrated spirit of altruism, laboriously distilled by successive moralists,—the very essence of that social science elaborated by Lord Chesterfield in whole volumes of anxious letters. It is clear that it would be impossible for any human being to become a Bore who should sink his own personality and refrain from calling on other people to listen to the details of his own affairs —loves, quarrels, money, health, or what not. There is nothing in this, you understand, at variance with the late Dr Jowett's indulgent saying that he believed Bores were generally good men. Very likely they are; and their only fault is that, instead of encouraging other people to lead out their hobbies, they have not the tact to keep their own locked up in the stable. Are you vain, selfish, gluttonous, amorous, avaricious? Have the goodness not to talk about it, and you shall find us quite pleased to be in your company. Are you brave, handsome, rich, successful, learned? For heaven's sake, let us find out all that for ourselves, or you will infallibly be avoided as a Bore. For it is the sad case that, although truth is, perhaps, the greatest, as it certainly is the most valuable and lovable of virtues, its possession is no safeguard against becoming a Bore. On the contrary, some of the most incorrigible Bores that can be named are in conduct conspicuously straightforward, and no one hesitates to accept their word. It is only when affectation and insincerity are so extreme as to meet their opposite—truthfulness— that they tend to shape a weak character into a Bore.

Consider Mrs Gann's two lodgers in the proem to the 'Adventures of Philip.' One of them, Andrea Fitch, the artist, was a terrible little Bore, yet his affectation was so complete that it turned the corner and became practical sincerity, for it deceived nobody except himself.

He was always putting himself into attitudes: he never spoke the truth, and was so entirely affected and absurd as to be quite honest at last; for it is my belief that the man did not know truth from falsehood any longer; and when he was alone, when he was in company—nay, when he was unconscious and sound asleep, snoring in bed—was one complete lump of affectation.

Andrea never injured a human being; on the contrary, as the story shows, his tender affection prevailed to deliver the object of it in the hour of her direst need. But can anybody doubt he was a Bore?

George Brandon, on the other hand—utterly selfish, dishonest, sensual, spendthrift — was a remarkably agreeable fellow, took an excellent part in conversation, and wrote captivating letters, but for superfluous classical quotations. He held as good an opinion of himself as his poor, silly fellow-lodger did of himself; he was continually scheming for his own advantage, which the other was not, yet no one dreamt of calling Brandon a Bore. Why? Because he had the tact—call it cunning if you will—to lead people to talk about their own affairs rather than to listen to his.

Here follows an instance of harmless insincerity employed to impart agreeable feelings to another. A gentleman of accomplishment in one of the learned professions met an equally distinguished authoress in the house of a friend. They had a pleasant talk, and the lady rose to leave first. Holding the door open for her, the gentleman said in leave - taking, "Now, Mrs ——, we won't let you go till you tell us when we are to have another book. How long are you going to make us wait?" Down-stairs went the authoress in the pleasant glow of being appreciated, for no one is so great as to be invulnerable to delicate flattery. But see the perfidy of the man! Carefully closing the door, he returned to his hostess and said, "I am so pleased to have met Mrs ——, but pray tell me the name of one of her books, for I have never read a line she has written."

Nothing could be less sincere, yet every one should be grateful to one who so adroitly oiled the cogs of intercourse. He sacrificed his own hand to that of the other, and won the game.

The hypothesis that the British Bore, as we know him, first manifested himself in the reign of Queen Anne is supported by the fact that the people of that age had no convenient designation for the genus. Neither Pope nor Swift, though both writhed under the infliction, found a convenient term to apply to it. The former was evidently groping for a word when he coined the Dunciad, but a numskull is very far from fulfilling all the attributes of a Bore. A Bore is very often a numskull, but duncehood does not necessarily imply the active properties of a Bore.

The first appearance of this pregnant monosyllable in literature occurs in the letters of Lord Carlisle and of Selwyn; but there it is used to express, not a creature, but a state or condition induced by tedium. Thus in 1767 Lord Carlisle writes: "I enclose you a packet of letters which, if they are French, the Lord deliver you from the bore!" Thereafter it became common as a verb in the correspondence of the eighteenth century,—expressive, apparently, of the intolerable anguish inflicted on their fellows by a class of men and women for whom, as yet, no generic term had been devised; and in that employment it has been admirably explained of late in the New

English Dictionary as "to weary by tedious conversation, or simply by the failure to be interesting."

But the nineteenth century had not long dawned before the want became too pressing not to be supplied, and writers began to apply the word "bore" to the agent—"the tiresome or uncongenial person: one who wearies or worries." They did so timidly at first, with due caveat of inverted commas; but the term took on; it filled a blank that had been felt for a hundred years, and it had come into such common use by the twenties that Byron declared

> "Society is now one polished horde
>   Formed of two mighty tribes—the Bores and Bored."

Disraeli rashly attempted a definition in 'Vivian Grey':—

The true bore is that man who thinks the world is only interested in one subject, because he himself can only comprehend one.

How imperfect is this limitation must be plain to any one who has devoted any attention to the subject. For one of the most justly dreaded varieties of the species is the jocular Bore—so fearful in his manifestations as to drive persons to such hazardous means of escape as are resorted to only in moments of extreme terror.

Now the jocular Bore is not necessarily a professional wag: that is a comparatively harmless creature. Any one may, indeed, suffer grievously in a single encounter with one of this sort, but it is his own fault if he does so a second time; for to be an avowed wag, except for hire, implies such a low degree of intellect as to make it easy for one of ordinary capacity to baffle him. No : the really formidable foe is the man who, having distinguished himself by attainments in science, politics, or art, merits attention on their account, but, by some inscrutable action of the bi-lobed brain, is impelled to buttonhole his victim while he tells a facetious story or recites a rancid epigram. More than one example of this lamentable combination will occur to the minds of my readers. We would willingly hear from such a one something about the new doctrine of the polar origin of life, the bearing of *Amphioxus* and *Aplysia* on the problem of evolution, the liquefaction of oxygen, the latest combination of political parties, or criticism on the pictures of the year,—anything he could spare from his vast storehouse of knowledge would be a welcome addition to our own little hoard; but our unkind fate is to listen and try to laugh when we are most disposed to shed tears of vexation. It is not possible, of course, to compile statistics of the motives actuating the people who are run over and killed each year in Piccadilly, for a man's latest thoughts perish with him; but there is good ground for believing that such accidents are chiefly owing to two causes—drink, and precipitate flight on the approach of a Bore of the kind above described.

Disraeli's definition must therefore be rejected, for the jocular Bore is often highly accomplished, and most entertaining when he can be brought to talk on his own subjects. It may be thought utopian, but there is really something plausible in the idea that this kind of Bore may be, if not stamped out, at all events considerably reduced in numbers by a rational appeal to themselves. They possess an intelligent side in a degree far above their fellows; let them reflect that the world is growing old and is not so easily tickled as of yore. The tales of Poggio, so richly appreciated in the fifteenth century, raise never a smile in the nineteenth, though their impropriety still stands their author in some stead. Let the jocular Bore, therefore, before he begins one of his stories, calmly put to himself the question, "Should I—A—derive pleasure from listening to this from the mouth of B?" Infallibly the answer, to be honest, must be an emphatic No. Whereupon A, unless he is a fool, will spare his listeners, and by so much redeem himself from the category of Bores.

But, in fact, Disraeli's synthesis of a Bore is imperfect in more than one respect. Infinitely more hurtful than the man of one idea is he who is ready, through want of definite occupation, to dabble with any subject under the sun, to ask questions without the faintest purpose of putting the answers to any practical use, and to skip from one topic to another, as if in equal dread of letting his victim escape, and of being himself condemned to a few minutes' silence. Steele struck far nearer the mark, long before Bores were scientifically classified, when he described idleness as the fountain of this kind of torment; and for every fellow who could afford to be idle in Steele's day there are hundreds in that condition now. He began No. 43 of the 'Spectator' with these wise words :—

There are Crowds of Men whose great Misfortune it is that they were not bound to Mechanic Arts or Trades, it being absolutely necessary for them to be led by some continual Task or Employment. Those are such as we commonly call dull Fellows: Persons who, for want of something to do, out of a certain Vacancy of Thought, rather than curiosity, are ever meddling with things for which they are unfit. . . . You may observe the Turn of their Minds tends only to Novelty, and not Satisfaction in anything. It would be Disappointment to them to come to Certainty in anything, for that would gravel them and put an end to their Enquiries, which dull Fellows do not make for Information, but for Exercise.

It would be difficult, even after nearly two centuries of later experience, to put in so few sentences a clearer description of a Bore. Is it not just such a one against whom you must be prepared when dining at your club, after a long day's work? You have ensconced yourself at a snug little table alone, and have read two or three pages of a lively article—say in that vigorous evergreen 'Blackwood's Magazine'— when the fatal "Hullo!" sounds in the air above you. That is the invariable battle-cry of the Bore, betokening his presence as surely as the warning hiss does the rattlesnake, and exasperating from its mingled tone of surprise and jocularity. You do not appreciate being greeted as a startling phenomenon, nor are you conscious of anything in your appearance to suggest facetious ideas. It is on the tip of your tongue to say, "My name is *not* Hullo, sir, but Binks," but that would only make matters worse.

"Hullo! Binks," your tormentor goes on, "who'd have thought of seeing *you* here! I say, have you heard the latest about Tom Hargrove and the little widow, eh?"

You give a hypocritical nod, raise your eyebrows, and shrug your shoulders significantly, cherishing a feeble hope that these symptoms of intelligence will give the wretch to understand that you are well posted in all the details of this bit of scandal. May heaven forgive you! you know little, and care less, about Tom Hargrove; are equally uninformed and indifferent about his relations with widows, little or big; and you are pining to return to your magazine. Meanwhile the club Bore, with legs astride, bending over you, supported by his hands planted on your table, is sweeping the horizon of the diningroom with keen eye, to see if there is any victim more meet for sacrifice than yourself. There happens to be no ram caught in the thicket, so he concentrates himself upon you.

"That was a nice show-up about the bracelet—eh?" he proceeds. "It was, indeed," you reply, with a sickly smile, for you feel how your frail defence will shortly crumble away under concentrated fire.

"You heard the true story about it, of course?" he persists. A lie trembles on your lip: if ever a lie were pardonable it were now, to avert impending calamity. But *will* it avert it? Even if you succeed in simulating thorough familiarity with all the ins and outs—the first, second, and all the succeeding editions of the story of Tom Hargrove and the widow —the Bore will produce another tale from his fardel, and, after piling lie upon lie, your ultimate fate is inevitable: you will be condemned to a lingering captivity. The foe marks your hesitation, and, masterspirit that he is, seizes his opportunity. "Waiter," he cries, pointing to a vacant table next to yours, "bring my dinner beside Mr Binks."

Quid multa? Why dwell on the harrowing details

of your surrender and sack? You shut your book with a suppressed sigh, and assume a fraudulent air of conviviality towards the ruthless conqueror. It is vain to cherish schemes of retaliation. France may nurse her fury by dreams of recapturing Alsace and Lorraine; Irishmen, at least some of them, may put up with the injustice of being less heavily taxed than Englishmen, because they believe that the day is at hand when they will have a Government of their own to lay greater burdens upon them. But for you there is no sweet prospect of revenge, for 'the club Bore is invulnerable in triple brass. You can only sigh for the scheme set forth in the 'Spectator,' under which your tyrant might have been tied to some handicraft —if unhealthy, so much the greater gain—and so have been denied the loitering and leisure in which Bores are generated.

Like the rest of the dangerous classes, Bores divide themselves into two groups—positive and negative— and the club Bore clearly belongs to the former. It is far the more formidable, just as the ruffian who batters his wife's head and puts his baby in the water-butt is a beast more to be feared than he who merely neglects to support his family; but precautions have to be taken against both kinds.

The definition, however, of negative Bores implies more subtle analysis than suffices for the positive sort. Human judgment, distorted by suffering, is not always to be relied on in this matter. Oliver Wendell Holmes is not only too sweeping in the assertion he puts into the mouth of the Autocrat of the Breakfast-Table, that "all men are bores except when you want them," but he overlooks therein the radical objectivity

of the Bore. There are times, of course, with all of
us when we would fain be apart, when we prefer to
dispense with the society of almost every one else.
Again, there are times when we desire intercourse
with one or more chosen ones, and the presence of
others is distinctly superfluous. The lover, for instance, will say in his haste that all men are Bores
who spoil a *tête-à-tête*. A man's mood or circumstances, in short, may be such that the unwelcome
presence of any other individual may be a subjective Bore to him, quite independently of the inherent
objective qualities of that individual, whom to class as
a Bore would be manifestly unphilosophic, and probably unjust.

It would be wrong to imagine, because the people
of the eighteenth century failed to coin a word to express the Bore, that therefore he was not well known
to them. The race existed in considerable numbers
and of prodigious dimensions. Dr Johnson was redeemed only by his love of occasional and prolonged
seclusion from figuring in this category ; indeed his
passion for argument, of all forms of conversation the
most wearisome, makes it almost impossible to exclude
him from the list. Loud, rude, and impatient, if people
got the better of him in dispute he insulted them ; if
he overcame them he turned them into ridicule. No
one was better able to pronounce judgment on a man's
social qualities than Horace Walpole.

The more [he says] one hears of Johnson, the more pre-
posterous assemblage he appears of strong common-sense,
of the lowest bigotry and prejudices, of pride, brutality,
fretfulness, and vanity.

What reconciled ordinary people to being in company with a man of so many forbidding attributes was the prospect of amusement in seeing others ground to powder. Sometimes the punishment was no more than just, as when a pert young fellow asked Johnson, " What would you give, old gentleman, to be as young and sprightly as I am ? " " Why, sir," was the thunderous reply, " I would almost be content to be as foolish." But at other times he would turn and rend inoffensive bystanders. This was to be something more than a Bore : it was dangerous, and wearied out his best friends — those of them at least who, like Mrs Thrale, had any independence of character. One can only wonder that they endured him so long, partly out of pity for his physical infirmity and poverty, and partly, no doubt, because the man cannot have been destitute of charm who could write as follows :—

To let friendship die away by negligence certainly is not wise : it is voluntarily to throw away one of the greatest comforts of this weary pilgrimage, of which, when it is, as it must be, taken finally away, he that travels on alone will wonder how his esteem can be so little.[1]

But if Johnson, in virtue of his work and forceful mind, be acquitted, what can be said to prevent his chronicler Boswell being deemed the very worst of Bores ? Restless, garrulous, flippant, inquisitive, drunken, he has written his character so large in his own hand, that Walpole's evidence is almost super-

---

[1] Were there nothing else recorded of Dr Johnson than what he did on waking one morning to find himself speechless and crippled by a stroke of paralysis, there were enough to command reverence for a mind which sometimes shone obscurely through a clumsy mortal envelope. Supremely anxious lest the calamity which he felt had visited

fluous. Yet Walpole has, with infinitely dexterous touch, given such a vivid picture of an incident in his house in Arlington Street that it is hard to refrain from quotation :—

Boswell, that quintessence of busybodies, called on me last week, and was let in, which he should not have been could I have foreseen it. After tapping many topics, to which I made as dry answers as an unbribed oracle, he vented his errand: "Had I seen Dr Johnson's 'Lives of the Poets'?" I said, slightly, "No, not yet"; and so overlaid his whole impertinence.

There is nothing wanting here to the letter-writer's art. Slightly as it is sketched, many pages of manuscript could have added nothing to our comprehension of the scene. We can see the pale, dark-eyed, frail Horace receive with icy courtesy the rubicund, fussy tattler, parry innumerable questions, assent to the patter of commonplace, and betray impatience by no more than the nervous fingering of an ivory paperknife on the table beside him.

It avails not to multiply instances of distinction

his body should also have impaired his intellect, he tested it by putting the silent prayer that sprang to his lips into Latin verse :—

> " Summe Pater ! quodcunque tuum de corpore numen
> Hoc statuat, precibus Christus adesse velit.
> Ingenio parcas, nec sit mihi culpa rogasse,
> Quá solum potero parte placere tibi."

Of which the spirit may be thus rendered :—

> " Great Sire ! by whatsoe'er decree
>   Has come the blow Thy servant bears,
> Although his lips must silent be,
>   May Christ lend audience to his prayers.
> Yet spare his intellect, O Lord !
>   Nor deem it pride that prompts the vow,
> For by that part Thou art adored,
>   And shalt be evermore as now."

attained in this walk. Jemmie Boswell may be taken as the typical, the standard Bore, by comparison with whom every other may be tested. For just as early in the history of human culture the Ionian school produced men of a range and scope of intellect that has never since been surpassed, so, almost before English society was conscious of the danger to which it was exposed, Boswell blazed upon it—precocious, invulnerable, complete in all the attributes of the Bore—the father of the modern race.

Yet Boswell himself would be incomplete as a type of the kind if he did not furnish an example of the right use of Bores. These fulfil functions in the social scheme, just as other objectionable animals play a part in the plan of Nature, not less useful because those who suffer from their attacks fail to discern it. What Pepys did for the seventeenth century, Boswell accomplished for the eighteenth, and it is for us in the nineteenth to enjoy the pictures which none but inveterate Bores could have painted.

So much—perhaps overmuch—on the historical part of the subject: now for what concerns us more nearly—the present distribution and armament of the race, and the condition of our defences against them.

Negative Bores are, strangely enough, to be most surely found in literary circles. It might have been expected that this form of culture would prove the most certain to purge a man of self-consciousness. The ocean of literature is so vast and so profound, it reaches towards such a distant horizon, that he whose business it is to contribute to it must surely be penetrated with the sense of his own insignificance. It is not so, as daily experience must prove, and it may

easily be seen that the smaller the bucket to be discharged, the weightier the writer's sense of his own
importance. No man was ever freer from self-assertion
than Sir Walter Scott, though he laid broader foundations for it than most moderns. See how shrewdly
he touched, how gently he condoned, the foible of a
smaller *confrère*, in a letter to Lady Abercorn :—

I am not surprised that Tom Campbell disappointed
your expectations in society. To a mind peculiarly irritable, and galled, I fear, by the consciousness of narrow
circumstances, there is added a want of acquaintance with
the usual intercourse of the world, which, like many other
things, can only be acquired at an early period of life.
Besides, I have always remarked that literary people think
themselves obliged to take somewhat of a constrained and
affected turn in conversation, seeming to consider themselves as less a part of the company than something which
the rest were come to see and wonder at.

This is a good illustration of the negative Bore—the
person to whom society is anxious to show consideration proportioned to his attainments, yet who is exacting and suspicious lest he receive less than he believes
his due. Nothing, it is feared, can be done to this
sort in the present; prayer and fasting on the part of
others avail nothing, and it is of his nature that the
culprit cannot be got to pray and fast for his own
shortcomings, though very likely he sits permanently
in sackcloth and ashes on account of the perverse
generation with whom his lot is cast. Nevertheless,
something may be done to protect and purify generations yet unborn, and it is clearly a disinterested part
to exert our understanding for them. Children should
be trained from tender years in that cardinal maxim

of whist which has been embodied in the execrable
rhyme,—

> " Regard your hand as to your partner's joined,
>   And play, not one alone, but both combined."

The bad whist-player who cannot be got to understand that he has to play, not thirteen, but twenty-six
cards, is the exact counterpart of the individual whose
thoughts cannot detach themselves from the colouring
of his own pursuits or circumstances. Ariosto Petrarch
Villon Jones has achieved some success in verse; his
satchel of sonnets, neatly printed on rough paper with
preposterously ragged edges, furnished with a title-
page of archaic design and a frontispiece representing
the Lothely Ladye in her most abandoned mood, has
touched the rare distinction of a third edition. The
flowing tide is with him; he is one of the lions of the
hour, and no one could complain though he should
mildly roar.   But, however conscious of, and, as it
may be hoped, grateful he may be for the attention
paid to him, it is distinctly a blunder when Mr A.
P. V. Jones thinks it safe or in good taste to neglect
all the ordinary means of sweetening intercourse with
his fellow-creatures.   Sonnets are, after all, pretty
well caviare to the general, and caviare, too, of a kind
with which the market is at present rather over- than
under-stocked : it is on ordinary men and women
whom we must all, even if we are gifted poets, rely
as travelling companions, and if they come to look
upon the gifted poet as a Bore he will be apt to find
his earthly sojourn become a trifle solitary. People
may continue to buy his books, but they won't put
up with Mr A. P. V. Jones at any price—least of all

at his own. The poet's stock-in-trade is his imagination; it is strange how often defects in that faculty prevent him from seeing into the minds of other people—of playing his own hand to suit theirs. The poet's boast is his culture, but true culture would have taught him to reckon with the souls of others as clearly as with his own. It is imperfect imagination and culture which give Mr A. P. V. Jones and his sort that dissatisfied, peevish mien which, although hostesses are pleased to receive them at their entertainments, makes men prefer to keep out of their path—makes them Bores, in short. Minds of the first order are quick with all-embracing sympathy, but those of inferior ranks are too likely to be tainted with self-consciousness. He who has either touched fame or preserved his obscurity may hold popular applause at its right value; but it often intoxicates one who has attained no more than distinction, and deprives him of common-sense.

There is no more common manifestation of the Bore than the way some people talk of their bodily ailments. Everybody with a disorder must be painfully conscious of it—there need be no doubt about that. An ordinary cold in the head is probably the uppermost idea in the mind of him afflicted by it, just as the exquisite rhythm of his own sonnets is ever the ruling reflection in that of Mr A. P. V. Jones. All the more pressing is the duty of marshalling one's ideas before offering them to the notice of an acquaintance. A sensitive person will do so instinctively—from delicacy of perception; a sensible one consciously—from a rational desire to please. Both will be influenced by a thought which might be put thus into words: " Of what *possible* greater concern can my catarrh be to So-and-so than the million and odd other catarrhs now being endured by the people of these islands?" Unhappily there are many persons neither sensitive nor sensible, and these be the very people out of which Bores are fashioned: there is nothing commoner than to meet people anxious to dwell at great length on all the phases of their disorders. Let us suppose an imaginary lady, who, not very many years ago, was of the sort a man might well be content to take a very long journey and endure much inconvenience to have the privilege of seeing. Her eyes were tender and deeply, darkly, beautifully blue; her complexion a divine amalgam of ivory and rose; her laughter low and soft; her talk that mixture of sentiment and persiflage which sways more minds than all the prosings of the schools. Time has laid its finger gently on this lady's charms—her cheeks are not hollow, her eyes not faded, the accents are the same; but the aches and pains which visit her fair frame have become the staple of her confidence; one wearies in listening to moans about the obstinacy of ailments and the futility of treatment: not to meet her would the long journey now be taken, but rather to escape the chance of taking her to dinner. She has, in short, become a perfect Bore.

It is rather odd that this infirmity should have escaped Molière's keen perception when he penned the amusing comedy - ballet "Les Fâcheux." His country was a full century in advance of ours in experience of the good and evil of civilisation; he not only anticipated us by two centuries in devising the term *fâcheux* to express what we mean by a Bore,[1] but he has collected into one short piece a very comprehensive assortment of different kinds. Some of the types are immortal—Alcidor, for instance, who bustles into the playhouse and, fixing on Eraste, who is only putting off the time before a rendezvous with Orphise, talks louder than the actors and explains the plot in advance.

> "'Tu n'as pas vu ceci, Marquis? Ah, Dieu me damne!
> Je le trouve assez drôle, et je ne suis pas âne :
> Je sais par quelles lois un ouvrage est parfait,
> Et Corneille me vient lire tout ce qu'il fait.'
> Là-dessus de la pièce il m'a fait un sommaire,
> Scène à scène averti de ce qui s'alloit faire,
> Et jusques à des vers qu'il en savoit par cœur
> Il me les récitoit tout haut avant l'acteur."

Lisandre, perpetually singing and tripping his last new *coranto*, is one of Disraeli's ideal Bores—the man of one subject; Alcippe we know, with his interminable explanation of disputed card-play; Caritides the pedant, and Dorant the hunting Bore—all these are good enough. But Molière fails in scientific analysis in the same way that Oliver Holmes failed in his comprehensive definition. Alcandre, who interferes with Eraste's *tête-à-tête* by asking him to carry a challenge, is unfairly classed among the *fâcheux*,—he is at most only an instance of a subjective and temporary Bore; and as for the valet, La Montagne, he is no more of

---

[1] How much the want of a convenient term was felt in English may be seen in a translation of Cardinal Richelieu's 'L'Art de plaire dans la Conversation,' published in London in 1722. The French and English versions are printed side by side, and on p. 95 the sentence, "Quoi! vous pouvez excuser ces fâcheux," &c., is translated, "You can then excuse these Troublesomes," &c.

a Bore than Sam Weller, and not half as much so as the sententious Sancho. The philosophy is delightful with which he soothes his master, ruffled by an encounter with the odious Alcidor:—

"Le ciel veut qu'ici bas chacun ait ses fâcheux,
   Et les hommes seroient sans cela trop heureux."

There is another mischance incident to human life which, though it be necessary to allude to it sometimes, is much more commonly dwelt upon by sufferers than there is any need for. It is usually called poverty, but really consists in no more than the necessity of denying oneself certain pleasant but superfluous luxuries. It would, of course, be a very fine world if every one were able to keep two pairs of carriage-horses and a good cook; but it is a great mistake for any one to suppose that, so long as he can keep a roof over his head and a coat on his back, it is a matter of the slightest interest to anybody else— anybody, that is, whose regard is worth retaining— whether his income be £500 a - year, or £5000, or £50,000. It is just as ill-advised to make the smallness of your means a topic of conversation as the affluence of them. This is specially the case in this country, where we are sadly deficient in the graces of expression. It is necessary of course, sometimes, though not half so often as is supposed, to mention one's inability to incur such and such expense. You happen to speak anxiously in the presence of a friend about your wife's health.

"My dear fellow," he says earnestly, "you ought to take that in time. Chests are not to be trifled with, especially in these days of influenza. Take her away at once, and, if you will follow my advice, let it be to take a villa there for the winter, and you'll never repent it."

"Oh, it's all very well for *you* to give advice," you reply with a mien of virtuous austerity, "but *I* can't afford it, you know. Why, look here, my rents are down five-and-twenty or thirty per cent (that comes off free income, mind), I have three boys at school, and then there's the governess at home," &c., &c. If your friend is well - bred and sympathetic you will very likely be tempted to enter at some length upon your misfortunes, but none the less will he be bored with you. This is essentially a moment to

> " Give thy thoughts no tongue,
> Nor any unproportioned thought his act."

It sounds heartless to say so, but men are impatient with poor acquaintances, not because of their narrow fortune, nor because they apprehend appeals to their liberality, but simply because the story is ungracefully told. Plenty of people are poor and yet not Bores, because they can bear and even talk of their poverty without wearying others, just as there are sweet old men with whom to be is a delight as great as the burden of being with others. It is the way the mantle is carried, not its texture or trimming, that makes the wearer look knightly or beggarly. The truth is, we English - speaking people have not the gift to trick out harsh truth in lightsome phrase. They possess that art in Naples. Children of the sun and sea-breeze, needy and mendacious more than the populace of most towns, they can tell the truth about their narrow means more poetically than any others.

There are no milk-carts in Naples, the cows and goats are driven in each day from the country and milked at the house-doors of customers. It often happens that a poor housewife has not the needful coppers to pay for the day's supply; *Passa la vacca!*—let the cow pass on—is then the word; and *passa la vacca* has become a well-understood metaphor among all classes for "I can't afford it." Such a phrase has a reflex effect upon him who utters it; he is snapping his fingers at untoward circumstance; there is a lordly nonchalance in his tone as different as can be from the beggar's whine. Yet when begging is his occasion none understands it better than the Neapolitan.

Verbal expression—spoken intercourse between a man and his fellows—is sure to degenerate without watchful culture. The English tongue, though inferior in harmony to some Continental languages, is pliant and melodious enough to bring minds into very intimate communion; but it must not be carelessly used, and it will not stand pranks being played with it. There are some people who think it engaging, or once thought it so, and have contracted a horrible habit to mispronounce words. You know by experience the vocables which they are accustomed to torture, and you wince at what is coming. Such people may be expected to talk of "mutting" for "mutton," "homblibus" for "omnibus," and so on. You are certain that when they leave you they will say "addoo" for *adieu,* or *eau reservoir* for *au revoir.* It is a very contagious trick, this kind of linguistic grimace, and it is just as offensive to warp words, which are indeed holy things, as if one should be perpetually screwing up the nose or putting out the tongue. Condillac knew how easily the edge of speech is blunted, and declared, in seeming paradox, that by studying to speak accurately one acquired the habit of thinking rightly.

Well, we have passed in review a few who have taken service in the great army of Bores; we have sorted them roughly into combatant and non-combatant ranks, noting the various uniforms by which they may be identified, and, taking account in an unprofessional way of their armament, have come to the somewhat Hibernian conclusion that the best way to encounter them is to keep out of their way altogether. It is certain you cannot meet them on equal terms: you may be as intrepid and agile as Lobengula's crack impis; the assegais of your wit may be of perfect edge and temper; but you have no armour that will protect you from the merciless fire of their Maxim guns. Study to keep out of range. "How can I do that, Mr Philosopher?" complains one; "my *wife* is the greatest Bore I know."

"Is she indeed, sir? Then you have no one but yourself to blame. It is your own fault."

"Oh, but I assure you that is not so. When I married her, twenty years ago, she was the sweetest and brightest girl in the country, and so sympathetic."

"Precisely, sir! she sympathised with all your projects, listened to all your long stories, gave up all her own little schemes; and how did you requite her? You were rude to some of her old friends because they did not happen to suit you; you sulked because she said long walks round the home-farm tired her; and music being her ruling passion, you told her you would not have those greasy, long-haired fiddler fellows in your house any more. Morning callers are not, as a class, a very lively lot, yet day after day you left her to receive them, while you went off to your club, or your House of Commons, or your match at Lord's. Poor thing, she played her hand to yours as long as the cards held out, but you would not respond: it is not her fault if the rubber ends in failure. What united strength you might have shown if you had bestowed a thought upon the suits in which she was strong, and been at half the pains to draw them out which she was at to support you! It is *you* that have made her a Bore, by neglecting or repressing every independent idea she possessed. Bores are made, not born; and if a man finds his wife a Bore, rely upon it she is one of his own creation."

There remains one other variety of Bore to be alluded to, and it is one that peculiarly abounds in, if indeed it be not the product of, the present day. This is the earnest-eyed, intense being whose normal mood is to ordinary human nature what Mr Burne-Jones's dingy-lipped, jointless maidens are to the glorious women whom the Venetian painters loved to limn. It exists of both sexes, and may be known by its talk, though capable of sustained spells of studied silence. This talk is at once confident and plaintive, reproachful and consciously meek, enigmatic and surpassingly simple. On the whole, it wears a mournful, inquiring, rather languid air; it is intended to give the impression that the talker is always in quest of the hidden meaning of everyday aspects—a kind of mental pin-hunting; but when least expected it wakes up and pours forth its soul with astonishing earnestness on such subjects as affinity, thought-reading, art (of the post-præ-Raphaelite school), and poetry (of the fleshly school). It is not easily moved to laughter, except by what it sees ludicrous in the Christian religion, and then it is not laughter of a nice sort—not such as it does one good to hear among young people. For, strange to say, this class of Bores consists as yet mainly of people comparatively young. You shall find them in the best houses—at least in houses where the cookery is of the best; for, loftily as these superior beings stand towards material pleasures, there is a notable vein of sensuousness through them all.

This is, of all others, the most irredeemable kind of Bore. How can one put up with a creature that is continually posing as one of a select school, who never for a single instant forgets that he has a part to play, or lets you forget how immeasurably you are his inferior? What! the world is old, but is it to learn not to laugh? Is any human being helped through his troubles by others refusing to be frankly grateful for what beauty is around them and what mirth may be had? Are these yearning, discontented souls to sit like spectres at our board, shaming us out of the belief that it is good to be young, strong, healthy, happy, and hungry; calling on us to believe that wisdom and dainty pleasure died with the invention of return-tickets; and that all that can be saved is reserved to a handful of sad-eyed, sallow-cheeked disciples of Schopenhauer? No: our course is clear. Rather than suffer this posed handful of modern Bores to interrupt one ray the blessed sun may shed across our path, we will accept and glory in the damaging title of Philistine: we will even run the risk of some prophet arising to revile us as "Dead-Sea apes."

THE CONDUCT OF FRIENDSHIP.

'TIS an intrepid hand that will stir this well-worn theme, or essay to throw fresh light upon a subject which has shared with its congener, love, the attention of the most observant minds since thought first found expression in literature. Yet, inasmuch as friendship and love are the fertilising streams without which the scene of life is no more than an arid, uninteresting plain—streams in which, unless the traveller can slake his thirst and bathe his limbs, the journey is but a cheerless, objectless toil, riches are but heaps of dazzling sand, and ambition is a disappointing mirage—it is impossible to reflect upon any human occasion, or estimate any achievement or circumstance of man, without acknowledging these relations as the very source of earthly happiness. Charlotte Brontë expressed herself more feebly than was her wont when she put into the mouth of Jane Eyre the sentence, " There is no happiness like that of being loved by your fellow-creatures, and feeling that your presence is an addition to their comfort."

It would have been more fully true to say that there is no happiness possible without it, for "what no one with us shares seems scarce our own."

It is far too late in the day to undertake inquiry into the abstract qualities of friendship and love; their analysis and explanation could hardly be carried further than has been done by philosophers in all ages. But it concerns us to watch how their nurture and conduct are affected by the altered conditions of society, its greater wealth, more diffused education, increasing numbers, and ease of locomotion; for, although these two kinds of communion may be held to be of spontaneous origin, and not to be generated by any precision of forethought or sagacity of plan, yet they require constant cultivation to maintain them in vigour. Dr Johnson observed to Sir Joshua Reynolds: "If a man does not make new acquaintance as he advances through life, he will very soon find himself alone. A man, sir, should keep his friendship in constant repair." To friendship and love alike may be applied the saying of one of Molière's *Précieuses*, "Les choses ne valent que ce qu'on les fait valoir."

This may be held heresy in the matter of love. Turn we then to the consideration of friendship, seeing that it is less hazardous, more deliberate, and less fleeting than, alas! the other has so often proved to be. On the other hand, it is, of the two, the more difficult to define; its colouring is less vivid, its outlines less distinct, its approach less perceptible, than those of passion.

Cicero had this vagueness in view when he said that although a man is sure to be able to inform you accurately how many horses, oxen, sheep, he possesses, yet question him as to the number of his friends, and his answer will be hesitating and indefinite: nevertheless, his friends might well be supposed to contribute more to his happiness than his cattle. But every man could declare how many women he was in love with: nay, if he were really in love, he would resent as impertinent or ridiculous the suggestion that there could be more than one.

There are men, though hardly are there women, who pass through life without friends, and there are men, and women more than men, who have never a sweetheart or lover. There are men, also, who change their friendships, not of design, but because of change in neighbourhood or occupation; yet each such successive friendship may be genuine and warm, just as there are those who have been passionately in love with one woman after another. It is a common and fond belief that there can be but one true love in a life; there is a less common, but not less fond, idea that first love is true love, and that all that follow are vain or base. It is more poetic, it ennobles and simplifies our conception of human nature, to hold this faith; but the hard, resistless truth is otherwise: man—let the case against him be stated as harshly as possible—is prone to allow his thoughts and senses to be detached from his first sovereign, and the allegiance exacted from him in later years by her successor is just as complete and absorbing as was paid to the other. Would that it were otherwise! for then much suffering would be saved to men and women. As in measles and scarlet fever, they might feel tolerable immunity after the first affliction.

But even friendship—the more sober and rational
kind of human intercourse—is not the simple matter
it might be supposed to be. It is a holy thing, yet
most capricious, and is no more under command of
the will than faith.

Montaigne, ruminating in his own deliciously frank
and leisurely way over the origin of his intimacy
with a dear friend, observes:—

If I am pressed to explain why I loved him, I feel that
it can only be expressed by answering " Because it was he,
because it was I " (*parce que c'estoit luy, parce que c'estoit
moy*).

They were the complement of each other, which
implied not identity of character or inclination, but
more nearly the reverse of it—one mind supplying
the deficiency of the other, and recruiting itself from
the abundance of that wherein it is conscious of
shortcoming.

Nevertheless friendship is largely the outcome of
circumstance. The pursuit of a common object, the
neighbourhood of homes, community of language and
environment—if these are not indispensable to friendship, they are at least the accidents by which it is
engendered and kept in being: it is, indeed, difficult
to imagine living friendship without one or another of
these conditions. The instance comes to mind at once
of Horace Walpole and Horace Mann, who, although
they never met for forty years, maintained a close and
constant correspondence. But, perfect as this communion seems in print, one cannot but suspect the
literary man of the world to have been posing in
these letters as one of a pair of friends. Mann was

useful to him as the recipient—the "addressee"—of letters which Walpole intended should be published some day, and spent much time in polishing and correcting long after they had been written. It was an artistic way of keeping a journal, obviating the tiresome egoism of that form of literary monologue and giving a spontaneous air to some of the most self-conscious pages that were ever penned. Walpole found it possible during a long life of abundant leisure to keep up the tone of intimacy which had taken its rise between the two men when they were young; but this is attributable rather to his literary instinct than to the depth of his affection.

They remain, these letters, among the most delightful pieces of English literature; but, on the whole, they leave a painful impression on the reader. They are masterly, leisurely sketches of a scheming, sordid society, in which frequent drunkenness and coarse libertinism were reckoned no darker stains on a statesman's private character than bribery and jobbery were on his public fame; and the limner of them was cynically content with the world as he found it, and indifferent whether he should leave it any better.[1]

Nevertheless, let us not do injustice to the "uncle of the late Earl of Orford." The solicitude he showed in exchanging thoughts with his friend deserves all admiration: it was the only means by which the

---

[1] There is almost as much truth as exaggeration in Walpole's summary of the state of things in the best society of his day: "There is no living in this country under £20,000 a-year; not that that suffices, but it entitles one to ask for a pension for two or three lives."

warm tide of affection could have been kept flowing
between those who had been so long parted, without
which it must have soon slackened and cooled. For
friendship, though in its origin involuntary, will not
endure without conscious cultivation. If the bond is
to survive changes of circumstance, of proximity, of
pursuit, of station in life, it must be sedulously
lengthened or strengthened in adaptation to them.
" I am a bad correspondent," says one, and thinks
he thereby excuses himself for not writing regularly
to an absent friend ; but, in truth, that is no palliation for neglect of the only known means by which
friendship may be made independent of separation.
If friendship is silent, rest assured that it is dead.
If two friends travel together, dine together, or are
in any way associated, they *must* talk ; the very fact
that they are friends ensures effortless conversation—
the difficulty would be to keep silence ; the effort, if
successful, would very soon put an end to their
friendship. It is true that when these two are at
a distance from each other, the effort to maintain
communion is a conscious one ; but, inasmuch as the
best correspondence is no more than written conversation, how slight is the exertion required ; how un-
pardonable, yet how frequent, is its neglect ! The
trouble of sitting down to write a sentence is certainly greater than that of uttering it, inasmuch as
literature is a weightier matter than speech ; but the
habit is easily acquired by Englishmen, who excel
more often as writers than as orators. The secret
of good letter-writing is the same as that of all good
literature—the writer speaks because he has something to say, not because he has to say something ;

and who can have a friend without having something to say to him, and a constant wish to say it?

Novantes said that every Englishman was an island, and it is open to some Irishmen to add that every Scotchman is a cross between an island and a hedgehog. There are two causes which chiefly deter our countrymen from correspondence: first, their innate dread of *épanchement* (we have no exact equivalent for this term except the derisive slang "gush"), and, second, their habitually careless and inaccurate speech. Slipshod expressions pass muster in familiar conversation, but they do not afford agreeable reading. The greater the pity, for there is no people on earth who habitually entertain loftier thoughts, or are more capable of disinterested attachment, than the English.

But there is another circumstance, peculiar to modern society, which tends as much as the extraordinary reserve of Englishmen to make the duration of friendship precarious—namely, the numerical increase of acquaintanceship. Never before in the history of the world has there been such a vast concourse of human beings as exists in and about London. A man's acquaintance is numbered nowadays not by the score, but by the hundred; and not only does the presence of such a multitude encourage the idea that if he loses one friend he can surely pick up two or three more, but it increases the effort necessary to retain the friends he has. The ceremony, once so scrupulously observed, of paying and receiving calls has been mightily relaxed; indeed there are some people who affect to be smart in virtue of having forsworn altogether the time-honoured custom. The decay of morning calls as a source of social enjoyment may not be cause for regret, but it is a sign that society is becoming so huge that additional care is required to preserve acquaintanceship and even friendship. There is an amusing exaggeration of the ease of finding new friends related in the life of the author of 'Friends in Council.' Sir Arthur Helps, than whom no one ever cared less for the pleasures of the table, observed one day to C. V. Bayley, a noted *bon vivant*, that he thought dinners were a bore. " My dear Helps," replied Bayley, " I entirely disagree: I would rather lose a friend than a dinner, for if I lose a friend, I can go down to the club and get another; whereas if I lose a dinner, the misfortune is irreparable, for nobody can eat two dinners on the same day."

In these observations it will be observed that reference is chiefly made to persons of the wealthier and leisurely class, because it is they who have the best opportunities of selecting and cultivating friendships. It is not that they are endowed with finer feelings or are capable of more intense affection—nothing can be further from the truth; but a life of toil absorbs so much physical energy as to leave little more than a capacity for fellowship, which is rarely intense enough to rank as friendship. The chances of employment expose all acquaintanceship among the working classes to sudden rupture; to maintain close correspondence thereafter is forbidden alike by habit and want of leisure; and in the evening of life, when the drooping frame brings a man to involuntary, unwelcome repose, too often it is the case that the vital powers have run so low as to be incapable of expansion in intercourse with those who might have been his friends ; all he wants is to be let alone. A Royal Commission was appointed lately to inquire into the condition of the aged poor, and devise means, if possible, to improve it. Among other subjects, evidence was taken on the practice of Boards of Guardians in dealing with old married couples who find their way into the workhouse. Under the law as it used to be, husband and wife were placed in separate wards ; but, as this seemed a harsh proceeding, the law was amended not long ago so as to give the Guardians power to lodge aged couples together. A witness of long experience in the administration of the Poor Law was asked if the poor folk valued the privilege, of living together in the workhouse.

"In the case of an aged man and wife entering the workhouse" (was the question), "do you find that they prefer to live together or to live separate ?"

"As a rule, they prefer to live separate. When an aged married couple come into the workhouse I desire the master to let me know . . . and I will go and see them. 'Well,' I will say, 'you are not in the rooms which are specially built, furnished, and everything else for you.' The answer of the woman probably is, 'I have had enough o' he ;' and very often it is the other way, 'I have had enough o' she.' It is more often on that side."

There is a pathetic lesson in such an experience. Friendship, even between husband and wife, must be cultivated, and cultivation implies leisure—a luxury denied to the lower working classes. Comrades as these people have been in the long battle of life, the hardships of conflict seem to have strained out of their nature all capacity for the sweetness of fellowship, all desire save to get rid of worry and be at rest. They remain to one another but a surly, stupid old man, and a querulous; ugly old woman; in neither case the kind of associate one would choose for relaxation. Yet had their lot been less hard—had there been intervals of drudgery when they could have talked over bygone days and devised plans for their common future, such pauses would have been links in a long chain, leading them back in memory to the dewy evenings when they used to meet in the green loaning and wander arm-locked through half the summer night. Truly we are creatures of circumstance, and the playthings of fate; truly Dives receives good things in his lifetime and Lazarus evil things, and it is hard to believe in the justice which not only awards purple and fine linen and sumptuous daily fare to one and fallen crumbs to the other, but also denies to the poor man the opportunity of cherishing that kind of intercourse which sweetens the harshest fortune. "The gods are just," insisted Dryden,

> " But how can finite measure infinite ?
> Reason ! alas, it does not show itself.
> Yet man, vain man, would with his short lined plummet
> Fathom the vast abyss of heavenly justice.
> Whatever is, is in its causes just,
> Since all things are by fate.   But purblind man
> Sees but a part o' the chain, the nearest links,
> His eyes not carrying to that equal beam
> That poises all above."

The parable of the Sower, like many of the poignant illustrations used by Christ to bring home doctrine to His hearers, has a far wider application than merely to the preaching of the Word. All acquaintanceship carries in it the seed of lasting friendship, but very little of it reaches good soil, where, favoured by the seasons, it may bring forth fruit. The most familiar friendships in a man's life are those sown in the natural seed-time—boyhood and youth—but though his schoolfellows may have been numbered by the hundred, those of them that become his fast friends may be counted on his fingers—most often on the fingers of one hand. The seeds of friendship scattered by the poor man fall, for the most part, "upon stony places where they have not much earth." The young growth flourishes apace, but when the sun is up—when the daily task is set and the whole strength of the man is wanted to keep body and soul together—it withers away. Political economists shake their heads at the agitation for an eight hours' day; but, looked at from the workman's point of view, it has aspects which are worthy of consideration. People are never done extolling the blessedness of work, and within reasonable limits it is undoubtedly a priceless medicine; but beyond these limits it is a curse, for it deprives a man of the power of cultivating friendship. Bacon's aspiration was probably not far amiss, for a life of leisure without loitering, which was glossed by Johnson "work without weariness." That seems to define the lot most favourable to the development and endurance of friendship, affording opportunity to cultivate acquaintance, the chance of common employment, the indulgence of like tastes, the pursuit of a common aim, without the lassitude and petulance sure to spring from idleness. Love may be—nay, must be, idle, at least on one side; but friendship shall be ever stirring and active: love, irrational and wayward, may be content with faith, but friendship cries, "Show me thy works!"

If the poor man's crop of friendship is burnt up because it has "no deepness of earth," the leisured man's seedlings often fare no better, because of the thorns which spring up and choke them. The very multitude of his acquaintance, as has been shown, is a hindrance to close friendship, so that Charles Lamb spoke truly of the rarity of early friendship enduring into middle age :—

Oh! it is pleasant as it is rare to find the same arm linked in yours at forty which at thirteen helped it to turn over the 'Cicero de Amicitiâ,' or some other tale of antique friendship, which the young heart even then was burning to anticipate.

Yet it might be otherwise. There are many thousands of young men of means in this country with nothing to do, or, at any rate, who do nothing, because they are not compelled to earn a living. They are, for the most part, amiable, good to look on, well-bred, well-groomed, fairly well-mannered, and capable, if the necessity arose, of doing brave service in the field. They have been at schools selected as the likeliest to afford them—not the best education, but the best set of friends for life. What are they doing to secure friendship? Nothing—it is said advisedly, nothing. Take one of them who is devoted to fox-hunting. In most cases, that takes him out of his own county for at least half the year; another quarter of the year is spent in London; then a month or two in Scotland or a few weeks at Monte Carlo leave him little time to cultivate the acquaintance of those who would be his country neighbours if he were ever at home. But, after all, that matters the less because there are, perhaps, no friendships so intimate as those of hunting men. His lot is surely one of the brightest that can befall a young fellow.

Presently there comes a change; he falls in love and marries, or he loses his nerve or some of his money, gives up hunting and sells his horses. What becomes then of his hunting friends? For a time he may keep on with the old set, but neither he nor they know what it is to exert themselves for one another; they find less and less in common; a vacant place is soon filled up, and when he arrives at middle age he finds himself " out of it," and perhaps becomes a bit of a bore. Unless he is lucky enough to find domestic consolation, it is strange if there does not come home to him the reflection of the Princesse de Belgiojoso: " I cannot imagine what joy there can be in living when the eyes of others no longer look love into ours."

This is perhaps an extreme case, but most of us will have no difficulty in remembering plenty of men on the down grade of years, who own not a single friend for whom they would make a sacrifice, or who would make a sacrifice for them. In friendship, as in love, the test of reality is the readiness to sacrifice—sacrifice of time, of money, of exertion, or whatever else. Sacrifice lies at the root of the primitive idea of devotion. Fashionable hospitality has travelled a long way from the original scheme; modern hosts fill their houses with those who are likely to amuse them or be useful to them, but of old no sacrifice was considered too costly to make for a guest. A traveller, so the story runs, arriving late at an Irish harper's cabin, asked for supper and shelter. There was no fuel in the house, and outside all was drenched with rain: the only dry combustible was the poor man's beloved harp—his only means of living; but he did not hesitate to condemn it to the flames, in order to cook a meal for the wayfarer. Imagine one of our Amphitryons making a bonfire of his Erard or Steinway grand for a like purpose.

But whatever may be the cost of friendship to one side or the other, it is of its very nature that a debtor and creditor account is out of the question, and this not the less because in friendship, as in love, *il y a toujours l'un qui embrasse, et l'autre qui tend la joue.*

The pursuit of literature is sometimes supposed to be more productive of friendship than other occupations; but that is probably because quill-drivers prattle more about their affairs than is the fashion of other folk, and it is their business to give a dramatic or romantic cast to things which in reality are sober, and even tedious. The coffee-house wits of the eighteenth century, though they depicted each other sweetly enough in literary miniatures, were often bored with their own society; and the narrative of their intercourse, which sparkles so brightly on their pages, is but the reflection of their happier moments enhanced by the kindly office of memory. The quarrels of authors are at least as conspicuous as their friendships. The fact is, that literary men as a class are less dependent on friendship than almost any other; they are patient of solitude, for their occupation is a solitary one; and there are not many natures so elastic as Sir Walter Scott's, who was as much at home to living men and women as he was among his library shelves, and coveted companionship of flesh and blood not less ardently than he did the luxury of study. Sydney

Smith spoke impatiently of Macaulay as "a book in breeches." There is a quaint passage in a very quaint book by Anatole France—'La Rôtisserie de la Reine Pédauque'—in which one of the characters who frequent that house of modest entertainment and motley intercourse prescribes letters as a remedy for afflicted love; and another, while admitting that may be true enough, doubts if they are any cure for an empty belly.

"Ainsi donc" (répliqua l'abbé), "le faut-il former aux bonnes lettres, qui sont l'honneur de l'homme, la consolation de la vie et le remède à tous les maux, même à ceux de l'amour, ainsi que l'affirme le poète Théocrite."

"Tout rôtisseur que je suis," répondit mon père, "j'estime le savoir, et je veux bien croire qu'il est, comme dit Votre Grâce, un remède à l'amour. Mais je ne crois pas qu'il soit un remède à la faim."

The literary, like the artistic, temperament is prone to jealousy, and its ancillary, suspicion. Where there is suspicion there is no place for confidence, and without confidence there can be no true friendship. Hence the most memorable literary friendships are those where one was content to be beyond question subordinate to the other. There be those who profanely hold that the delight of lovers arises entirely from the flattery of mutual preference; and this is undoubtedly one of the legitimate gratifications of friendship. I am pleased that my friend should prefer my society to that of many other men, and it is extremely pleasant to me when he shows that it is so. So in the case of the historic friendship of Johnson and Boswell, each was agreeably flattered by the attention of the other. Johnson's appetite for admiration was insatiable; Boswell had an inexhaustible supply at the disposal of his hero, and felt amply repaid by the credit of associating with one whom he invested with the attributes of a demigod. How savagely, yet eloquently, the great man resented indifference to his talents was shown in his memorable letter to Lord Chesterfield :—

The notice which you have been pleased to take of my labours, had it been early, had been kind; but it has been delayed till I am indifferent and cannot enjoy it; till I am solitary, and cannot impart it; till I am known, and do not want it. I hope it is no very cynical asperity not to confess obligations where no benefit has been received, or to be unwilling that the public should consider me as owing that to a patron, which Providence has enabled me to do for myself.

Johnson never forgave the slight he had received, or fancied he had received, and years afterwards when Lord Chesterfield's 'Letters to his Son' were published, he condemned them as teaching "the morals of a whore, and the manners of a dancing-master."

Johnson used often to deplore the neglect to nourish affection between those who ought to be and might be the closest friends. In a letter to Mr Bennet Langton he said :—

You are busy in acquiring and in communicating knowledge, and while you are studying, enjoy the end of study by making others wiser and happier. I was much pleased with the tale you told me of being tutor to your sisters. I, who have no sisters nor brothers, look with some degree of innocent envy on those who may be said to be born to be friends, and cannot see without wonder how rarely that native union is afterwards regarded. It sometimes happens, indeed, that some supervenient cause of discord may overpower the original amity, but it seems to me more frequently thrown away with levity, or lost by negligence, than destroyed by injury or violence.

Perhaps the most comprehensive analysis of friendship would be, after all, no more than an expansion of one of the most eloquent essays ever penned—one of which constant repetition through nearly two thousand years has not prevailed to smirch the freshness, nor the changed conditions of human society to darken the significance—that part of his Epistle to the Corinthians in which St Paul explains the attributes of charity. Our ears have become enamoured of its rhythm, which is lost in replacing the Latin word "charity" by the more literal, yet ambiguous, English monosyllable "love"; but indeed the sense is hardly less full if friendship be read throughout this chapter. What can be said of friendship more than that it suffereth long and is kind, envieth not, seeketh not her own, is not easily provoked, thinketh no evil; beareth all things, believeth all things, hopeth all things, endureth all things?

Of all the pieces of political pedantry that ever have been perpetrated, none has exceeded that clause in the code of St Just which abolished marriage as a sacrament and substituted friendship, ordaining it a public institution. Every citizen on coming of full age was to be bound to make legal declaration of his friends, and if he had none he was to suffer banishment; on the other hand, those whom he proclaimed his friends were to be held responsible for his conduct, and if he committed a crime then they were to be banished. Thus was every citizen to be placed between the devil and the deep sea: if he could announce no friendships, he would be punished; if one of those who claimed his friendship were to break the law, the punishment would fall upon himself.

Hitherto account has been taken only of friendship between man and man, and an attempt has been made to show that it is of a profound yet delicate nature; much greater are the hazards besetting that of man and woman. The difference of sex, in itself a well-nigh insuperable hindrance to disinterested attachment between persons of nearly the same age, is accentuated in youth by difference of education, and in maturity by limitation of aim and scope. How far the first is necessary may be matter for reflection, and the last opens up a disputed field on which one may have neither the occasion nor the wish to enter. Let it be granted for the sake of peace that it is no more reasonable to forbid a woman to sit in Parliament because she is born to have children than it would be to forbid a man because he is born to have the gout. The kind of woman who shows herself aggrieved because the present laws prevent her entering Parliament or the County Council may have just cause of complaint, but in proportion as she is earnest in making it known she parts with her indefinable charm, and becomes an individual with whom a man is more likely to find himself in competition than in intimacy. The problem of friendship between them is not one that will probably arise for settlement.

Nevertheless, this exclusion, for good or ill, of women from public life, from politics and commerce —from the arena, namely, wherein men most often measure their strength—shears away, as between man and woman, a great province of employment in which the woman's interest can never be other than altruistic. Of course there is much literal truth in the apparently cynical saying that most men who enter Parliament do so to please their wives, who want to go to London. It is as true now as when Horace Walpole wrote to Horace Mann — "I revive after being in London for an hour or two like a member of Parliament's wife," and it derives support from the well-known fact that there is a smaller proportion of bachelors in the House of Commons than in any other profession or assembly of men. In that sense, indeed, a wife's interest in her husband's occupation is not pure altruism, but then the matter under consideration is not the close fellowship which ought to and often does unite the aims of husband and wife, but the possibility of friendship between unattached men and women, and the extent to which it is interfered with by the exclusion of women from those occupations which men pursue with most ardour. Husband and wife naturally have many common material interests, it is an unnatural state of matters when they have not, and if, in addition, they share intellectual or spiritual views, so much the better; they will be bound by a closer tie.

But it is otherwise with man and woman who, though not in wedlock, feel that mutual attraction which sometimes proves strong enough between persons of the same sex to overcome the obstacles of difference in education and object in life. The difficulty of education lies on the threshold, though its force is not generally felt till after some length of acquaintance. In the early days a man and woman who suit each other will find plenty of suggestion for

the exchange of thought in the outward aspect of
things—the glow of summer suns, the changeful moods
of Nature, the simpler impressions of art, the doings
of other people, fondness for animals; but as they
are longer acquainted, one or other, or both of them,
will seek further into the nature of things and specu-
late about the hidden springs of motive, the range of
understanding, the laws of the physical and spiritual
world. When these are reached the friends are very
apt to part company; either they take diverging paths
or else one lags too far behind the other to keep up
companionship.

The man, so far as he has retained anything of his
schoolboy tasks, is conscious of a voice in inanimate
things which finds no sympathetic echo in the woman,
for from her the Greek poets have been sedulously
sealed away. His deepest thoughts have a tinge of
classical melancholy, which is as far as possible from
the tone imparted by a girl's education; she cannot
comprehend his allusions, for indeed such sentiment
is inexplicable except by common understanding, and
she is apt to be shocked by the semi-paganism of such
lines as these:—

> "Sad eyes! the blue sea laughs as heretofore,
>   Ah! singing birds, your happy music pour;
>   Ah! poets, leave the sordid earth awhile,
>   *Fill to those ancient gods we still adore,*
>   It may be we shall touch the happy isle."

The whole scheme of a boy's education (as distinct
from instruction) has been laid apart from the girl's;
except some recollection of arithmetic and grammar,
they retain no common impression of what they have

learnt; their heads have been differently handled, their thoughts run in a different mould — what wonder, then, if there is found to be a centrifugal force in their intercourse—a lack of harmony without which friendship is not?

Failing education, some help may be derived from instruction in the same subjects. It is still the case that in this country it is the rule that girls — the exception that boys—should be instructed in music. A man and woman equally accomplished in this art, and understanding music enough to be capable of thoroughly enjoying it, have a common ground on which lasting friendship may be, and often has been, established; but, failing some such convenient excuse for intercourse, the young growth is very apt to wither away because " there is no deepness of earth."

But there is another respect in which the training of young people of the wealthier class not only builds up a barrier between their lives, but sends the whole current of their thoughts into separate channels. From the day a boy goes to school he is aware of the existence of a certain kind of evil of which a girl never suspects the existence until she has grown up. The boy knows it is evil, but he learns also that in the eyes of the world there will be no disgrace incurred if he yields to it; that, on the contrary, public opinion condones it. It is the subject of constant conversation among the young, and often of arch allusion among older men, and thus, unless he is of peculiar constitution, it occupies a great deal of his thoughts. The finger cannot be laid on any circumstance of modern society which so completely severs the outset in life and separates the tone of mind of the two sexes. And it endures through life; for though a woman's purity is acknowledged to be beautiful and worthy of worship, it is held to be inevitable —looked for as matter of course, like the purity of a crystal. We prize it, but we do not wonder at it, for it is secured by sedulous training and the habit of watchfulness; it implies no mortal encounter with evil. But a man's purity does stir our marvel, for it means a living martyrdom. It is like a soaring Alp, now gleaming cold and wan above us, through rifts of cloud, and anon glistening far, very far off, on the sunlit horizon.

What wonder, then, if lives thus set moving upon different planes and fenced off by different social codes of morality, should very rarely link themselves in the golden band of friendship? The chances against this happening would probably not be lessened by the plan advocated by some people of letting women compete with men in the professions. There is some truth in the French philosopher's observation: " Les femmes doivent la moitié de leur supériorité à cet avantage de n'avoir point de profession."

But it must be admitted that one great difficulty in the way of friendship between man and woman would be got over if women took part in the business of the law, politics, and commerce. A recent decision of the Geographical Society, whereby women were excluded from Fellowships in that learned body, does not point to any innovation in this respect, or to a state of things in which the two sexes would meet in natural intercourse day by day. As matters stand now, in order to cultivate friendship with a woman, a man has to make special arrangements to meet her—at least they would be called arrangements if they were made with another man, but being made with a woman they are spitefully classed as assignations—a term of sinister meaning. "One must often consider," said Helps, "not what the wise think, but what the foolish will say."

It is only fair to admit, however, that the wise and foolish would very likely come to the same conclusion in this matter—namely, that in attempting to lay the foundations of friendship by these means, a man and woman stand in imminent peril of a far more serious state of affairs. A woman's beauty is, after all, the most formidable of all barriers to disinterested friendship.

> "Beauty, my lord, 'tis the worst part of woman,
> A poor weak thing, assaulted every hour
> By creeping minutes of defacing time ;
> A superficies, which each breath of care
> Blasts off, and every humorous stream of grief
> Washeth away as rain doth winter snow."

When love comes in at the door, friendship flies out of the window, and seldom finds its way back. Not often from the ashes of a dead love will the phœnix of friendship arise; commonly the only form that stirs there is the pale brooding ghost of departed bliss— the only sound that moves, the sigh of shattered faith. "Nay but," says one, "there are many instances in disproof of that. Take Madame Récamier, for instance; did she not turn many of her lovers into friends, and did they not live for years in perfect amity?" Well she *claimed* to have done so, but it is difficult to believe that she did not feed their attachment with thin, delusive hopes. It costs so little effort to send a tender glance from eyes so eloquent as hers; and though *la belle Juliette* affected to ignore the source of her power, none knew better than she that it lay in her beauty. She inadvertently betrayed that, when, one day in her declining years, somebody complimented her on retaining her good looks so long:—

Oh, ma chère amie [she said], il n'y a plus d'illusion à se faire. Du jour où j'ai vu que les petits Savoyards dans la rue ne se retournaient plus, j'ai compris que tout était fini.

Madame Récamier—beautiful, accomplished, gentle, and sympathetic—was absolutely passionless,[1] but had a never-resting desire to please. Witness her behaviour with Prince Augustus of Prussia, nephew of Frederick the Great, during his imprisonment at Geneva in 1807. He was then nine-and-twenty. Fourteen years previously she had entered into the ghost of a marriage with a man twenty-seven years older than herself, and they had never thereafter lived together as husband and wife. For three months she permitted the Prince to pay ardent court to her, and at length yielded so far as to write and ask her husband's consent to a divorce in order that she might marry her lover. And then when this husband, who had never suffered his marriage to interfere with his business, his pleasures, his punctual attendance at the incessant guillotine orgies of the Reign of Terror, a husband who had exercised none of a husband's rights or duties,

---

[1] "Tandis que la femme aimée, au cœur pudique, confiante et sans désir, est assez comblée de voir à côté d'elle son ami, de lui abandonner au plus sa main pour un instant, et de le traiter comme une sœur, sa sœur chérie, l'homme, fut-il doué du ciel comme Abel ou Jean, souffre inévitablement en secret de sa position incomplète et fausse; il se sent blessé dans sa nature secondaire, sourdement grondante, agressive; les moments en apparence les plus harmonieux lui deviennent vite une douleur, un péril, une honte; de là les retours irrités et cruels."—*Volupté :* Sainte-Beuve.

whom she had not seen for years—when this nominal husband wrote a cold assent, coupled with a whining remonstrance on the ground of his own kindness to her as a child, and reminding her that it was her own susceptibilities and repugnance that had prevented him making their marriage indissoluble, and caused the peculiar nature of the relations between them, she drew back in terror from the only course which could have brought happiness to the Prince and honour to herself, and at last, after keeping him in suspense for more than a year, wrote him a letter intended to extinguish his hope.[1]

There is something almost forbidding in the cool calculation with which she counted the debit and credit of the Prince's proposal. One is not disposed to judge a woman harshly in the matter of flirtation—when the account comes to be reckoned up between the two sexes, there will be found a heavy balance of reparation due by man—but the history of these spring

---

[1] "Le Prince Auguste, bourrelé d'inquiétudes, tomba malade; une affection grave, la rougeole, le mit dans un grand danger. Madame Récamier, de son côté, revenue dans sa famille, pesait avec plus de sang-froid et une raison plus libre toutes les chances, toutes les séductions, tous les inconvénients de l'avenir qui lui était offert. Pénétrée de la plus profonde reconnaissance pour la loyale tendresse et le dévouement du Prince Auguste, elle sentait bien, en sondant son propre cœur, qu'elle ne répondrait qu'imparfaitement à l'ardeur des sentiments qu'elle inspirait, et sa délicatesse se troublait à la pensée d'accepter un aussi considérable sacrifice d'un homme auquel elle ne rendrait pas en échange un attachement égal au sien. Ses scrupules religieux, que le langage d'une passion profonde ne faisait point taire en présence du prince, s'étaient fortifiés par la réflexion; l'effet de la rupture de son mariage sur le public l'épouvantait, et l'idée de quitter à jamais son pays ne lui causait pas moins d'effroi. Elle écrivit donc au Prince Auguste une lettre qui devait lui ôter toute espérance."—*Souvenirs et Correspondance de Madame Récamier*, i. 145.

months at Geneva is not pleasant reading: one watches this pair in their daily excursions along the shores of the lake, or floating on its limpid waters, one of them paying the tribute of a warm, generous nature, the other content to receive it, but unready to give anything in exchange. The story goes on too long not to have a different ending: it cannot be right that a noble nature should be encouraged to prostrate itself so entirely before another, and be cheated of its legitimate reward.

Madame Récamier was incapable of love, and, graceful figure though she be, moving among the blood-steeped personalities of that woful time, she is too careful in preserving her balance, too little forgetful of herself, to suffer us to dwell affectionately on her memory.[1] David's portrait has faithfully preserved that charm which drew so many men towards her, but it would move us more deeply if we knew that she had lived for another rather than for herself.

Nevertheless there is another and a nobler aspect of this woman's character and conduct—a judgment on her motives under which, though her treatment of Prince Augustus cannot be condoned, it appears in painful contrast with her usual integrity. It is clear that she wished to form with the men whom her

---

[1] "Je poserai donc la question, ou plutôt elle se pose d'elle-même malgré moi pour Madame Récamier, et pour elle comme pour Madame de Maintenon, comme pour Madame de Sévigné (la Madame de Sévigné non encore mère); je répondrai hardiment: *Non.* Non, elle n'a jamais aimé de passion et de flamme; mais cet immense besoin d'aimer que porte en elle toute âme tendre se changeait pour elle en un infini besoin de plaire, ou mieux d'être aimée, et en une volonté active, en un fervent désir de payer tout cela en bonté."—Sainte-Beuve.

beauty brought to her feet—with Ballanche, the Montmorencis, Chateaubriand, and others—a durable friendship, over which the clouds of passion should cast no shade, to breathe with them a rarer atmosphere than masculine nature can commonly endure. Ballanche, in one of his early letters to Madame Récamier, showed that he had penetrated the secret of her relations with his own sex—

Vous étiez primitivement une Antigone, dont on a voulu, à toute force, faire une Armide.. On y a mal réussi : nul ne peut mentir à sa propre nature.

Not the less keen was the anguish she inflicted on those men than if she had been a heartless coquette. She was an old woman when Chateaubriand moaned in language far more sincere than compliment—

Gardez-vous bien mon souvenir. Je n'ai qu'un seul espoir gravé dans mon cœur—c'est de vous revoir.

So it is probably just to credit Madame Récamier with a degree of success in an attempt, which many others have tried ineffectually, to convert lovers into friends—an attempt which is far less hopeful when the passion has been mutual. When one of a pair of lovers grows cold, the other feels the solid earth melt away beneath his feet. Confidence, as essential to friendship as it is inseparable from love, is utterly destroyed for the time, and it is rare indeed that the temper of the discarded one is so plastic as to admit of its restoration. Let it be supposed that it is the woman who has changed; like Madame Récamier she may wish to retain her old lover as a friend, but how great are the difficulties to be surmounted—how rarely is it possible for the pair to settle down into new relations! Even if she has not deserted him for another, the man's confidence has sustained a shock which most often proves a deathblow. There seems to be no foothold for trust, no material left out of which to construct friendship. His sorely wounded vanity also embitters him; for a man is a sensitive vain animal, and it testifies strangely to the peculiar nature of his vanity that you shall hardly find a man under middle age with so mean a body or so exalted a mind, that he will prefer that a woman should distinguish him more for his mental than his physical qualities. There is no man, in short, who, being in love and therefore anxious to appear at his best, will not be at greater pains to conceal his baldness than display his intellectual powers. Yet it is rare for an Englishwoman to consider a man's person as anything more important than an envelope for the mind.

On the whole, however, it is perhaps more often the one who has been deceived than the deceiver who will remain most anxious to make friends.

> "Forgiveness to the injured does belong,
>   But they ne'er pardon who have done the wrong."

The discarded one will be only too ready for reconciliation, for hope dies hard, and it is long before he can persuade himself that things may not be again as they have been before.

But we are insensibly being drawn into a dissertation on love, which only concerns our present purpose in so far as it affects the prospects of friendship.

Happy are they (and they are many) whom circumstances have allowed to slip imperceptibly from the relation of lovers into that of friends, to whom sadness only comes from the thought expressed by Hartley Coleridge:—

> " We only meet on earth
> That we may know how sad it is to part."

Men cannot enjoy supreme happiness here without running the terrible risk of surviving it. "It is a hazardous kind of happiness," Mr Andrew Lang has written, "that attends great affection. Your capital is always at the mercy of failures, of death, of jealousy, of estrangement."

Circumstances may prove too strong for us, and we may lose that which we rightly prize most highly. But let us not earn the bitterness of losing it through neglect of the simple means which tend to secure it, for that is what brings some of us to long to pass a sponge over the record: ay, or to lay a cloth wet with tears so closely over the features of the past that it shall never breathe again. Yet we cannot afford to look no more on the departed: we shall never see the like of it again here below.

> " Our broken friendships we deplore,
> And loves of youth that are no more ;
> No after friendships e'er can raise
> The endearments of our early days."

If we were to forget them, what sweetness would be left in life ? We profess our belief in a Sun of Righteousness, but all that is known of the sunrise to many of us in this murk valley of the Shadow of Death is the brightness reflected from the faces of those who have reached a higher standing than it seems possible for us ever to do.

THE CRAVING FOR FICTION.

IT is not altogether easy to examine the psychical
and mental forces which prevail to give fiction
the immense preference it possesses over other forms
of literature, and to estimate its effect on social and
intellectual growth, without seeming to assume the
superior airs of a lecturer to a Young Men's Christian
Association. But, in truth, the subject is so remarkable in some of its features as to deserve philosophic
consideration of the origin and results of the appetite
for romance.

Hedonism, then—the doctrine of Aristippus, which
sets pleasure as the right aim of existence—seems
to be the spirit ruling the readers of books : pleasure,
that is, not of a grossly material kind, for the disciples are often as free from the thrall of the senses
as from the discipline of strenuous research; but
pleasure not the less because it is directed and con-
trolled by culture and knowledge, for there is no
pleasure less liable to pall than reading, no pastime
more sure to satisfy.

It is so difficult for us to imagine a world without books that we are apt to forget that it is only within the last three or four centuries that the materials for reading have come within reach of the majority of Europeans. In 1340, when Richard of Bury penned that sentence which has since found sympathetic echo in so many minds, there were no printed books—no books, that is, in our understanding of the term.

These are masters [he said] who instruct us without chastisement, without anger, without fee; if you repair to them, they are not asleep; if you would consult them, they do not hide themselves; if you blunder, they complain not; if you betray ignorance, they laugh not.

How would good Richard, poring over manuscripts limited in number and difficult of access, have esteemed our lot in these days? The difficulty now is not to get books, but to decide on a choice from the overwhelming multitude that pour from the press. It is hardly possible for the most voracious bookworm to devour more than 150 books in the space of a year; one who achieved that number might accomplish about 9000 in the course of his life. Probably nobody ever did so, and it would, after all, be an insignificant fraction of contemporary publications, for about 20,000 separate works are annually added to the shelves of the British Museum — more than twice as many as any man could possibly peruse in a lifetime—amounting in a normal life-period of seventy years to the prodigious total of 1,400,000 books. And this leaves wholly out of account the vastly greater mass of journalistic literature which consumes part of everybody's time and attention.

Seeing, then, that almost every reader is not only free to select for himself, but actually under obligation to do so, it is not without interest to inquire what, in the majority of cases, is the nature of that selection, and to trace, if possible, the influence under which people make it.

The returns of every free library prove how enormously the demand for fiction preponderates over that for any other kind of literature.

The annual report for 1891 of the committee managing the free libraries of Birmingham shows that during the course of that year 855,096 volumes were asked for and issued. These were divided into twelve classes: (1) theology and moral philosophy; (2) history, biography, voyages, and travels; (3) law, politics, and commerce; (4) arts, sciences, and natural history; (5) poetry and drama; (6) magazines and periodicals, those of a special character being classed under the subject to which they belong; (7) prose fiction; (8) miscellaneous, including dictionaries and cyclopædias; (9) patents; (10) juvenile books; (11) embossed books for the blind; (12) music. Now, of the 855,096 volumes inquired for, no less than 519,595 were novels and magazines, leaving 335,501 for the other ten classes of literature.

This is the more remarkable when the composition of the Birmingham libraries is analysed. It might be supposed that fiction is more in request because the committee have more of that class on stock than of others. But this is not so. Out of a total of 169,230 volumes on their shelves only 31,996 are classified as prose fiction and magazines. It appears then that, although the committee have provided fiction and magazines only in the proportion of about one to five of other books, literature of that class is in demand in the proportion of five to every three of other classes. There is this additional fact to be remembered: that whereas many books are only required for purposes of reference, novels are read from beginning to end.

Such is the evidence of the public appetite for reading in a community like Birmingham, a great industrial centre, where, of course, works on technical subjects must be in pretty general demand. But the results are still more remarkable if the returns of libraries in districts not so exclusively industrial are examined. The table showing the number of volumes issued during the same year, 1891, from the lending department of the Battersea free libraries shows that out of 178,261 volumes lent no fewer than 146,515 were novels, four-fifths of the whole—four novels to every single work in all the other classes.

If would be easy to multiply proofs of the preference shown by readers for imaginary narrative over all other kinds of books, but it is unnecessary; one has only to run over the contents of the nearest railway bookstall to find assurance that those persons best acquainted by experience with the statistics of supply and demand are convinced of the futility of providing much else for the recreation of travellers.

Now, there is not the slightest intention of suggesting that all this is wrong and deplorable—to sit in ashes and cast dust on our beards because a depraved public finds more solace in imaginary love-stories than in works upon political economy or moral philosophy. It would be dishonest in one who has read all Miss Broughton's novels (and hopes to read many more) and only half of Shakespeare's plays, who pounces on all that comes from the pens of Mr Andrew Lang and Mr Anthony Hope, yet has never penetrated far into 'Paradise Lost,' to hint that there is much amiss in the fact revealed by the returns of free libraries, that (leaving newspapers out of account) out of every four persons engaged in reading at this moment three are reading novels, or, at all events, five out of eight. If this contributes to the general contentment, be it far from the philanthropist to interfere. If people prefer to read of the imaginary acts and conversations, not of an immoral tendency, of characters who never had existence, no objection need be raised on moral grounds. Dr John Brown, in a footnote to that masterpiece of pathos 'Rab and his Friends,' tells a story of a countryman who was asked to explain why his dog looked so grave. "Oh, sir," he replied, "life is full of sairiousness to him: he can just never get enough o' fechtin'." Life is "sairious" enough to everybody, and it is not to be regretted if the majority prefer fiction to "fechtin'." So let folk have all the mental relaxation that can be afforded them: society will be all the brighter and happier for it.

But there is no harm in speculating *why* it is that most people are entertained by narratives of what never took place rather than by history or biography; why they should be more deeply stirred in perusing the 'Prisoner of Zenda'—an admirable bit of fooling —than M. Jusserand's essay on the captivity of James I. of Scotland or Motley's 'Rise of the Dutch Republic'; and whether this remarkable characteristic of modern civilisation is really conducive to genuine recreation, or, like certain indolent habits, interferes with it.

That a preference for fictitious narrative is contrary to natural human instinct is an assumption that may be supported by known facts. Man is essentially an inquisitive animal.

Man's craving [says Mr E. Tylor] to know the causes at work in each event he witnesses, the reason why each state of things he surveys is such as it is and no other, is no product of high civilisation, but a characteristic of his race down to the lowest stages. Among rude savages it is already an intellectual appetite whose satisfaction claims many of the moments not engrossed in war or sport, food or sleep.

It is true that among primitive races this craving has to be put off with myths. People of whose origin no authentic record has been preserved are fain to invent fables to stand in its place. Thus in the eighth and ninth centuries the Scots were puzzled to account for their own name. Why, they wondered, should a people known as Scots inhabit a country known to them as Alba and to the Romans as Caledonia? Presently some learned man invented an eponymous legend to the effect that they were descended from a daughter of Pharaoh of Egypt, a princess whom, to suit the exigency of the case, he named Scotta. This naïve myth was eagerly grasped at, believed, and stood in place of history till, quite recently, ethnologists produced something more substantial. Even Milton, intellectually head and shoulders above his generation, could not bring himself to cast aside the fabled origin of Britain from Brutus.

Those old and inborn names of successive kings, never any to have bin real persons, or don in their lives at least som part of what so long hath bin remember'd, cannot be thought without too strict an incredulity.

He shrank from the feeling that, if he were to lose hold of the tradition, incapable as it was of proof, there would be nothing to which thoughts of the origin of his country might attach themselves. He preferred to believe what might not be true, rather than be left without anything to believe. But can it be doubted that, had he possessed the sources of information accessible at this day, a man of his mental fibre would not have sought delight in the truth rather than the tradition?

It would be natural, then, to expect that inasmuch as discovery and diligent comparison of records have prevailed to clear away the ancient myths which stood our ancestors in stead of history, that considering we possess a veritable narrative of much that they burned to know, and had to go to their graves without finding out, it would be in the study and extension of those subjects that much of our reading would be employed. But it is not so. At most, people like their history as they do their bread-and-butter—in thin slices. Perhaps it is the fault of historians, but there can be no doubt they are not in it with the novelists. Many sharp things have been said about them. Prosper Mérimée bluntly confessed that he hated all history except the anecdotes. Fielding, writing at a time when novels commanded only a small fraction of the interest which is taken in them now, declared that nothing was true in history except the names and dates, whereas in fiction everything was true except the names and dates. That is to mean, I suppose, that the master of romance is able to impress the imagination with a true picture of human character, whereas the historian, cramped by a sense of the necessity of recording actual events, presents his characters as if they were automata. He is apt to fit his personages to the incident, instead of being able, like the novelist, to invent or mould any incident to bring out the points in his characters. It is, in fact, the difference between science and art, between photography and painting. The object of the historian, as a scientist, is to produce an impression, colourless perhaps (for colour is subjective, and every historian professes to be impartial), but crammed with as many confirmatory details as possible. His intention should be, not to please, but to inform, and he aims at the scrupulous fidelity of a photographic plate. Every one knows the depressing effect of an exhibition of photographs. But the framer of romance enjoys an immeasurable advantage over the historian. His canvas is full of glowing tints, and just as it is lawful—nay, indispensable—for a landscape-painter to suppress some details, preserving only those which contribute to a brilliant and pleasing impression of the scene, leaving out a telegraph post here and placing a suitable group of figures there, bringing into bright relief the space where he desires attention should be concentrated, and spreading convenient gloom over whole tracts of canvas, so the skilful novelist knows how to keep his reader's attention by condensing tedious negotiations, skipping uneventful periods, enhancing merit, and making infamy more intense. One exclaims, "How lifelike!" because vivid contrast of character and brisk action constantly bring to mind familiar traits and experience, whereas a dispassionate critic would pronounce it unlike real life, for there the action is oftener tardy and the motives ambiguous or obscure.

The result of all this is that, although we are all
ready to smile at the credence yielded by savages to
their myths, few of us are unwilling, and none are
ashamed, to devote an enormous proportion of our
time to reading what we don't believe, and are not
intended to believe.

When the Queen of the Fairies persuaded Thomas
of Ercildoune to mount and ride with her, she brought
him to the parting of three roads—the stony, thorny
track of righteousness, the broad and easy way of self-
pleasing, and a third path along which she beckoned
him.

> "Oh, see ye not that bonnie road
>   That winds about the fernie brae?
> That is the road to fair Elfland,
>   Where thou and I this night maun gae."

That is the road down which so many of us wander
under the enchanter's spell, whereas it may be we
should find surer enjoyment in bending our steps
elsewhere.

But it may be said that we are no longer inquisitive,
like our forefathers, on the subject of history, because
the broad facts of it have been drubbed into most of
us at school. Everything has been explained; our
curiosity is stimulated by no enigmas in that field;
we need not invent myths, neither need we trouble
ourselves to know what everybody knows or can know
if he likes.

But how about the secrets of natural science, many
of which are secrets no longer? and why are we so
different in regard to them from men in a less
advanced state of society?

Take as an example that topic which, in our climate,

crops up more incessantly in conversation than any other—the weather. In Eastern lands a man, meeting his friend of a morning, observes that "God is great," a proposition which, in that old-fashioned society, no one is disposed to dispute. But among ourselves it is "It's a fine day," or "Cold this morning," that comes most readily to the lips; yet few people concern themselves with speculating why it is fine, or cold, or wet, or dry, or realise how immensely the daily interest of life is contributed to by observation of natural phenomena and acquaintance with their cause. It was otherwise in primitive times: all over the habitable globe men used to, and in some places do still, invent elaborate theories to account for fine weather and for foul; baffled in the endeavour to do so by natural causes, they imagined rain gods, sun gods, thunder gods, frost gods, supplicated them and propitiated them with costly or bloody sacrifices. But now that science has unravelled a great part of the mystery, the majority of men are wholly indifferent to the cause of weather. Lord Rosebery dwelt not long ago on the amazing cheapness of literature, and observed that one could buy the whole of 'Pickwick' for 4d.; it is a vast privilege, but surely it is still more remarkable that for 2s. 6d. one can buy Scott's 'Elementary Meteorology,' containing the solution of that problem of the weather which hitherto through all the ages has been the most perplexing and engrossing of enigmas to mankind. "The wind bloweth where it listeth, and thou hearest the sound thereof, but canst not tell whence it cometh, and whither it goeth"—a saying most true in the ears of those who heard it, but now that we can gather knowledge from a single octavo volume, enabling us to say exactly whence the wind cometh and precisely whither it bloweth, no one seems to care much about the matter.

It is the same with other branches of natural science. No one but he who has experienced it can realise how vastly a man's horizon is extended, how his resources of keen enjoyment are multiplied, by an elementary knowledge of geology or botany. It is, I believe, in the country where people of leisure are most apt to fall victims to the painful affliction of ennui, but it is hardly possible to lay the finger on a part of the map where the lover of plants will not find occupation, or the amateur geologist something on which to exercise his faculties.

Then how greatly the resources of one loitering in a town are extended by acquaintance with the different orders of architecture and their modifications. Yet there are tens of thousands of visitors to London who are content to be unable to define the difference between Westminster Abbey and St Paul's Cathedral.

It has been said by those who have had experience of it that no one understands the thrill of genuine enjoyment who has never voluntarily followed an in-tellectual pursuit: it is equally true that no one can receive all the pleasure afforded by natural scenery until he has learned in some degree to interpret its history; neither can any one enter into the spirit of a town without comprehending on what principles it has been built. And if this be the truth, then it is in the exercise of these natural faculties of observation and inquiry that a man will most surely find delight, and most surely sacrifice it by lulling them to sleep.

Granted that familiarity with the adventures of Guy

Mannering, Redgauntlet, and Dirk Hatterick adds zest to a tour on the shores of Solway, not the less is enjoyment ensured by an acquaintance with the New Red Sandstone and the Silurian beds.

Sir John Lubbock has wisely spoken :—

Those who have not tried for themselves can hardly imagine how much science adds to the interest and variety of life. It is altogether a mistake to regard it as dry, difficult, or prosaic; much of it is as easy as it is interesting. In endless aspects science is as wonderful and interesting as a fairy tale.

This source of endless interest and gratification lies open to every reader in countless admirable handbooks on every possible branch of natural knowledge.

For a time—but one cannot go on drenching his faculties and dulling the edge of his inborn appetite for knowledge with continual draughts of sweet but innutritious matter without a loss of natural power. After a time the mind recoils from effort, and the reader only

> "loves to hear
> A soft pulsation in the easy ear,
> To turn the page, and let the senses drink
> A lay which will not trouble him to think."

There are many busy workers following out the clues of truth—more in this age, perhaps, than in any previous one—but there are also many possessed of the priceless boon of leisure who might contribute aid to the work, and thereby earn for themselves unexpected enjoyment, but stand aside, absolutely indifferent, and prefer to occupy their minds with the fictitious predicaments of persons who never existed.

Any one who is in the habit of telling stories to

amuse children must have observed how often the question is put to him, " Is it a true story ? " and have noticed how the little countenance falls and the interest flags if he is unable to answer in the affirmative. The story loses half its interest unless the child can believe that it really took place. Perhaps it is a sign that the world is growing old that so many people are indifferent to the truth of a narrative and prefer fiction. Men of science have pricked so many fallacies that we are oppressed with the weight of sound information, and exclaim with Festus, the hero of Bailey's neglected drama—

> " Night brings us stars, as sorrow shows us truths :
> Though many, yet they help not ; bright, they light not ;
> They are too late to serve us ; and sad things
> Are aye too true. We never see the stars
> Till we can see nought but them. So with truth."

But there is one purpose of fiction which may be traced to the earliest times of which we have any record, and endures to this day. Moral philosophers, recognising the human appetite, which can be allayed only by story-telling, took advantage of it to convey wholesome teaching.

Æsop's fables are an early example of this system : being somewhat threadbare after 3000 years of use, we are apt to overlook the extraordinary knowledge of human nature condensed into these elementary stories. The cock that found a jewel, but preferred a barleycorn ; the goose that laid the golden egg ; the dog that dropped the bone he was carrying because in his own reflection he fancied he saw another dog carrying a bigger bone,—all these are everlasting illustrations of the motives of human action.

Imagine how the sage kept his audience in rapt attention when these old tales were new. Travellers describe how professional story-tellers in the East have so much power of gesture and facial expression that they hold the attention even of those listeners who cannot understand the language.

Many of the lessons taught by the Founder of Christianity were conveyed in the form of fiction. Some of the parables may have had foundation in facts, but probably most of them were merely illustrations of various types of character. Mrs Jameson tells us how, when she was young, she entertained no more doubt of the substantial existence of Dives and Lazarus, of the good Samaritan, and of the wise and foolish virgins than she did of that of Herod and John the Baptist. She relates how, in later life, she scandalised a good old woman by trying to explain to her the nature of a parable, and that the story of the prodigal son was not a fact.

We may be quite sure that, in order to arrest the interest of his hearers, our Lord neglected none of the arts of romance: observe in the story of Dives and Lazarus the clothing of purple and fine linen, the daily sumptuous fare, the dogs licking the beggar's sores—all so many details contributing to the vividness of the scene, which it is certain lost nothing in the telling.

English novelists maintain the tradition of the salutary offices of the story-teller to this day. If it is not along the steep and difficult way of spiritual wisdom that they lead us, neither is it the flowery paths of profligacy, and the traveller in quest of " fair Elfland " is not allured by poisonous flowers and fruits, such as in certain other lands are made the ordinary garniture of romance. We have passed through the riotings of the Restoration, and witnessed the frowsy and crapulous irregularities of the early Georges without losing all the sternness of decorum bequeathed by our Puritan sires. The limits set to English writers of the nineteenth century are drawn so as to shut out the chief stock-in-trade of modern French novelists — analysis of illicit love. An experienced priest once said that of the confessions he had received (and they were very many) ninety-nine hundredths referred to infringements of the seventh commandment, and the same may assuredly be said of French novels.[1] English novel-writers, on the other hand, have managed to produce, within the limits prescribed to them, a mass of literature wherein, while there is doubtless much that is of dubious worth, it is the rare exception to find the sin that most easily besets men alluded to otherwise than as a deplorable calamity. The unhappy consequences of that and of other sins—murder, theft, falsehood—are generally so strongly insisted on as to deepen the aversion with which it is the intention they should be regarded. Nor is it only the seven deadly sins which are thus presented: the minor frailties of human nature are systematically treated as to appear odious — selfishness, vanity, avarice, bigotry, backbiting—so that in fact a high moral ideal is kept before the novel-reader as constantly

---

[1] There is, of course, a limited class of French romance written down to the requirements of young unmarried ladies ; but, seeing that French girls of the upper classes are brought up far more strictly than those of our own country, these books are generally the reverse of seductive.

as it is from the pulpits of our churches; more effectually too, it may be added, for, as a nation, we have fewer imperfections as writers than as orators.

This much, then, must be set to the credit of our story-tellers: that they consistently enlist the sympathies of their listeners on the side of virtue, and in the interest of our social code it is well that it is so. It is disquieting to imagine the dangerous effect upon manners which a book, written in English with the witchery displayed by the Abbé Prévost in 'Manon Lescaut,' might have. As a work of art that romance is consummate; the reader is plunged into a state of tender enthusiasm for a couple of characters whose conduct in real life would ensure their exclusion from all society now held to be respectable.

Again, how deftly some novelists use a weapon which formal preachers seem to disdain. Satire— in its more humane form sarcasm—is by no means a monopoly of the comic papers. If a foible deserves to be exposed or an extravagance shamed out of existence, there is no surer or more merciful way of doing it than by the object-lessons of characters in fiction. Never was kindlier moralist than Sir Walter Besant, but those who have followed the fortunes of the 'Monks of Thelema' must have shivered at the castigation bestowed on extravagant philanthropy in the person of Alan Dunlop, and on the affectation of the school of higher culture in that of Paul Rondelet. This is a weapon, however, which must be used with much forbearance and skill, for the public is sensitive, and evinces quick jealousy of a novel with a moral.

The intellectual attitude of the modern novel-reader

is highly complex; his delight is to read what he does not believe, and knows he is not intended to believe, and yet he is not contented if it is incredible. Sir Walter Scott does not take us very deep into the question when he pronounces that "the mythology of one period passes into the romance of the next, and that into nursery tales of subsequent ages," for, as has been shown, myths originate in an attempt to account for unknown causes of visible phenomena or an existing state of things, and romance will not satisfy the succeeding age if it offends *scepsis scientifica*—a robust form of incredulity which withholds belief to assigned causes (even in fiction) when these are at variance with the known nature of things.

The myths of barbarous or semi-civilised people may be roughly divided into three grades; and to illustrate these, one of each may be selected from those fables constantly invented to explain obscure natural phenomena.

First comes the kind consisting of simple assertion, without pretending to excite admiration, fear, or any other emotion, intended merely to gratify curiosity. Such was the story told by the Algonquin Indians to Father Le Jeune, a Jesuit missionary of the seventeenth century.

'I asked them what caused eclipse of the moon and the sun; they replied that the moon was eclipsed and appeared dark because she took her child into her arms, which obscured her brightness. "If the moon has a child," I said, "she is married, or has been so." "Certainly," they answered; "the sun is her husband, who marches all day, and she all the night, and when he is eclipsed it is because he has taken the child into his arms." "But," I argued, "neither sun nor moon has arms." "Oh, *you have no imagination*," they rejoined ; " they hold their bows always bent before their faces, that is why you can't see their arms." "And what do they intend to shoot at ? " I asked. " Ah, how can we tell ? " said they.

Next in order comes the narrative myth, in which the listener is intended not only to receive instruction on matters exciting his curiosity, but to be interested in the incidents of the story. The medieval Slavonic legend of the mysterious advance of the plague is a vivid instance in point. Mr Tylor has given a translation of a greatly condensed version, in the original of which the interest would be intensified by minute details of scenery, features, and language.

There sat a Russian under a larch-tree, and the sunshine glared like fire. He saw something coming from afar ; he looked again : it was the Pest Maiden, huge of stature, all shrouded in linen, striding towards him. He would have fled in terror, but the form grasped him with her long outstretched hand. " Knowest thou the Pest ? " she said ; " I am she. Take me on thy shoulders and carry me through all Russia ; miss no village, no town, for I must visit all. But fear not for thyself ; thou shalt be safe amid the dying." Clinging with her long hands, she clambered on the peasant's back. He stepped onward, saw the form above him as he went, but felt no burden. First he bore her to the towns. They found there joyous dance and song ; but the form waved her linen shroud, and joy and mirth were gone. As the wretched man looked round he saw mourning, he heard the tolling of bells ; there came funeral processions ; the graves could not hold the dead. He passed on, and coming near each village heard the shriek of the dying, saw all faces white in the desolate houses. But high on the hill stands his own hamlet ; his wife, his little children are there, and the aged parents. His heart bleeds as he draws near. With strong gripe he holds the maiden fast and plunges with her beneath the waves. He sank: she rose again, but she quailed before a heart so fearless and fled far away to the forest and the mountain.

Now in this story a long advance has been made in one respect from the primitive nature myths towards the spirit of the modern novel. Sympathy is aroused on behalf of the hero; one feels impatient to know whether he rose again as well as the Pest Maiden, and lived to rejoin his family in the village which he had saved, and the unsatisfactory feature in the narrative is that we are left in doubt on that point. But in another respect this legend predicates a less abstract art than those fables which, though here placed in a third group, are often, in point of time, found in earlier stages of human development than the others. In myths of this third class there are many connected with the daily spectacle of sunrise and sunset. Some of them are elaborate and beautiful, implying a high degree of sensibility both in the teller and his hearers; but sometimes the incidents recorded are such as could not have taken place more than once, and therefore can never have been accepted as literally true even by simple and easily satisfied intellects. People might believe that the stir, the hues, the balmy odours of morning were caused each day by Tithonus leaving the embraces of Aurora, for that might be repeated daily throughout eternity; but the North American legend of the Red Swan, which Longfellow has woven into his poem of " Hiawatha," though purporting to explain the displays of sunset, can never have been accepted as anything but figurative, for it involves the daily death of some of the characters in it. Those who listened to the Russian myth of the Pest Maiden very likely believed it, for it explained an exceptional occurrence, and professed nothing except what happened on a single occasion. But in the story of the Red Swan we trace evidence of something akin to the mental condition of modern novel-readers, who prefer amusement to exact information. Only the novel-reader, while willing to dispense with a faithful explanation, will not put up with an incredible narrative.

The truth about the popularity of novels is that most people, being discontented with their environment, find relief in contemplating an ideal society where tedium is unknown and disappointment is generally circumvented; and, on the other hand, there is afforded to those who are moderately virtuous and prosperously at ease the pleasure of contrast in narratives of crime, hardship, or disaster, without the responsibility of relieving or the exertion of sharing these conditions. The hedonist who is not so well off as he feels he ought to be tickles his imagination with the power and pleasure derived from wealth by the Count of Monte Cristo. The man who finds himself unable to derive much exhilaration in the conversation of his own valet takes much enjoyment in reading the quaint sentences in which Sancho Panza or Sam Weller framed their philosophy. Has a woman been denied the gift of beauty? she is free to identify herself for the time with the fortunes of Di Vernon or Tess of the D'Urbervilles. Is a man tied to the colourless routine of a counting-house? what a stirring playground is open to him in the never-flagging adventures of Dumas's 'Trois Mousquetaires.' And for all of us it is delightful to trace the action of life-like, or at least lively, characters exposed to the same temptations, predicaments, losses, and apprehensions which it has been our own lot to encounter.

For all such harmless illusion we cannot but be grateful to those who provide such abundant entertainment to wile the journey through life. They stand, each at the door of his wayside tavern, beckoning us aside from the dust and fatigue of travelling, and we can easily choose those who are sure to bring us among amusing and instructive people.

But it is not safe to tarry too long with this phantom company, or we shall find ourselves out of tune with real men and women; unbraced for the stern difficulties, the dark perplexity which, at one time or another, we all have to encounter.

The dilemmas of real life are never so artistically arranged as they are in a novel or a drama: the living characters move awkwardly enough sometimes; they fail to satisfy our critical sense, made excessively fastidious by the perfect adjustment of parts in fiction. One is often in doubt whether living characters are good or bad; but it is easy to decide between Cinderella and her sisters, or the three daughters of King Lear. The novelist keeps the seamy side of the character of his hero or heroine carefully out of view; those who feed their judgment chiefly on romance are prone to forget how truly speaks the nameless lord in " All's Well that Ends Well ": " The web of our life is of a mingled yarn, good and ill together; our virtues would be proud if our faults whipped them not, and our crimes would despair if they were not cherished by our virtues."

The fact is that, minutely as novelists affect to paint character, there is a great deal that must not even be sketched in. It is part only of a few of real lives that endure being put on the canvas at all; over the rest a discreet veil must be drawn. It is all very well to be moved to tenderness by the misfortunes of Effie Deans, and to glow sympathetically over the devotion of Jeanie; but how many an Effie Deans there is who earns nothing but reproach, condemnation, and avoidance because no friendly hand has intervened to keep out of sight her unlovely or ungraceful attributes. Many a lass may have borne a part not less noble, not less worthy of admiration than Jeanie Deans, but has failed of her meed of praise because she squinted, or dropped her *h*'s, or picked her teeth with a hair-pin.

Reading a good novel is rather like paying a visit to a friend who is much richer than yourself: everything in his house is so luxurious and well arranged; his wife and children lay themselves out to find amusement for you; his servants are all on their best behaviour; so that when you return home you are apt to be offended if things are not so faultlessly adjusted in your own establishment.

It requires a conscious mental effort to remember that the most impressive characters in romance never had actual existence, but have been trimmed and furbished and posed into artistic perfection, with which frail and awkward human beings can never successfully compete. Even railway directors—a most material and humdrum class of men—bow before the sway of the unreal, and are so possessed of the actuality of Old Mortality as to advertise excursions, not to

Craignethan on the Clyde, but to Tillietudlem.[1] Not
less astute in this than the priests of Buddha, who
exhibit hair, bones, and feathers as veritable relics
of the 550 fabulous births of Gautama, each in the
form of a different animal.

In fact, to enjoy fiction thoroughly one must throw
himself so completely into the action of the plot as
to believe, for the nonce, in the reality of the characters. "Harp and carp," said the Queen of Elfland
to Thomas the Rhymer,—

> "'Harp and carp, Sir Thomas,' she said,
>   'Harp and carp along wi' me ;
> And if ye dare to kiss my lips,
>   Sure of your body I will be.'
>
> 'Betide me weal, betide me woe,
>   That weird shall never daunton me ;'
> Syne he has kissed her rosy lips
>   All underneath the Eildon tree."

And then the spell was complete.

And when it is seen how potent is the spell—how
many and many a mind is incessantly lulled by the
perusal of skilfully woven romance, how fiction is read
by some people to the exclusion of every other form
of literature except the daily papers—is it unreasonable to feel some apprehension lest the mental faculties become enervated and the intellect hampered
when the realities of life come to be dealt with?
The lesson of fiction is that life is nothing without
love and marriage: it brings people to the threshold,

---

[1] There is actually a station on the Caledonian Railway of this
name, and the North British route from Edinburgh to Carlisle and
the South is called the Waverley.

where real anxiety and trial begins, and leaves them
there.

But real life is not accomplished with the end of
its love-passages.   It is little to a man's credit that he
should act heroically when he is in love, for then,
despite himself, he takes more thought for another
than for himself.

> " You love : no higher shall you go,
>   For this is true as Gospel text ;
> Not noble *then* is never so
>   Either in this world or the next."

But to equip him for the real wear and tear of life
his mind should be stored with examples of those who
have encountered constant vexation, and have tri-
umphed over disappointment, perplexity, failure, and
even disaster.   It is well for him to read the Waverley
Novels, but it is far better to read Lockhart's ' Life of
Scott,' for that marvellous biography brings him acquainted with a life led as nobly in foul weather as
in fair ; of overwhelming losses surmounted by a stout
spirit ; and a kindly nature unsoured by disappointment or distrust.

One grudges to observe the amount of time spent
on sentimental love-stories, while such lives as those
of the great artists Michel Angelo and Benvenuto
Cellini go unread.   There is nothing in fiction more
absorbing than the lives of these two men.   Each of
them, as a boy, had to encounter that most formidable
of all external obstacles—an angry father armed with
a rod ; in vain were repeated floggings to dissuade each
of them from entering upon that career upon which
each was destined to throw immortal lustre.   Rivalries,
jealousies, oppression, conflict form a series of vicissi-

tudes with which it may profit a man better to store the memory than with the rogueries of Roderick Random or the dilemmas of David Copperfield.

Thousands of persons are familiar with the spiritual fumblings of Robert Elsmere, as explained by Mrs Ward's consummate art, but comparatively few have followed the wondrous story of the Italian Renaissance—a movement only second to Christianity in its influence on modern life and thought, an era which Paul Bourget (himself a novelist) has epitomised in a single masterly sentence :—

Cette minute de floraison unique où la créature humaine semble avoir été si complète, entre le moyen âge, qui fut le règne de la force trop forte, et notre siècle, où la culture confine sans cesse à la maladie.

Again, let it be said that if novel-reading is the surest as it is the easiest means of intellectual recreation, there is no cause to interfere with or discourage it; but the true hedonist—he whose avowed aim is pleasure—will find it to his profit to consider whether he is getting good value for the time spent in it, whether he is not neglecting other sources of delight not less sure and more enduring. If he applies to novels an infallible test of the value of any book—is it worth reading notebook and pencil in hand?—he will be surprised how few, how very few works of fiction stand the proof. That this test is infallible rests on the well-known fact that pleasure consists not in the present, which is fleeting, but in anticipation and retrospect. Memory is treacherous and requires refreshing, and, unless the recollection of what is read is ensured by notes, reading is a task as fruitless as that of the daughters of Danaus; it serves to spend our limited capital in time without enriching the ever-diminishing store of future.

Perhaps it will be expected that, after deprecating excessive devotion to fiction — after suggesting that the human intellect has passed out of that stage in which it may worthily be much occupied with myth— I should point out some other course that may be steered with more profit through the sea of literature. The attempt to do so has been the task of abler hands, but of all those who conned the lists published a few years ago of the "hundred best books" how many conformed to the instructions, and with what result?

If any young person of leisure were so much at a loss as to ask advice as to what he should read, mine should be exceedingly simple: *Read anything* bearing on a definite object.   Let him take up any imaginable subject to which he feels attracted, be it the precession of the equinoxes or postage stamps, the Athenian drama or London street cries; let him follow it from book to book, and unconsciously his knowledge, not of that subject only but of many subjects, will be increased, for the departments of the realm of knowledge are divided by no *octroi*.   He may abandon the first object of his pursuit for another; it does not matter, one subject leads to another: he will have learnt the habit of acquisition; he will have gained that conviction of the pricelessness of time which stirs a sigh as each day comes to its close.

But to show that, in extolling the pursuit of truth above the contemplation of fabrication, no disrespect is intended to our clever writers of fiction as guides to the higher pleasure, these observations may be brought to a close by reference to an early example of that very class of literature, in which the same lesson is more dexterously conveyed — namely, the fable of the dying husbandman who bade his sons dig in the vineyard for a hidden treasure. They did so—most diligently, and, as they thought, in vain; but in after seasons the reward came in the tenfold produce of the vines.

THE FIRST ENGLISH FREETHINKER.

THE brilliance of the intellectual Renaissance in Italy, the potency of its effect upon the philosophy, literature, and art of Western Europe, and the renown attained by the foremost men at all stages of the movement, have blinded us to the eminence of thinkers and writers who lived before the close of the middle ages. Apart from and besides the imperfection of such records as remain, the attention of succeeding generations has been diverted from the silent labour of earlier students by the intense and sudden vitality awakened in those of the fifteenth century. Just as, standing before a great conflagration on a dark night, the spectator beholds none of the objects in the landscape immediately beyond the blaze, so in order to view the operations carried on in the civilised world during the thirteenth century, one must pass to one side of the centre of action, and disregard, for the moment, the stir and tumult in the foreground. And even then, in estimating the proportions and nature of the different figures disclosed, allowance must be made for the glare reflected on them from the nearer flames.

It was the age of princes and of priests. Military force and ecclesiastical power alternately strove for mastery and allied themselves for rule. The titles of kings and cardinals of that time are associated with great works of art, while of those who wrought them, even the names have perished. No one who has traced the development of Gothic architecture from the sturdy Saxon translation of Roman building through the masculine beauty of the Norman, down to its consummation in the honest splendour of the thirteenth century, can fail in the conviction that great intellects were untiringly at work during all the rigours and perils of these four hundred years—nay, that in the matter of noble building, neither in this country nor in Germany or France have their equals since been seen. The most ambitious efforts of modern architects are no more than copies of the old master-pieces.

Take the most complete expression of the intellectual energy of the thirteenth century which we possess, the only great building designed and completed during the noontide of Gothic art and unaltered since, the Cathedral of Salisbury, and you may read that it was founded by Bishop Poore in 1220, that the cloisters and chapter-house were built forty years later by Bishop de la Wyle, and that the tower and matchless spire were completed by Bishop Wyville, more than a hundred years after the foundations were laid. But you shall learn nothing about the minds that conceived, or the hands that carried out, the noble designs: only the bare names of these perfect workers may here and there survive in the account-books of the Chapter. Nevertheless, their works remain, testifying that men thought and wrought mightily before the revival of learning.

The coincidence that Roger Bacon bore, in a time before surnames had come into general use, the same surname that was to be carried to fame four centuries later by " the wisest, brightest, meanest of mankind," has cast into deeper eclipse the reputation of one of the most penetrating thinkers who have from time to time revolted against false teaching and unsound systems of science. Hardly for every hundred persons who have a general idea of the life and works of Francis Bacon of Verulam shall one be found who could give an outline of those of Roger Bacon the Franciscan. Yet with the fruit of four additional centuries of learning and civilisation at his command, the secret of the later Bacon's philosophy was none other than the earlier Bacon had imparted to ears that would not hear—that the road to knowledge lay, not through scholastic argument and self - confident routine, but by way of cautious induction and patient experiment.

There exists one other hindrance to popular familiarity with Roger Bacon's teaching, inasmuch as there hangs over his writings the veil of a dead language. A very small part of them have been translated out of the original Latin, nor is there, indeed, any pressing reason for undertaking this at the present day. It is pathetically interesting to follow the workings of a powerful mind tearing at the trammels woven by generations of mysticism and scholasticism, and sympathy is deeply stirred for the dauntless spirit suffering persecution at the hands of prejudice and vanity; but the battle has since been fought and won, the truths contended for are now so unquestionable, the knowledge so painfully strained at has been brought within such easy reach of all who care to possess it, that, except as a study of faithful human endeavour, these writings are not now of great profit to the general reader.

But it is otherwise with the author of them. It is well worth calling to mind the earnestness, patience, and courage of the humble Franciscan friar.

M. Emile Charles, who has written by far the best monograph extant on Roger Bacon,[1] complains of the conspiracy of silence which wrapped his memory for more than two hundred years after his death. When in the sixteenth century human intelligence was pouring through channels reopened by the Renaissance, men became aware that a prophet had been allowed to pass away without honour, and John Leyland set himself to collect the scattered remains of Bacon's writings. But there was no remembrance of the philosopher's life, nor hardly any written record, save fragments of narrative and disconnected allusions in his own works, slender materials out of which to compile a biography. Anthony Wood says he was born a younger son of a good family near Ilchester in Somerset; there is evidence under his own hand to show that this must have been about the year 1214. Early in his teens, perhaps in the year 1228, he went to study at Oxford, where he came immediately under the influence of a learned namesake, Robert Bacon,

---

[1] Roger Bacon, sa Vie, ses Ouvrages, ses Doctrines. Par Emile Charles. Paris, 1861.

probably a near relative of his own. It was in the company of this individual that Roger first flashed into public notice. Matthew Paris records how Henry III., then at the beginning of his political troubles, visited Oxford in 1233, in order to meet his malcontent barons. Robert Bacon, having been appointed to preach before the king, had an interview with Henry after the sermon, and told him roundly that there was no chance of peace so long as Pierre Desroches, Bishop of Winchester, and head of the foreign party in England, remained his adviser. His Majesty took this plain-speaking in wonderfully good part, whereupon, says Matthew Paris, "a certain clerk, to wit Roger Bacon, already renowned for wit, dared to address the following audacious pleasantry to the king: 'Sire, dost thou know the dangers most to be feared by those who sail upon the sea?' 'Those know them best,' replied Henry, 'who are accustomed to make voyages.' 'Well, I will tell thee,' answered the clerk; 'the greatest dangers come from stones and rocks (*les pierres et les roches*).' He referred in this to Pierre Desroches, Bishop of Winchester."

This anecdote is the only mention made of Roger in the chronicle in which it is preserved. Oxford had at that time the reputation for liberty of opinion and unconventional teaching beyond all other seats of learning, and mathematics, elsewhere neglected, were diligently studied there. The last-named circumstance was one which greatly contributed to the subsequent character of the young student's philosophy.[1]

---

[1] The term "mathematics" was used in the thirteenth century in a sense far more extended than it bears now. It embraced the study of geography, geometry, astronomy, chronology, arithmetic, and music.

But even more plainly than the effect of sound mathematical training upon Roger, there may be traced certain influences to which he was thus early exposed at the University. Robert Grosseteste, Bishop of Lincoln, was one of the ruling spirits of Oxford and the leading mathematician of his age. In the strange combination of an ardent student with a fearless social reformer he trod the same path which his pupil was to follow, and roused similar opposition to that which young Roger was destined to encounter. Grosseteste's dearest friend was Adam de Marisco, also a profound mathematician, who, though of much milder nature than the Bishop of Lincoln, had also to pay heavily for incurring the displeasure of the Papal Court. He was a wealthy man, and it was not till he was well advanced in years that he joined the Mendicant Order of St Francis.

In the thirteenth century Paris was the metropolis of letters in Western Europe, and it was a common thing for ambitious students to pass thither after a period of instruction at Oxford. Bacon, whose ardour and proficiency in study had already brought him into notice, was but following the example set by his friend and patron Grosseteste, and no doubt fulfilling his advice, when, about the year 1234, being then twenty years of age, he went to Paris. He seems to have remained there for not less than sixteen years, by which time he had attained the degree of doctor in theology, which could not be conferred on any one under the age of thirty-five. The reputation for learning which he had gained at Oxford was certainly not dimmed in the greater world of Paris: it is said that he held some official rank as lecturer, and that his classes were well attended; but in the tenor of his teaching may be traced in the pupil of Grosseteste a growing spirit of revolt against scholastic authority and pedantry. The wrangling between the Begging Friars and the University filled him with disgust, and, when referring in a later day to the doings in the learned world, he uttered no word of reverence, still less of affection, for the weighty names of Alexander of Hales, Albertus Magnus, Thomas Aquinas, and others who were foremost in the fray. The root of the whole mischief lay, so Bacon believed, in the miserably corrupt translations of Holy Writ, of Aristotle, and of other masters, upon which the arguments on either side were founded; so, leaving aside metaphysics, he threw himself ardently into the study of languages, and acquired the power of reading the original manuscripts in Chaldean, Hebrew, Arabic, and Greek.[1] At the same time he worked hard at alchemy, mathematics, and optics, and was incessantly conducting experiments in physical science.

He had one chosen leader and companion in his labours, to whom he refers as *dominus experimentorum.* Of this individual's fame, if he enjoyed any beyond the devotion of his disciple, nothing now remains; and his works, except a single letter addressed to the knight Sigurd de Fontancourt on the subject of the magnet, have all perished. It was to this Maitre Pierre—Petrus de Mahariscuria, a Picard—that Bacon declared he owed all his proficiency in science. In the following passage he promised to tell us all about him, but the fulfilment of the pledge has not come down to our time:—

[1] Compendium Studii, c. viii.; Opus Tertium, c. xi.

No one can obtain the service of first-rate mathematicians except my lord the Pope, or some other great prince,[1] especially the services of him who is worth more than any of them; of whom I have written fully in my 'Opus Minus,' and shall write more in its proper place.[2]

Elsewhere,[3] in urging the superiority of experiment over argument in the attainment of knowledge, he declared there was only one scholar who understood this truth—namely, Magister Petrus.

Biographers of Bacon greatly differ in fixing the date when he entered the Order of St Francis. Anthony Wood says it was before he first left Oxford for Paris; but his subsequent declaration to Pope Clement IV. is inconsistent with the vow of poverty which he must then have taken. Writing in 1267, he said :—

During the twenty years that I have specially laboured in the attainment of Wisdom, abandoning the vulgar path, I have spent upon these pursuits more than two thousand pounds, not to mention the cost of secret books, of various experiments, instruments, tables, and the like.[4]

It is clear that during these twenty years, at all events, he must have been a free man with money to spend; and if they be reckoned from the time he went to Oxford, say in 1228, it will be seen that he had nearly reached the prime of life before he surrendered his liberty.

[1] Professor Brewer has compared this passage with a sigh from the later Bacon : "These are *opera basilica,* kingly works, towards which the endeavours of a private man may be but as an image in a cross-way, that may point the road, but not travel it."

[2] Opus Tertium, c. viii.   [3] Ibid., cc. xi. and xiii.

[4] Ibid., c. xvii.

The exact date, however, does not greatly concern us now: what is of more moment is the object such a man can have had in view in entering the Mendicant Order. Robert Grosseteste and Adam de Marisco had both taken the vow of poverty; the former was the first head of the Franciscan House at Oxford: but if the motive was obscure in their case, it remains doubly so in that of Roger, whose restless spirit brought him constantly into conflict with authority. Perhaps the reason might be in the state of his private affairs. His original patrimony having been spent, as he explained, in books and experiments; his family, once affluent, having been ruined, as we know, by adherence to Henry III. in his long conflict with the barons,—he found himself without means. The remuneration for his lectures in Paris, seeing that he was a free-lance in learning, was probably the reverse of liberal or regular. To a bankrupt student one of the Mendicant Orders, in which all private property was prohibited, would offer a welcome asylum, and early association would incline him towards the Franciscans rather than the Dominicans. M. Charles has suggested another cause for sacrificing his freedom. Only three kinds of power existed capable of lifting a solitary student over the difficulties in his path— the king, the Pope, and one of the religious corporations — for there was no public in those days to extend sympathy to the searcher for truth. The only way for Bacon to reach the ear of either of the two first was through the agency of the last named. Among these the Franciscans, or Minorites proper, were then the leading Order, for Albertus Magnus and Thomas Aquinas had not yet raised the renown of the Dominicans. Further, Bacon might be attracted to the Franciscans because of their independent spirit, which was to culminate in the following century in their revolt against Pope John XXII. He became, therefore, a brother of the Order of St Francis of Assisi, the first step in a road leading him to irremediable misery.

We have Bacon's own statement that during this sixteen years' residence at Paris he wrote nothing but a few scattered tracts; but we have the same authority for knowing the intensity with which he applied himself to learning :—

While I was in another condition [that is, before he entered the Franciscan Order] people were astonished that I could endure the excessive labours which I undertook.

Through all these years of youth and prime there shines no gleam of amatory romance, nor even of friendship, save such as arose in the common pursuit of learning. No woman is mentioned in any part of his surviving writings, except his mother, of whom he speaks as still alive in 1267. If these writings faithfully reflect his life, from the day he first set foot in Oxford he kept two objects, and two only, in view—the discovery and diffusion of truth, and the exposure and expulsion of what he called " the pestilential causes of human error."

Bacon returned to Oxford about the year 1250, bringing with him the familiar and complimentary *sobriquet,* conferred in Paris, of *doctor mirabilis.* There is ever sadness inseparable from revisiting one's old college, but for Roger there must have been more than full measure of melancholy. In the brightness of life's morning he had left the old city, a free man, with all the confidence of youth and the ardour stirred by the first draught of knowledge; it was high noon before he trod the well - remembered streets again. They were filled with new faces; his own countenance was hardened by disappointment, his shoulders bent by close study: the world on which he had embarked with such high hopes had turned out to be full of imposture and make-believe science. The Oxford he had left was no more the same for him. Grosseteste of Lincoln, who, he afterwards declared, alone had true learning,[1] the gentle and wise Adam de Marisco, the intrepid reformer Edmund Rich—all had passed away; while outside Oxford his birthplace was desolate—his mother and brothers, ruined in the civil disturbances, were exiles from the Somersetshire home.

Roger was not a man to make new friends easily; his manner was too dogmatic, his spirit too little patient of control, his temper, perhaps, like Dante's, not of the sweetest. His profound learning, however, commanded respect, and it may be assumed that he found little difficulty in attracting pupils to his lectures. There stood, until 1779, a tower on the Berkshire shore of the Isis, known as Friar Bacon's study: it is shown in an engraving in Skelton's 'Oxonia Antiqua Restorata.' The secrecy of his pursuits in that secluded retreat, and his researches into unlawful arts and astrology, soon brought upon him the jealous scrutiny of his superiors. He was accused, as Wadding, his earliest biographer, states, of certain suspicious novelties (*quasdam novitates suspectas*), from which, when commanded, he refused to desist. Bona-

---

[1] "Solus scivit scientias."—Opus Tertium, c. x.

ventura, the Seraphic Doctor, had succeeded Jean de Rochelle as General of the Franciscans, and had set his hand sternly to restore discipline in the Order. In 1257 Bacon was interdicted from lecturing, and ordered to quit Oxford and place himself under supervision at Paris. We have only knowledge of one friend whom he left to deplore his exile, a certain Friar Thomas Bungay, who, remarks the magnanimous compiler of the *Historia Ecclesiastica Magdeburgensis*, " had profound knowledge in mathematics, either by inspiration of the devil or by the teaching of Robert Bacon." [1]

This was the beginning of tribulation for the unhappy friar. For the next ten years Bacon was, if not actually incarcerated, at least subjected to restraint which would have been humiliating to an idle schoolboy, and must have been little short of intolerable to an intellect burning to achieve and communicate knowledge. We do not know what detail of irksome discipline he may have had to endure; we can only guess at the means and opportunity he may have secured for study, and the degree of intercourse with learned men which may have been permitted to him. At all events, we know that during this period of ten years he was forbidden, under pain of severe fasting, to write anything that should pass beyond the walls of his house of bondage, and no one was ever more thoroughly of Seneca's opinion that knowledge is but a corpse unless it can be communicated to others. What was the use of learning if he might not teach ?

One bright thread was woven in this dark web of suffering. There was a servant lad in the convent,

---

[1] Hist. Eccl. Magd., i. 3.

named Jean, of whom Friar Roger made a friend and disciple. Jean became the repository of all that his master could impart, the confidant of all his aspirations, the accomplice in all his schemes. The sympathy of this humble follower must have been the one means which saved him from utter despair or madness.

At last, when the cloud was darkest, when Bacon was entering the decline of years, and it seemed as if the knowledge he had so painfully amassed was to pass with its possessor into the land where all things are forgotten, there came relief. In 1264, the year when Henry was defeated by Leicester at the battle of Lewes, Pope Urban IV. had sent Cardinal Guy de Foulques as his legate to England to mediate between the king and the subjects whom he had lashed into rebellion. His mission, as is well known, was contemptuously rejected by the barons, and ended in a failure, but it was of indirect advantage to Bacon. De Foulques was an eager patron of learning: his attention having been called by his chaplain, Raymond de Laon, to the extraordinary erudition of the Franciscan friar, it was quickened into sympathetic interest when he learned that the family of Bacon had been ruined by their adherence to the king's cause in England. Guy was not of a temper to forget or pardon the insults put upon his legation by the popular party in England: he determined to assist the poor scholar whose relations had suffered as royalists. It was not long before he was in a position to do so effectively. In 1265 he was elected Pope, under the name of Clement IV. Raymond had told him, erroneously as it turned out, that Bacon had composed a great work on philosophy and natural science. Raymond had also, it appears, advised Bacon to address a letter to Clement, which was put into the hands of a gentleman called Bonnecor to carry to the Pope, together with many oral explanations which it was not considered prudent to commit to writing. Soon after, in 1266, came the gracious response. It is pleasant to imagine the rapture which burst upon Roger's troubled life when the following letter was put into his hands:—

To our beloved son, Brother Roger, called Bacon, of the order of Friars Minor:—
We have received with joy the letter of thy devotion, and have also paid heed to the explanation thereupon which our dear son, the knight G., called Bonnecor, laid before us by word of mouth, no less faithfully than wisely. In order that we may better understand thy purpose, it is our will, and in virtue of our apostolic authority we command, that thou shalt send to us as soon as possible that work fairly written out, which, when we were in a less exalted office, we desired thee to communicate to our beloved son, Raymond de Laon; and this notwithstanding the command to the contrary of any prelate whatsoever, or any ordinance whatsoever of your Order. And further, that thou shalt explain in thy letter the remedies which seem to thee applicable in certain circumstances, of which lately, at a very critical time, thou madest mention.
Given at Viterbio, the second year of our pontificate, x Cal. Julii [June 22].

Now, at last, the tyranny of prejudice and professional interest was at an end; with the authority of God's Vicegerent in his hand, Bacon might disregard the maddening restraint of his superiors, and, carrying out the explicit instructions of a higher power, let in

a flood of light upon the ignorance and corruption of
his enemies.

But the greatest genius cannot express itself without
out common materials.   There is nothing to show that
Clement directed that the rules of the convent, which
he enjoined upon Bacon to disregard, should be relaxed
in order that he might apply himself to his appointed
task.   Bacon explained to Clement, in the forefront
of his work, the delay which, greatly contrary to his
desire, ensued upon receipt of the command.   In the
first place, no such book as Raymond had described
was in existence.   Before joining the Franciscans he
had written nothing but a few essays not worth men-
tioning; and since that time, seeing that he had been
forbidden under severe penalties to communicate anything he might write to persons outside the convent,
where had been the object in writing?   Otherwise he
would assuredly have written much for the information of his scholarly brother and other dear friends.
He proceeds to say [1] that when the welcome command
at last arrived, he met with other causes of delay
which wellnigh made him despair.   It was accom-
panied by an injunction from the Pope, probably
conveyed verbally by Bonnecor, not to reveal the
secret of what he was going to do.

My chief impediment lay in my superiors; for whereas
you had written nothing to them in the way of dispensa-
tion for me, I have been unable to reveal your secret to
them, which, in face of your command to secrecy, it was
my duty to conceal.   They threatened me with indescribable violence in order that I should obey their will like the
other brethren. . . . Certain particulars of this opposition

---

[1] Opus Tertium, c. iii.

I will peradventure explain to you in their due place, and draw them up in my own handwriting because of the importance of the secret.

It must be admitted that there does not seem here evidence of wanton tyranny. Bacon, as a sworn brother of the Order, was bound to conform to its rules; his superiors were only acting according to their light in enforcing them. It could hardly be expected that they would take the unsupported word of a quick-tempered insubordinate friar as good assurance that the head of the Church had so strangely departed from constitutional order as to address himself to one under their rule, directing him to disregard that rule and write a treatise on forbidden subjects. Probably they thought him not a little insane, and that a bread-and-water diet would tend to restore him to reason.

But Bacon goes on, in execrable Latin it must be confessed, to give a second reason for delay, which it is certainly strange that Clement had overlooked. Member of a Mendicant Order, Bacon was penniless; the Pope knew that his mother and brothers were in the same plight, in exile, and utterly unable to help him. How was he to employ copyists, obtain manuscripts for reference, make experiments, without money? It would take, he said, sixty Paris pounds for the necessary expenses.

This obstacle was enough to upset the whole business (*quod suffecit ad subversionem totius negotiæ*). . . . I do not wonder that these expenses never occurred to you, for, seated on the summit of the world, you have so many and so great things to consider that the cares on your mind must be incalculable.

He then describes how he implored the aid of many great people, " of some of whom you know the features, but not the characters." He told them that he was employed on a certain business in France for the Pope, which he might not reveal, but which required funds :—

But how often I was deemed a rogue, how often I was repulsed, how often inflated with vain hopes, how often I was completely bewildered, I cannot express. Even my friends would not believe me, because I could not explain to them the nature of the business. Perplexed, therefore, beyond description, I compelled (*coëgi*) poor people and servants to spend all they had, to sell some of their possessions and pawn others, and I pledged myself to give you a detailed account of these expenses, and that I would obtain from you full repayment.

It says much for the kind hearts of the poor that he got anything on such extraordinary security; but he collected the required sum, and got to work at last.

When one considers the scope of the treatise he had undertaken, the narrow means which he had at command, and the short space of time he took to complete it, one cannot but be filled with admiration of a great intellectual feat. Bacon was now fifty-three; his all-absorbent mind had for nearly forty years been accumulating facts, theories, judgments, and foreign languages. But his knowledge had not been committed to writing; a few notes may have been laid by in his cell, and that was all. He had suddenly been called on to set forth all he knew, fairly written out—*scriptum de bona littera.* A startling summons, in truth, which any ordinary student might reasonably have demanded years to fulfil. Not so Bacon. It was not the least remarkable part of his encyclopædic intellect that it enabled him to utter thoughts in consecutive and consistent order, as fast as copyists could follow; and the ' Opus Majus,' filling 474 pages in folio, was completed with almost incredible despatch. Whewell summarised its contents as follows: 1. On the four causes of human ignorance —authority, custom, popular opinion, and the pride of supposed knowledge. 2. On the cause of perfect wisdom in the Sacred Scriptures. 3. On the usefulness of grammar. 4. On the usefulness of mathematics.[1] 5. On Optics. 6. On experimental science.

Even [wrote Dr Whewell] if the work had no leading purpose, it would have been highly valuable as a treasure of the most solid knowledge and soundest speculation of the time. . . . It may be considered as at the same time the Encyclopædia and Novum Organon of the thirteenth century.

The work having been happily brought to completion—and the happiness of its author can only be estimated by comparison with the foregoing years of misery—it might have been expected that Bacon would have hastened in person to lay it before his august patron. We know not what cause stood in the way, whether conventual discipline or another; in effect it was committed to the faithful Jean,—not, as some biographers have stated, Jean de Londres, the mathematician honourably mentioned elsewhere in Bacon's writings, but Jean the servant, the humble disciple, whom he had been instructing for six years, and could now trust to deliver, in addition to the precious volume, oral explanations of such passages

---

[1] For the subjects included in mathematics see footnote, p. 206.

as might be obscure.[1] Jean was but twenty, yet his master gives to Clement an enthusiastic certificate of his honesty, purity, and abundant knowledge, and predicted for him an illustrious career. We know not whether this was fulfilled in the person of any one of the many learned men named Jean of the generation succeeding Bacon.

Well, Bacon had got the great work off his hands, but he could not rest. The way to Rome was long, and set with many perils. His solitary messenger might miscarry, his precious freight never reach its destiny, so Bacon set to work immediately on another treatise, of which the only copy known to exist at this day is but a fragment in the Bodleian Library—moreover, a very badly copied fragment. This 'Opus Minus' was an abridgment of the first work, in which, also, some of the subjects treated before were further explained, and the evils of schoolmen were exposed at greater length.[2]

But Bacon did not rest satisfied with the completion of this second work. He undertook a third, 'Opus Tertium,' which, though designed as an introduction to the other two, is the most attractive of all to the modern reader, for it is that which tells most of the author's life and difficulties.

When it is considered that these three great works were begun and finished within little more than a year, it is difficult to find a parallel to such a stupendous effort in the annals of literature. It may be

---

[1] Opus Tertium, c. xix.

[2] The 'Opus Minus,' 'Opus Tertium,' and 'Compendium Studii Philosophiæ' were first printed in 1859 in the Historical Manuscripts Series, under the able editorship of Professor J. S. Brewer.

thought putting a heavy strain on Bacon's veracity to accept his assurance [1] that no part of them was in existence before he received the Pope's command,—that he had composed nothing except a few tracts (*aliqua capitula*), thrown hastily together at the instance of friends from time to time; but there is, in truth, no reason to doubt it. Any writings which he had beside him in his cell must surely have been known to the convent authorities, and they would have been ready enough in after-years to expose the falsehood of the assurance, repeated more than once in the works themselves, that they were only begun in obedience to the Pope's letter. That letter was dated 22d June 1266; it could not have been received in Paris until some weeks later: then arose the delays so bitterly complained of; money had to be collected and materials obtained. The writer could scarcely have got to work till late in autumn. Yet in the 'Opus Tertium,' the last of the three, he refers to the current year as 1267, which leads us to the astonishing conclusion that the whole of this triple series was begun, continued, and ended in not more than fifteen months. Truly a prodigious feat in literature.

Soon after the completion of 'Opus Minus,' Bacon, doubtless by direction of Clement, was released from surveillance, and returned to Oxford. But a terrible discomfiture of his hopes took place in the following year, 1268, when Clement IV. died. There was no fresh election of a Pope till 1271, when Gregory X. assumed the tiara. This pontiff, the nominee of Bonaventura, General of the Franciscan Order, was not likely to show special indulgence to a recalcitrant

---

[1] Opus Tertium, c. ii.

friar. It behoved Bacon to walk warily, and, as he
valued liberty to study, to attract no attention by pub-
lishing anything that might give offence. He began a
fresh work which might expand and place in better
order the subjects which had been so hastily thrown
together in his other books. The 'Compendium Philosophiæ' was designed as a complete and leisured ex-
position of the whole field of science. But ever while
Bacon mused the fire burned. He could not be content with stating the truth as he knew it, he must
also expose ignorance as he saw it. To fulminate was
as necessary to him as to illuminate. It might be
held necessary to show the corruptness of translations
from Greek and Arabic; but it had been wiser to refrain from denouncing the translators as false pre-
tenders and pouring ridicule upon the doctors, some
of whom were still alive, who relied on these translations.[1] Not content with this, he set in the very
forefront of his new book [2] a tirade against the abuses
in high places of both State and Church, not fearing
to lash the Papal See itself; and, sweeping the religious Orders into one common contempt, declared
that Christians were far behind Pagans in all that
conduced to wisdom and inventive science.

This was all very true, no doubt, in the sense that
there is always plenty of material for the moralist and
satirist in every age. But Bacon was distinctly im-
prudent in making a personal grievance of it. He
perceived rightly enough the false methods and vicious
material that had to be got rid of before any advance
in learning could be made; it seems now that he might
have borne testimony to the truth not less effective

---

[1] Compendium Phil., viii.   [2] Ibid., i.

without making so many implacable enemies. But he was not a man to save his skin at the price of his principles: peradventure his warnings had never been heeded if he had refrained from pointing out the chief offenders, for authority was all-powerful in those days.

Jerome d'Ascoli, a doctrinal martinet, succeeded Bonaventura in 1274 as General of the Franciscans. Nicholas III., of the family of Orsini, became Pope in 1276. Bacon's proceedings at Oxford brought upon him afresh the disciplinary eye of the authorities, and in 1278 he was taken to Paris and tried before the Grand Chapter for heretical teaching, and condemned to imprisonment. He appealed to the Pope, but Jerome anticipated him.[1] Others had caught from Bacon the dangerous infection of speculation; the authority of the Church had to be vindicated, the rebellious inquirer to be silenced, so the prison doors closed on the rash prophet. "I was imprisoned," he afterwards said, "because of the incredible stupidity of those with whom I had to do."

But not for ever. After fourteen years the *vox clamantis* was to be heard once more in the old strain. In 1292 died Pope Nicholas IV., no other than the pitiless Jerome d'Ascoli, and in the same year Raymond Gaufredi, who had succeeded him as General of the Franciscans, summoned a Grand Chapter of the Order in Paris. There is documentary evidence, not complete, indeed, but reasonably convincing, that Gaufredi, who had already released many persons imprisoned by Jerome for heretical opinions, effected at this meeting the liberation of Bacon.

He was now an old man of seventy-eight, yet his

---

[1] Wadding's *Annals*, anno 1278.

indomitable spirit had survived the sorrows of captivity. He could still strive to save the world which had treated him so harshly. He designed another and a last great book, the 'Compendium Studii Theologiæ,' and finished several parts of it. It begins, like its predecessors, with deploring the prevalence of ignorance and prescribing for its cure, and then he proceeds :—

I propose to set forth all the speculative philosophy now in use among theologians, adding many necessary considerations besides, with which they are not acquainted.

The year in which this troubled life was laid to rest cannot be exactly fixed. There is nothing but vague tradition in support of the statement that he died at Oxford, and was buried in the church of the Franciscans there.

It profits not to enter in this place upon an examination of Bacon's philosophy, writings, and discoveries. The labours of Jebb, Whewell, Brewster, and Charles have provided inquirers with a full analysis of these, and my purpose has been limited to presenting as clear a picture as may be drawn through the mists of six centuries of a life remarkable for singleness of purpose and penetration of intellect. Nevertheless, there are certain salient points in Bacon's teaching which jar so harshly with that which he ever held chiefly in view —namely, the truth—that some allusion to them is necessary to understanding his character.

While he attached no credit to magic or necromancy, and devoted some pains to exposing their absurdity and impossibility, he was a firm believer in astrology. His writings on this subject formed part of the charges on which he was condemned by the chapter of Jerome d'Ascoli. Now there is a radical difference between the relations of medieval astrology with modern astronomy and those of alchemy and chemistry. Bacon was an industrious alchemist, and pursued the two grand objects which ever flitted before students of that craft — the elixir of life, and the secret of transmuting metals. But there was nothing inconsistent with true philosophy in those ideas. They represented ends highly desirable to be obtained. So long as men worked on the plan of four irreducible elements — earth, air, fire, and water — there was nothing unreasonable in attempting to turn lead into silver and copper into gold. Had Bacon's appliances and opportunities enabled him to ascertain, as we have ascertained, that there are not four but sixty - four elements (or, as Lord Rayleigh has now discovered, sixty-five),[1] he would have directed his energy into more fruitful channels. And as for the elixir of life, who is there at this day so bold as to prescribe the limit beyond which it is impossible to carry resistance to bodily decay ?

In truth, the science of chemistry owes a great deal to the alchemists. Much of our knowledge of the properties of matter was acquired in conducting the pursuit of a chimera, and from the experiments necessary to disprove the existence of the chimera. The pursuit started with an *a priori* fallacy, but was itself a kind of roundabout process of negative induction.

But his belief in judicial astrology is less creditable to Bacon's intelligence. It involved the acceptance of a cruder hypothesis than was required in alchemy.

---

[1] A sixty-sixth, helium, has been identified since this was written.

The alchemist began with a hypothesis, and proceeded to experiments in the hope of discovering the secret. The judicial astrologer began with the naked assertion that the heavenly bodies exerted a direct influence upon terrestrial beings, and proceeded to dogmatise on purely imaginary grounds. There was no shame in being ignorant of the fact, which Copernicus first revealed, that the earth is itself one of the heavenly bodies; but it is a slur on Bacon's intellectual standing that he lent credence to the system under which the planets, arbitrarily named after the heathen gods, were invested with the human attributes which these deities personified, and variously affected the course of lives and events, according to the varying perspective in which they appeared when viewed from the earth. It is true that the belief was of immemorial standing, and that rules for casting horoscopes had been framed by writers of the greatest erudition. But were not these the very circumstances that should have put Bacon on his guard? Did he not himself denounce authority, custom, popular opinion, and the pride of supposed knowledge as the fourfold root of error?

Nor did he make matters any better by the limitation which he set to the power of the stars over man's freewill. In the *Opus Majus* he explains the difference between himself and those astrologers whom he derides as false mathematicians; for whereas they held that all mundane events were the direct result of certain conjunctions of the heavenly bodies, Bacon insisted that the influence, though powerful, and predisposing human beings to certain lines of conduct, good or evil fortune, accident or mode of death, was yet capable of being modified or overcome by resolute will and sagacious precautions.[1]   According to this scheme, a man born under the influence of the planet Mercury would be predisposed to baldness, but might avert that inconvenience by using the proper hair-wash.   It does not require very deep insight into the modern system of reasoning to recognise in Bacon's treatment of astrology an autocratic dogmatism no whit less baseless than that of his opponents.   No greater fallacy lies in the original assertion of sidereal influence than in the arbitrary limitation thereof.

Howbeit, if Roger Bacon must be blamed for yielding assent to an almost universal belief, the later and greater Bacon cannot be absolved from betraying his own philosophy in a similar way; for if he did not greatly encourage the study of judicial astrology and the doctrine of portents, he quotes some of the phenomena, without condemning the system.

Popular tradition has attributed many discoveries to " Friar Bacon " to which in truth he could have no claim.   In the *De Mirabili Potestate* he imparts the secret of imitating thunder and lightning by means of a mixture of saltpetre, charcoal, and sulphur, whence the legend of his invention of gunpowder.   But he himself mentions in the *Opus Majus* how children of various countries made squibs of this material, which was well known long before his day.   Bacon has also been credited with the invention of spectacles; but M. Charles traces this to his use of a reading-glass, which,

---

[1] See Scott's Introduction to ' Guy Mannering,' where this doctrine is explained by the Astrologer.   " The influence of the constellations is powerful ; but He who made the heavens is more powerful than all, if His aid be invoked in sincerity and truth."

being flat on one side and convex on the other, was laid on the written page and facilitated reading by magnifying the text. Although the first spectacles were made towards the close of the thirteenth century, there is no evidence that Bacon was their inventor. He undoubtedly knew the use of the lens, but Layard found a convex lens of rock-crystal in the ruins of Nimrod's palace; and Cuvier, in attributing to Bacon the invention of the microscope, was unable to show that he understood how to apply a combination of lenses.

But, partly by experiment and partly by availing himself of the researches of the Arabian Alhazen, Bacon undoubtedly carried the science of optics to a point beyond which it did not rise till the days of Kepler. He frankly owned what he had borrowed from the Eastern sage, which is just what Vitellion, a contemporary Polish *savant*, did *not* do, thereby gaining renown to which he was not entitled.

It has been commonly said of Roger Bacon that he lived three centuries before his time, but this is an observation founded on a misconception of human progress. None can say what he might have accomplished in direct invention and discovery had he not been hampered by ecclesiastical authority, and deprived, during the best years of his life, of the means of carrying out experiments. He was born into an atmosphere loaded with what Erasmus, in a later day, complained of as irreligious religion and unlearned learning. The part of his mission which he performed was to detect fallacies in accepted systems, and clear the way for workers in a happier age. Error had been accumulating in Europe through all the centuries following the fall of the Roman Empire. It lay deep as volcanic ash on buried Pompeii on every subject of human inquiry; and, if the truth were to be brought to light, some one must be found with hardihood to break the crust. Such pioneers are only too likely to meet a martyr's fate. Bacon's career, weighed as that of an individual, may be reckoned a failure, but only inasmuch as he failed to convince the world of the falsity of its system of learning. Regarded in its true light as an episode in the advance of knowledge, it must be deemed part of the mighty movement, destined in the lapse of years to overthrow the whole fabric of medieval scholasticism. The gospel he proclaimed fell as seed by the wayside; the clue which he uncovered seemed to slip unheeded from his dying hand: but still, the seed had been sown, the clue had been found, and it is to the despised Franciscan friar that the glory is due of having been the protomartyr of the new learning, at once the knell of dogma and the *réveillé* of free inquiry. Roger Bacon was the first Englishman to claim freedom for human intellect and proclaim its scope.

WOODLANDS,

WITH A POSTSCRIPT ON LONDON TREES.

" Linquenda tellus et domus et placens
Uxor, neque harum quas colis arborum
Te, præter invisas cupressus,
Ulla brevem dominum sequetur."

HORACE was less likely than any one else to be insensible to the pathos of one of the most touching sights that can be witnessed—that of an old man laying out plantations of which he cannot hope to enjoy the shelter; and in the lines quoted above he has touched on the consideration which, more than any other, might discourage the planting of trees—

" Thy lands, and home, and charming wife
Must all be left with parting life,
And, save the bough abhorred
Of monumental cypress, none
Of all the trees thy care hath grown
Follow their short-lived lord."

It *would* have discouraged and put an end to it altogether were men influenced only by selfish motives; but happily the instincts of race are as strong as those of the individual, and we are eager to do many things of which the fruits can only be enjoyed by generations unborn. It may be claimed for our country gentlemen that they have diligently (though not altogether discreetly, as is proposed to be shown) carried out the advice given by the Laird of Dumbiedikes to his son, "Be aye stickin' in a tree; it'll be growin', Jock, when ye're sleepin';" woods are reckoned as indispensable to the furnishing of a country-house as carpets and pictures; and, on the whole, the efforts of the last three generations to repair the waste of their spendthrift forerunners have been creditable and fairly successful. Leaving Ireland out of account for the moment (for in that country agrarian questions have interfered with replanting the land), the vast increase in the people's wealth has told with marked effect on the landscape, so that, considering the density of our population and the high value until quite recently of agricultural land, it is remarkable how much of the latter is devoted to the growth of timber.

Indeed, to one surveying the noble prospect from Richmond Hill or Wimbledon Common, it might well seem that he was in a thoroughly silvan country. Ridge rises beyond ridge of foliage on the south, west, and north-west, so closely that there seems no space for the breadths of pasture and grain revealed on a closer acquaintance. Yet when it is shown that of 76,323,203 acres in the United Kingdom only 2,788,000, equal to 3.29 per cent, are under wood, it is apparent that of all European States ours contains the smallest proportion of forest. How puny it seems compared 'to the mighty tracts of Russia in Europe, which, out of a total area of 1,244,367,357 acres, returns no less than 527,426,510, or 42.38 per cent, as woodland! The extents in the other principal countries of Europe are as follows:—

	Total Area. Acres.	Woods. Acres.
Austria . . .	74,106,022	24,150,213
Hungary . . .	79,617,286	22,552,646
Belgium . . .	7,275,916	1,208,875
Denmark . . .	9,347,443	507,016
France . . .	130,557,281	20,746,914
Germany . . .	133,441,960	34,353,743
Holland . . .	7,800,505	562,009
Italy	70,787,236	10,266,310
Norway . . .	76,716,965	19,167,200
Sweden . . .	100,260,443	43,953,504

In spite, however, of the trifling extent of British woodland, ours does not strike the traveller as a treeless country; trees are scattered so generally over the surface of these islands—of England at least—as to give the impression of a greater wealth of wood than in countries really possessed of a larger proportion, where the forests are generally massed on mountain flanks. Trees are still the chief feature in the scenery of our plains. The hill districts, for the most part, are bare enough; their native pines have long ago been cleared away; countless sheep browse the grass so closely that nothing taller than a rush-bush can rise. But it is from woods and waters that our lowland landscapes mainly derive their grace. Statistics take no account of wayside or hedgerow timber, of the foliage that fringes innumerable streams or flings cool shadows over the sunburnt sward of the churchyard. Coal is so plentiful and cheap with us, that there is no need to lop trees for firing, a practice to which much of the monotony of French scenery is due.

And it is not only in rural England that trees enrich the landscape. In London itself—grimed, fog-smothered, overgrown London—it is as difficult now as it was in Leigh Hunt's day to find a street, standing in some part of which—either at one end or looking down some side-opening—one cannot rest the eye on foliage. " Gently there !" perhaps the reader exclaims, believing that he can name a dozen streets where not the ghost of a tree is visible; nevertheless, one who is condemned to live more than half the year in London went a long time without finding such a street on the north side of the Thames. Any one who cares to repeat the experiment will discover that the same instinct that prompts men to embosom their country-homes in greenery has caused them to stick in a tree wherever a courtyard or a street somewhat wider than usual affords a chance of its growing.[1]

It was not always so. As in other countries, so in this, the first object of civilised man was to get rid of the trees. During the four centuries of Roman occupation the dense forest clothing almost the whole surface of the island was broken up, and entirely cleared away from large tracts. The denudation was most complete in the Scottish Lowlands and northern England, because there strategic reasons long remained paramount, whereas in the southern and midland provinces the foreigners dwelt long enough to spend money and time in planting and preserving woods.

---

[1] Savile Row and two or three of the short streets between Picca-dilly and Conduit Street afford no prospect of a green bough.

Thus the "haning" or preservation of growing wood was the object of some of the earliest Scottish legislation, the forest laws of William the Lion having been devised almost as much for the protection of trees as of game.

Gif the forestier or wiridier [verderer] finds anie man without the principall wode, but ʒit within the pale, heueand dune ane aik tree [hewing down an oak], . . . he sould attach him.

Four centuries later, in 1513, the Parliament of James V. enacts

that everie man, Spirituall and Temporall, havand ane hundreth pounde land . . . quhair there is na wooddes or forrestes, plant woodde and forrest and make hedges . . . in place maist convenient; And that they cause everie tennent of their landes . . . to plant vpon their on-set (holding) ʒeirly, for everie marke land, ane tree.

Many traces of this legislation may be recognised to this day in the scenery of Scotland. In every district round old houses or house-sites stand aged ash-trees, the planting of which was specially encouraged for the manufacture of pike-staves, the pike being the national weapon of Scotsmen, as the yew-bow was of Englishmen.

In spite of this legislative forethought, trees continue to disappear from Scotland, till at the time of the union with England all but a few shreds of the ancient Caledonian forest had been swept away. But the eighteenth century witnessed a great change. Scotland had hitherto been a byword for poverty among the nations; one war with her powerful rival used scarcely to draw to a close ere she had to prepare for another; her people had neither leisure nor means to develop the resources of their land. But with the Union came peace, and with peace wealth began to accumulate, so that by the year 1812 it was reckoned that there were 400,000 acres of woodland in Scotland, consisting partly of the remains of natural forest, and partly of new plantation. A pathetic monument of the good intentions of one great Highland chief in this respect still remains. Just before the rising in 1745, Cameron of Lochiel received a quantity of young trees for planting around Achnacarry, his principal seat; when the summons came for the clan to join the standard of Charles Edward, the plants were hurriedly heeled-in in long lines to await the return of peaceful times. But the men who were to have set them out " came back to Lochaber no more "; the saplings struggled into growth in the trenches as best they could, and there they stand to this day, a double row of beeches, their silvery stems so closely crowded that a man may hardly force his body between some of them, and under the dark canopy of foliage, of which the outer fringe trails in the swift-running Arkaig, there broods a green twilight the long summer through.

Of the natural wood remaining in Scotland in 1812, 200,000 acres, if we are to believe in the accuracy of the returns, had disappeared fifty years later. Still, planting has been carried on with energy in the north, so much so that, although Dr Johnson avowed that in his Scottish tour he had only noticed three trees big enough to hang a man on,[1] it is a Scottish county that now contains the largest extent of wood

---

[1] One of these, a sycamore at Ellon, was blown down in 1873.

of any in the United Kingdom. The four counties
which head the list in the Agricultural Returns for
1888 are as follows:—

	Acres of wood.
Inverness	162,795
Surrey	114,375
Hants	111,863
Aberdeen	106,677

All this good work has been carried out without
legislative interference, for it does not appear that
any statute affecting the lands of private owners has
been passed for either kingdom since 6 James VI. c.
84, which re-enacts "sindrie louabil and gud Acts" of
that king's predecessors. But in 1885 a Select Committee of the House of Commons was appointed, on
the motion of Sir John Lubbock, "to consider whether
by the establishment of a Forest School, or otherwise,
our woodlands could be rendered more remunerative."
The inquiry having been interrupted by the general
elections of 1885 and 1886, it was not till 1887 that
the Committee reported. Out of a total area of
76,323,203 acres in the United Kingdom, the Committee estimates that 2,788,000 acres were woodland,
distributed thus:—

	Acres.
England	1,466,000
Wales	163,000
Scotland	829,000
Ireland	330,000

They declared themselves

satisfied that . . . the management of our woodlands
might be materially improved, . . . and that some considerable proportion of the timber now imported—to the

[annual] value of £16,000,000 [1]—might, under more skilful management, be raised at home.

The Committee points out that, whereas nearly every other civilised State possesses one or more forest schools, there exists in this country (although it boasts a Department of Woods and Forests) no organised system of forestry instruction, except in connection with the Indian service. They unanimously agree in recommending the establishment of a Forest Board, of which the main functions should be the establishment or direction of forest schools, or, at least, a course of instruction and examination in forestry.

To most people the estimate formed by the Committee of the expenses of this establishment will appear fantastically disproportioned to its importance: in stating that it would probably not exceed £500 a-year (a cost which they suggest may be considerably reduced by fees for diplomas) they seem to be anxious to lull the apprehensions of the Secretary to the Treasury. Clearly, if technical training of woodmen could be secured at such a trifling expense, it could easily be done without troubling the Government at all, by the class most directly interested—namely, the landowners. But if it be the case that in our woodlands, and in land capable of growing timber, the nation possesses a source of much dormant wealth, then, in view of the haphazard, wasteful management, the ignorance and want of system proved to exist by the evidence received by the Select Com-

---

[1] There are imported annually, in addition to timber, forest products of the value of about £14,000,000 ; but of course much of this is of a nature that could not be produced in this country.

mittee, it is not surprising that the aid of the State should be invoked to provide instruction how to develop it.

Far short, however, of insisting upon the interference of the Government and the establishment of a national forestry school supported out of public moneys, it would not seem unreasonable to look to the State for an example in the management of its own forests. Unhappily, it offers none but the worst. Witness the account of the New Forest given before the Select Committee by Mr Lascelles, the Deputy Surveyor. In this great tract of forest-land, extending to between 60,000 and 70,000 acres—

There are to be seen [he said], by the student of forestry, over 40,000 acres of waste land lying idle and worthless. But by s. 5 of the Act of 1877 *no planting may be done there.* He will see several fine plantations of oak, which are not only ripe and mature, but which are going back rapidly, and he will wonder why the crop is not realised and the ground replanted, till he is referred to clause 6 of the same Act, by which he will see that ground may not be cleared of the crop. Last, and worst of all, he will see some 4500 acres of the most beautiful old woods in the country, most of which are dying back and steadily going to wreck and ruin. But here again absolutely nothing can be done. . . . It is sad to see them dying out, when all that is required to preserve them for future generations is to imitate the wisdom of those who made them at first, and by simply protecting— by enclosing them and removing dead trees—leave nature to perpetuate them. . . . Those who framed the New Forest Act of 1877 desired to conserve these old woods, but their zeal seems to have carried them so far as to defeat the object they had in view ; and I cannot but think that, had forestry been a science commonly taught in the past, as I trust it may be in the future, owing to this inquiry, no such clause could ever have found a place in an Act of Parliament dealing with woodlands.

Parliament in a melting mood is prone to pile it rather high. Two motives, equally amiable, inspired the Act of 1877—namely, philanthropy and love of scenery. The first prevailed to have the rights of the commoners prodigiously increased at the expense of the Crown; the extension of common grazing put an end absolutely to the process of natural reproduction of wood. The second promoted an attempt at landscape-gardening on a heroic scale—a luxury to which a wealthy empire may be held fairly entitled; but the method prescribed defeated the object in view. No one who has followed the footsteps of Charles Kingsley through the glades of that venerable forest, who has sheltered himself from the midday heat under the massive shade of its immemorial oaks, or watched the sunbeams slanting between the grey beech boles, and lying in golden lakelets on the carpet of fallen leaves, would sanction use of sacrilegious axe among these silvan patriarchs. There are ancient groves and isolated groups here and there through the forest over which Parliament does well to throw its ægis, but there is also a vast deal of useless rubbish which should be cleared away to make room for vigorous growth. To forbid all interference with old and decaying trees is about as reasonable as to object to the necessary repairs on Windsor Castle because it would be much more picturesque in a state of ruin; yet that is the course passionately advocated by Mr Auberon Herbert.

We want to prevent [he says], *under any excuse whatever,* the cutting of trees in them [the old groves], the fencing of them round, which has long been an official project for bringing them completely under official control, and, above all, the planting of new and fanciful species of trees which are not indigenous to the forest.

Now, in favour of the last of these conditions a good deal may be said. It may be reasonably contended that the whole area should be strictly maintained as a forest of English trees (though Mr Herbert seems to have forgotten that it is doubtful if the beech is a native of this country) to the exclusion of all foreigners. At the same time it must be remembered that this would make it almost useless as a school of economic forestry, of which not the least important function is the testing of exotic species. But the first condition—that of non-interference—condemns the forest, as similar treatment condemns a cathedral, to the sequence of two disasters—complete dilapidation leading to drastic restoration; and the second, by which fencing as a protection from grazing by the commoners' beasts is prohibited, would prevent natural reproduction, which constitutes the essential difference between forest and plantation.

Even on the purely æsthetic and sentimental grounds advocated by Mr Herbert, there is more to be gained from intelligent management than from his system of deliberate neglect; for what landscape yields more constant views of beauty and interest than a woodland, with fold upon fold of trees in all stages of growth, and the ever-varying scenes of forest industry—felling, carting, barking, burning?— a woodland, mark you, as distinguished from a plantation. The British woodman's sole idea is cutting down and replanting; but in Continental forests,

though breadths are periodically felled, the old trees
are replaced, not by formal planting, but by the
natural growth of self-sown saplings. Woods thus
treated possess in all stages of their growth beauty
which mere plantations can never rival, but this
system is absolutely incompatible with common rights
of grazing and turbary.

In the management of the New Forest, Parliament
in its wisdom has prohibited both systems. The idea
was to keep the forest in the state it was at the time
the Act was passed; the irreverent action of time and
storm has been utterly ignored. The net result is
that out of about 63,000 acres comprised in the New
Forest, 17,600 consist of plantations made under former
Acts of Parliament; 4600 of old and decaying wood,
to replace which, as it dies out, no provision has been
made; the remainder, upwards of 46,000 acres, lies
practically waste, being common pasture of the poorest
possible description. It has been decreed that this
great tract of land shall be kept, as Mr Lascelles expresses it, as a " vast pleasure-ground, combined with
a cattle farm "; which makes it utterly worthless as
a school of forestry.

Another State woodland, the Forest of Dean in
Gloucestershire, extending to 25,000 acres, is managed
on commercial principles—that is to say, the wood is
grown and cut with a view to the market rather than
the landscape; but for some years the management
has shown no profit—indeed, for the two or three
years preceding 1887, Sir James Campbell, the manager under the Woods and Forests Department, stated
that the sales had not covered the expenses. This is
the reverse of encouraging to those who see in the

great unreclaimed wastes of Scotland and Ireland a field for profitable forestry; but it is well to remember that the Forest of Dean is mainly composed of oak, partly treated as coppice, the price of which is liable to heavy fluctuation, and partly for the growth of trees which are exceedingly slow in coming to maturity. No private landowner would now dream of planting oak with a view to profit, and in days when our war-ships are built mainly of iron backed by teak, the policy which led the State to maintain oak forests is obsolete.

One other great State woodland there is in our country—namely, Windsor Forest—covering 14,000 acres; but this is an example rather of splendid arboriculture than economic forestry.

Turning once more to the Report of the Select Committee, we read that, in their opinion,

apart from the question of actual profit derived from tree-planting, its importance as an accessory to agriculture is shown by the effects which woods have in affording shelter and improving the climate, . . . whilst on public and national grounds timber cultivation on a more scientific system should be encouraged. Landowners might make their woods more remunerative were greater attention paid to the selection of trees suitable to different soils and to more skilful management after the trees are planted.

One chief hindrance to our woodlands being re-munerative may be stated at once—we are arbori-culturists and sportsmen, not foresters. A large proportion of the land returned as woodland is really pleasure-ground and game-cover. Thousands of land-owners follow on a smaller scale the example set by the State on a larger in the New Forest and Windsor

Forest. Mixed planting is generally practised, in sharp contrast to what Continental foresters call "pure forest"—that is, a woodland composed of one species of tree. This is in itself a hindrance to profitable management, because pure forest is much more easily tended than mixed plantation, and the timber is more readily marketable.[1] Two causes chiefly have led to mixed planting becoming almost universal in this country: the first is the use of fast-growing trees as nurses to others, and in order to keep down the weeds. Want of system leads to irregularity in thinning out the nurses, which often remain to compete with what was intended to be the permanent wood, and the result is a mixed plantation. The other cause exists in the idea that a variety of foliage yields more picturesque effects than a uniform kind, and planting with us is still inseparable from a notion of luxury and ornament.

Even on those estates where trees are grown as a crop, the system of "cut and replant" (or *not* replant, as the case may be) is at painful variance with the Continental custom of "cut and come again"—*i.e.*, that of natural reproduction. M. Boppe, Inspector of French Forests, in his report of a professional tour in this country, describes the generally unfavourable impression made on his mind by the economic

---

[1] I leave this paragraph in its original form, although it has been severely commented on by high authority. I am not in a position to deny that mixed planting—that is, the intelligent mixture of two or more selected species—has been found more remunerative in Continental forests than the growth of pure forest; but I adhere to the opinion that helter-skelter planting—the cramming of the ground with many sorts of trees put in at random—as commonly seen in this country, is neither profitable nor ornamental.

management of British woods, though he speaks enthusiastically of our skill in arboriculture as shown in the production of fine specimens and ornamental planting.

When the time arrives for the trees to be cut down, or should they be uprooted by a hurricane, the forest disappears in its entirety, owing to the total want of young growth which is necessary as a link between the old forest and the new one which ought to be created. . . . We saw the remains of a noble forest [in Scotland] which some twenty years ago had been cut down and converted into railway-sleepers. The sight of the huge stumps, blackened by time, with their gnarled roots twisting themselves over the ground, gave us the idea of some vast charnel-house. This scene of utter ruin was indeed a sad spectacle, though the present proprietor is doing his best to cover again his estate with timber. With a better system he might have been spared both time and expense.

Happily M. Boppe is able to point to isolated instances of better management in the same district.

It is easy in Scotland to perpetuate a forest by natural means, and of this a practical proof was given us in two forests which we visited : one near Grantown, in Strathspey, the other at Beauly. In these the results obtained under the skilful and intelligent direction of the gentlemen who manage these forests for their employers form a striking example of what may be done in the way of reproducing forests by natural means. In fact nothing had been neglected which even the most critical forester could desire. The gradation of age was here complete, and the reservation of specially vigorous trees, of known pedigree, duly carried out. The *modus operandi* consists in the exclusion of sheep and deer, in judiciously thinning out the growing crop, and in the removal of mature, seed-bearing trees by successive fellings as the young forest grows up and acquires more vigour.

It is tantalising to think of the hundreds of thousands of acres which might be so treated in Scotland alone, to the enhancement of her beauty and the improvement of her climate; but it is almost hopeless to look for a general and early change in this direction, which would imply that landowners must forego their yearly rents from deer-forests, sheep-grazings, and grouse-moors. Deer and sheep will not permit trees to grow, and trees, in their turn, make the land uninhabitable by grouse.

The question remains, Is it worth while invoking the interference of the Legislature to promote the instruction of foresters? The Select Committee answers " Ay," and point to the almost universal absence of skill and system among those charged with the management of woods. Mr Britton, a wood-valuer on a large scale, well acquainted with Wales, Herefordshire, Oxfordshire, Worcestershire, and the principal timber-producing counties, was asked his opinion about the quality of management. " Generally speaking," he replied, " there seems to be no system. I am acquainted with a great many of the land-agents in all these counties, and they are not men who understand the management of woods; and, of course, the workmen, or woodmen as they call them, have no one to give them instruction with reference to thinning." Asked if he found that many land-agents possessed a practical knowledge of forestry, " Very few," he answered; " in all my experience, I think I could pretty well count them on my fingers' ends. . . . The general result I have come to is that very few land-agents know anything of forestry, or very little."

It requires but a moderate knowledge of the craft to

enable one travelling through this country to recognise the natural result of this state of things. Woods
utterly neglected are a common sight; in some, the
want of regular thinning has caused the trees to be
drawn up into wretched weakly things; to others resort is had without method to supply timber for estate
purposes; saplings, being allowed to grow up with two
or more leaders, make deformed and worthless trees,
which timely use of the knife might have trained
into serviceable and sightly timber. In short, the
general treatment is such as might be expected, seeing that land-agents generally are encouraged to
regard woods as an expensive luxury, a fad of the
landowner.

In certain counties, useful and economical practices
prevail which are wholly unknown in others, to which
it is worth taking some pains to introduce them. For
example, the convenient little fagots, locally called
"pimps" in Surrey, made of small brushwood bound
together with a green withe, are unknown in the
North. They do not seem even to have made their
way into London, of which the countless fires are
kindled by the much less effective fagots of split wood.
About twenty years ago, a landowner, in one of the
counties of southern Scotland, obtained a couple of
Surrey "pimps" and made his forester employ some
superannuated hands in imitating them; and each year
since, on that estate, several cartloads of small branches,
which would otherwise have gone to waste, have been
worked up into pimps—the best and most convenient
kindling possible for household use. But the example
has not been followed by his neighbours, who still use
split wood and shavings, though the labour of splitting

the wood is much greater than binding the brush into "pimps," not to mention the waste of good material. The pimps soon find favour with housemaids, for they have this advantage over fagots of split wood, that they kindle much more readily, bursting into a blaze at once, whereas a fire laid with the larger sticks often requires rekindling.

This is a trivial instance of the economic use of forest product, of which the knowledge would, no doubt, be diffused by the establishment of forest schools; but considering how far and how frequently people travel, it seems unnecessary to call on the State to provide them. Continental experts, trained in countries where coal fires in private houses are unknown, and every stick is husbanded for fuel, look with amazement on our neglect of what is so precious in their sight. Some time ago fuel in Paris rose to a high price; one of the French comic papers had a caricature of a gentleman presenting a lady with a wedding-present, the most costly he could procure—namely, *un fagot de bois.* Much of what we allow to go to waste might be made to afford employment to a number of hands in the country, and, so far, help to stem the resistless current that sweeps our rural population into the towns. Take, for instance, this matter of "pimps"—admitted it is a trivial one, but admit also that kindling material is a necessity in every household: probably it cannot be had for town mansions at less than a halfpenny for each fire. The following account is based on the moderate estimate that "pimps" can be made at the rate of thirty per hour (an industrious worker can produce a third more):—

Expenditure.	£	s.	*Receipts.*	£	s.
Wages of a worker at 3s. a-day, 310 days	46	10	74,400 pimps, being the output of one worker, 8 hours a-day for 310 days at the rate of 30 fagots an hour, to be sold at 2s. a hundred, carriage paid	74	4
Cost of brushwood	*nil*				
Carting brushwood, 310 carts at 1s.	15	10			
Knives, gloves, &c.	2	0			
Carriage, say	5	0			
Balance profit	5	4			
	74	4		74	4

Showing a net profit of £5, 4s. on an outlay of £69, or about £7, 10s. per cent, which must be considered a handsome return from material now burnt as waste.

To return to the question submitted to the Select Committee, " Whether by the establishment of a Forest School or otherwise our woodlands could be rendered more remunerative ": it is clear that the creation of a new Government Department would tend to a better diffused knowledge of economic forestry and more uniform scientific management of woodland ; but two circumstances have to be taken into account before the recommendation of the Select Committee is acted on. First of all, then, is the fact that forestry in this country is at present of less importance than in any other, owing to the small proportion of woodland to the total area, and to the habit of treating much of the existing woodland as chace and pleasure-ground. It would be a novel departure to create a Department for the administration of that which, practically, has no existence. Secondly, the work to be done by the Department is such as could and should be done by private enterprise. The expense, as shown above, has probably been much under-estimated by the Select

Committee, but even if it should prove to be five or six times greater, amounting, namely, to £2000 or £3000 a-year, what impediment would that offer to the landowners of Great Britain if they were as anxious as they ought to be to make the most of their woods? There exist already the English and Scottish Arboricultural Societies: if they were reconstituted under Royal charter and supported more liberally by those who would derive most benefit from their action, what is to hinder them from undertaking the functions which the Select Committee seek to throw on the State, viz. :—

> (*a*) To organise forest schools, or, at any rate, a course of instruction in forestry.
> (*b*) To make provision for examinations.
> (*c*) To prepare an official syllabus and text-book.

To appoint examiners in the following subjects—
> (*a*) Practical forestry.
> (*b*) Botany.
> (*c*) Vegetable Physiology and Entomology, especially in connection with diseases and insects affecting the growth of trees.
> (*d*) Geology, with special reference to soils.
> (*e*) Subjects connected with land-agency, such as land-drainage, surveying, timber-measuring, &c., and to grant diplomas to students qualifying in these subjects.

It is a sound principle which resists the interference of the State, unless it can be shown that private enterprise requires control and direction in the public interest, and this is the more necessary when assistance is invoked on behalf of a class whose leisure, education, means, and opportunities combine to enable them to do all that is necessary in the matter by a little salutary and concerted exertion.　While, therefore, gratitude is due to the Select Committee for having collected evidence to show, beyond the possibility of doubt, that British forestry is at a lamentably low level, and that hardly any effort is being made to redeem what might be a source of public and private wealth from the state to which it has been reduced by ignorance, indolence, and indifference, it is not possible to indorse their proposal to create a new Department of the Government to revivify it.

The first step in the right direction would be taken by summoning a meeting in London of landowners and others interested in the matter, to discuss the position and to take counsel with the managers of the English and Scottish Arboricultural Societies, with the view of securing their co-operation in undertaking the work which the Select Committee has rightly described as necessary, the neglect of which is discreditable. The present condition of matters is unsatisfactory enough, but admits of, even invites, improvement; for while climate and soil are exceptionally favourable in this country to the production of timber, both useful and ornamental, it is rare to find a country gentleman who is indifferent to the appearance of his woods, though it is still rarer to meet with one who has both time and technical knowledge to devote to their proper management: but Evelyn long ago applied Cato's saying to this matter, *Male agitur cum domino quem villicus docet*—it goes ill with the master who has to learn from the hind.　In forestry the danger of a little knowledge is as imminent as in other matters, and the hurtful effects of it are enduring.　The affection of landowners for their trees would be invaluable, were they able to rely thoroughly upon their wood-reeves for unerring management. If there were a trained body of students, properly certificated by competent examiners, it would be easy to appoint men to a charge for which they had been specially trained. At present, no such possibility exists; when a vacancy occurs, the employer generally applies to the nursery-man who supplies the estate with plants, and a man is selected for the post, instructed, indeed, in the routine of nursery work, planting and felling, but with no knowledge of geology, botany, or entomology to enable him to grapple with local difficulties of soil and climate. A single instance may be given illustrating the unfortunate results of good intentions on the part of the proprietor, to direct which the wood-reeve possessed no technical understanding. A gentleman in the south of Scotland, having retired from the army, lived constantly on his estates and devoted much attention to their improvement. He laid out much money in plantations, and his favourite tree being the oak, he spared no trouble to obtain what he believed should be the best acorns. Large quantities of these were collected for him from the finest trees in the south of England, where, if anywhere, noble oaks are to be found. A properly instructed forester would have informed him that there are two varieties of oak in Britain (it is doubtful whether they are species or only varieties)—namely, the common English oak (*Quercus robur pedunculata*) and the durmast oak (*Quercus robur sessiliflora*), the former prevailing in the southern and midland English counties, the latter in Wales, northern England, and Scotland. The southern form is distinguished by having footstalks

to the acorns, and none to the leaves, which are broad
and irregular in outline. The durmast oak, on the
other hand, has footstalks to the leaves, which are
elongated and regular in outline, and none to the
acorns. The timber of each is of equal value, but
the durmast produces it much more rapidly and is of
straighter, freer growth than the other, and makes a
much finer tree. Moreover, while the durmast oak
thrives finely in the south, the southern variety is a
complete failure in the north: it is not indigenous
there, the damp climate and soil disagree with it, it
requires more sun to ripen its wood, and under unfavourable conditions it becomes a prey to innumerable diseases and parasitical insects. Thirty, forty, and
fifty years have gone by since these woods were planted,
and the present owner of them has to deplore that the
energy and good intentions of his predecessor were
not better directed.

A good example of the contrast between the two
kinds of oak may be seen in Knowle Park, near Seven
Oaks. Scattered throughout that noble demesne are
quantities of fine English oaks; but an avenue, planted
apparently about 200 years ago, leads up to the house
from the north, and is composed entirely of durmast
oaks, which compare most favourably with their
southern relatives.[1]

A few words in conclusion as to indigenous British
trees, which form a much more limited list than is
generally supposed. The oak (two varieties), ash,
wych elm, white and aspen poplars, alder, mountain-

---

[1] The old oaks in the Forest of Arden are the durmast. Those
planted to replace losses by storm and decay are generally of the
pedunculate variety.

ash, common maple, birch, hornbeam, several species of willow, and the holly almost exhaust the number of those classed by timber merchants as "hardwood"; while of the conifers we boast but three—the Scots fir, yew, and juniper. The sycamore, lime, Spanish chestnut, and the so-called English elm (*Ulmus campestris*) are probably part of the inheritance left us by the Roman rulers. The beech may possibly be indigenous in the southern part of the island, though no traces of it have been identified in British peat-bogs, the great reliquaries of Post-Tertiary woodland; but the beech and sycamore have become so much at home and sow themselves so freely that they may almost be reckoned true natives. The English elm, for so long characteristic of Midland scenery as to have earned the name of the "Warwickshire weed,"[1] betrays its exotic origin by never, or hardly ever, ripening seed in this country; it propagates itself entirely by suckers, which it has the faculty of sending forth to amazing distances. It is this that has given it undisputed possession of so many hedgerows. The only native British elm is the wych elm (*Ulmus montana*), a common tree in the old forest, judging from the frequency with which its Celtic name *leamh, leamhan* (pronounced "lav," "lavan") survives in northern place - names—*e.g.*, Leven, Levens, Lennox (formerly written Levanach), Lomond (*leaman* being the older, unaspirated form).

To urge upon landowners in this country the expediency of more systematic treatment of their woodland is to invite them to undertake that which they are not only well able to carry out, but, it is believed, are

---

[1] In the northern part of the county it is contended that the oak is the right "Warwickshire weed."

naturally disposed to do, and to anticipate State interference in a matter which they are in a position to effect for their own and the public good.

POSTSCRIPT ON LONDON TREES.

It will be long before the summer of 1893 is forgotten in England. Its effect upon vegetation of every degree was very notable. The long, warm spring brought trees and shrubs into flower three weeks or a month before their usual time; the summer heat which followed ripened off the seed of such species as bear fruit in our latitude, after which some of them completed their annual growth and prepared for the repose of winter; others, stimulated by excessive sunshine into abnormal activity, matured a second growth, which, in the case of young specimens of *Abies* (*Picea*) *nobilis*, from five to thirty years old, and probably older, is not inferior to the first growth either in length or quality. Others, again, anticipating the functions of the coming spring, burst out in a second crop of bloom. This was especially the case with those plants which bear flowers on the old wood, such as laburnums, rhododendrons, and clematis of the *montana* section. These are early-flowering species, of which the habit is to make growth after the blooming season. This growth, duly ripened, becomes the old wood of the succeeding spring; but, under the extraordinary conditions of the summer and autumn of 1893, it seemed to have been impossible for some individuals of these species to restrain the activity which should have been stored up for another season, and so we were treated to a second inflorescence.

But it is especially in respect of London trees—those which we have, those we might have, and those which we must do without—that the summer of 1893 left us some important lessons to learn: dry and hot all over England, it was especially dry and hot in and around London, and drought and heat are conditions to which London trees are continually liable; another, unhappily one which increases with the annual growth of our huge city, being coal smoke.

Now, in spite of these adverse conditions, and, it must be added, in spite of our disregard of them in the choice of species to plant, London is better supplied with trees than any other town approaching it in size.

A direct physical influence may be traced to the presence of many trees in a town. Everybody knows —it is the Londoner's just boast — that London is the healthiest town in Great Britain, if not in the world. Not only so, but it actually bears favourable comparison with some of the country districts.

If, then, there were no more than a reasonable suspicion that foliage does sensibly contribute to the health and comfort of Londoners, as it undoubtedly does to their pleasure, it would be of some importance to consider to what extent this ingredient of our well-being has been secured, and what kinds of vegetation succeed best in the atmosphere of large, smoke-canopied towns.

Can there be imagined any function more important in a town like London, where 4,000,000 pair of human lungs, not to mention those of horses and dogs, are continually pouring forth carbonic acid and devouring oxygen, where, moreover, every lighted fire is engaged in the same process, and houses are being built at the rate of a thousand a month. It becomes of the utmost moment to our huge population that not only our parks and squares, but, so far as may be, even our streets should be furnished with verdure in a healthy state.

In a healthy state, be it observed, for unless the tissues of vegetables are maintained in a state of active vitality, a morbid process sets in, whereby they not only cease to exhale oxygen for our use, but actually produce carbonic acid to our detriment. It is not enough to have trees, we must have vigorous trees, and the conditions of a large town are such that the number of species able to grow vigorously is extremely limited. Far more constant attention is required to keep trees healthy in London than suffices in the country. Now any one may see with half an eye that, neither in the selection of species for planting, nor in care of them when planted, is enough consideration shown by those responsible in London. The Office of Works, with its numerous staff and ample command of money, does its part fairly well (though in the matter of wide-stretching verdure Hyde Park will not brook comparison with the Bois de Boulogne), but the condition of some of the squares in private management is nothing short of lamentable.

London trees have two chief enemies to contend with, the first of these being twofold, namely, summer heat and drought—heat multiplied many times by refraction from buildings and pavement, and drought intensified in effect because every part of the metropolitan area is drained to the uttermost.

The second enemy of town trees is fog polluted by the discharge from countless chimneys. The contents of London fog chiefly deleterious to vegetable life are, sulphur dioxide, hydrochloric and other acids, and finely divided carbon known to sorrowing house-wives as smuts. A clean stem is essential to the health of most trees; green bark acts in a similar way to the leaves, and the cells and vessels of the bark are concerned with the circulation of sap. When these become clogged with smut their function is interrupted, the tree languishes and ultimately dies; its circulatory system has been deranged. In like manner, when leaves become covered with blacks, the respiratory system is disordered with similar un-happy effect. Obviously, then, the trees best adapted for London planting are those which renew their bark rapidly and rely on their leaves for respira-tion during only half the year. Unhappily, the last consideration proscribes nearly all evergreens. Dr Maxwell Masters, a high authority on this subject, warmly recommends the holly for use in towns, because " the glossy leaf-surface of these evergreens, the thick texture of their leaves, and their accumulation of deep green chlorophyll enable them to maintain themselves in the struggle." But it must be confessed that of the thousands—millions of hollies which have been planted in London, very few present a satisfactory appearance. In some favoured spots they have done fairly well; among these are Hamilton Place Gardens at one end of Hyde Park, and Kensington Gardens at the other. Even there, they are no more than caricatures of the glistening, deep-green spires, thickly set with coral berries—the very ideal of vigorous life—which beautify so many Hampshire lanes and Highland glens. But what can be said in favour of the sparsely-clad, dingy, dying specimens, affording no pleasure to man or beast, such, for instance, as compose a group about fifteen feet high at the north end of Cadogan Gardens? Languid, unhealthy vegetation such as this is positively injurious to the atmosphere. It would be better to do without it altogether, and be content with greensward, without trees or bushes of any kind. The hollies last alluded to, and many others elsewhere in London, are suffering not so much from suffocation as from starvation. The soil of shrubberies in the squares is stirred every year and tender rootlets ruthlessly disturbed which were better left at rest, but it never seems to occur to the managing committee to apply much-needed manure. Hollies are voracious feeders, and the timely application of bones, well-decayed stable manure, or even leaf-mould, would very soon tell its tale upon their constitution. This point is specially commended to the attention of town gardeners.

Dr Masters commits himself to the remarkable assertion that it is the soil of London, rather than the air, which prevents rhododendrons thriving. If that were all that were amiss, nothing would be simpler than to supply suitable soil, just as is done for the magnificent collection which makes such a fine display every year near Hyde Park Corner. But these plants cannot endure the London atmosphere for more than two consecutive seasons. Sulphurous acid destroys the source of blossom. Fresh plants are brought each spring from the country nurseries, and their verdant, luxuriant foliage and multitudinous flower-buds are in striking contrast to the stunted, dingy green of the bushes which have passed a couple of winters in London, and offer little prospect of bloom. Where there is command of plenty of money, as is the case for the management of the public parks, it is an excellent system to replace the old plants with new ones each succeeding spring; but that is the only way rhododendrons may be grown in London, and the expense puts it out of the question for the adornment of private squares.

All coniferous evergreens lie under the same ban for planting in large towns where coal is the chief fuel, for not only are most of them impatient of overdrainage, but their resinous exudations become quickly and hopelessly clogged. There may still be seen in the Apothecaries' Garden on Chelsea Embankment one of the oldest cedars of Lebanon in London. The sap still circulates feebly through its aged veins, but its demise may be looked for any day, and no cone-bearing evergreen could, if planted at the present day in that position, attain to anything like the proportions of this relic of a better state of atmosphere. It is hard to forego the whole race of firs, pines, and cypresses, with their infinite variety of form and hue, and their beneficent exhalations, but there is no help for it as matters stand with us, and consolation must be sought in some other adage than Virgil's—

" Fraxinus in sylvis pulcherrima, pinus in hortis."

There is, indeed, one tree of this family which thrives well in London; it is deciduous, and, when in leaf, as little like a pine as a tree can he. This is the Maidenhair tree (*Salisburia adiantifolia*), the Gingko, or sacred tree of Japan. It is very seldom planted, but there is a fine one stretching its graceful sprays above a wall in Flood Street, Chelsea.

The aucuba is generally classed as an evergreen, because its foliage is persistent through the winter, but although this plant succeeds better than almost any other among crowded houses, it is of little service to hygiene. The purifying functions of leaves are discharged only by virtue of the chlorophyll that makes them green; the yellow blotches which cover the greater part of the leaf-surface of the aucuba being totally destitute of that substance, the agency of that shrub on disengaging oxygen is almost *nil*. It was, therefore, a blunder to plant it in that pretty glen at the east end of the Serpentine, where a much worthier plant, the common box, grows so freely.

In considering the condition of London plantations there remains yet another adverse circumstance to be taken into account. The first thing a builder does on laying out a new street is to strip the *humus* or upper soil and sell it as loam to nurserymen and gardeners. The level is then restored or heightened with brickbats, mortar rubbish, tin cans, and even organic refuse. A promising bed, this, to which to consign tender roots! The wonder is, not that our trees are no better than they are, but that they are no worse.

The planting of town gardens is generally let by contract to some nurseryman, who, naturally enough, is anxious to get some of his stock off his hands—more so than that the plants should be suitable for the purpose. The ground is filled with fine, fresh-looking stuff, and has an exceedingly attractive appearance when the contractor has to be paid. But it looks very different at the end of the first winter. The plants die off by degrees, and have to be replaced by others—an excellent system for trade, but detrimental to the dignity of our squares.

Then how unspeakably dreary square gardens become when the turf is parched. It is very seldom that any cost is incurred in watering it. This, when it is done, is usually performed from the end of a hose: the surface is deluged, and then allowed to bake to brick-like hardness in the sun. Whereas the right way of watering grass is carried to perfection in the Bois de Boulogne and other parks of Paris. Water is turned on through a hose, perforated throughout its length with small holes. This hose lies along the grass, and scatters a refreshing shower for hours at a time, without the need of any attention.

It is seldom that any of the householders immediately interested can be got to apply experience to managing the garden; generally some one is told off to collect an annual subscription, and he is deemed to have done his work well if he asks for £2, 10s. instead of £5. But if people could be got to realise that pure air is as important as pure water, and that it is only healthy trees that can purify the air, then they would perhaps pay a reasonable tree-rate as ungrudgingly as the water-rate.

The inhabitants of Berkeley Square probably do not pay more for garden keep than those of Eaton Square, yet who can measure the difference in result. The noble group of planes in Berkeley Square act as a well of life to the neighbourhood: while in Eaton Square, from neglect of the simplest attentions of forestry, half the trees can never hereafter be other than misshapen and decrepid. There is one, indeed, a plane-tree about forty years old, near St Peter's Church, which, by accident, has preserved a right-growing form; but the nearest tree to it, probably planted on the same day, has never received the timely succour to redeem it from deformity. What a magnificent town landscape might have been created here if the whole of that great square had been treated in coherent design as one grand avenue! The Victoria Embankment offers a splendid example of what careful forestry may perform under adverse conditions. The ground there reclaimed from the tide was filled up with the usual worthless or deleterious rubbish, fit only to sustain a crop of nettles and burdock. But the plane-trees, planted along the roadway, after some twenty years' growth, have amply rewarded the care bestowed in supplying good soil and pruning each to a single leader. They will never, probably, be very fine trees, because the soil staple is so poor, but at least they are the best that can be had under the circumstances—shapely specimens of their kind; the pruning which, in the judgment of persons accustomed to rural woodland, seems to have been carried too far, has in fact been a necessary regulation of annual growth.

On the other hand, it was a mistake to plant Shaftesbury Avenue with planes. The plane is a forest tree, admirably fitted for town planting wherever it can be given head-room, but is quite out of place in a rather narrow thoroughfare, within very few feet of the houses on either hand. For such places (and there are innumerable streets in London which might be adorned and sweetened in this way) a tree of humbler growth is required, or one that will endure severer clipping without becoming unsightly. Trees of the stature of the pepper-trees, so characteristic of town scenes in Athens, are what is wanted, which decorate the streets without darkening the windows. The Catalpa is such a tree, and thrives fairly well in the metropolis, yet the only conspicuous use made of it hitherto by the Office of Works is in Palace Yard, Westminster, where, seeing that there is plenty of room for stately piles of foliage, trees of larger growth should have been employed.

Another tree well suited for lining streets is the False Acacia (*Robinia pseudo-acacia*), which is unsurpassed for freshness and grace of foliage, and responds beautifully to free use of the knife, as may be seen in the hedges of it so common along the railways of Italy. The Ailantus, also, though a vigorous grower, may be kept within strict bounds without becoming unsightly, and probably the common laburnum would be found useful in furnishing such situation.

The best time for observing the relative merits of trees in London is the end of summer and in early autumn. The heat will generally be found to have told with dismal effect on some of the species most commonly planted. The limes often cast nearly, in many cases all, their leaves by the end of August, for the viscous exudation which these trees put forth makes them quite unsuitable for the London atmosphere, though they still flourish well in the suburbs. Elms of both kinds—the native wych elm and what is called the English elm (*Ulmus campestris*), though in truth it is no native, but an importation from southern Europe—look almost as unhappy; for although the last-named species retains much of its foliage, it is always darkly discoloured, rusty, and destroyed by insects. Another tree, which it goes to one's heart to condemn, but which experience proves to be utterly unfit for town life, though it is the pride of our suburbs, is the horse-chestnut. It must have root moisture, and that is just what it cannot have in London; the few specimens that drag out a lingering existence in the squares are not only unsightly, but probably, owing to their diseased condition, actually injurious to the atmosphere. Moreover, coming very early into leaf, it is often cut by late frosts, from which, in London, it does not possess enough vitality to recover. Its early leafing makes it a favourite in Paris, where it rarely suffers from frost, where, too, the glutinous buds are not clogged by coal smoke; but even there it suffers in hot seasons from drought, and is often shabby before July.

The ash thrives well in London, but it has two qualities which ought to prevent its general use there. First, it lingers behind other trees in putting out its leaves, and hastens before others to shed them; and, second, it is a bad neighbour to other vegetation, sending its roots far and wide to suck all virtue out of the soil. But the Flowering or Manna Ash (*Fraxinus ornus*) is better in both respects than its taller cousin, and the weeping variety of the common ash is so distinct, so beautiful in summer, and thrives so well, that it thoroughly repays cultivation.

A walk through the parks and streets in the early days of September 1893 revealed the excellence of a few species in resisting the influence of London atmosphere.

The planes had suffered very little. Some of the leaves had turned yellow, but none were shrivelled; most of them were in glossy verdure, and the stems, owing to the habit of this tree in shedding the outer bark annually, were clean and healthy. Taken all round, there is no tree to which London owes so much of what beauty it can boast as to the oriental plane, and it should be, and indeed has been, freely used wherever it can be allowed head-room. Its one drawback is that it is late of coming into leaf, but that is atoned for by its retaining its foliage far into the autumn. The species with which Londoners are so familiar is not, as is commonly supposed, the American or Occidental Plane, nor is it the true *Platanus orientalis*. It may easily be distinguished from the former, which is a worthless tree in the climate of Britain, by carrying two or more fruit-buttons on the flower-stalk (the Occidental Plane bears but one), and from the latter by the shape of the leaves, which are palmate, not cuneate. The London tree is a native of the East known to botanists as *Platanus acerifolius*, or the Maple-leaved Plane.

Poplars of all sorts stood the heat well, which is all the more remarkable on the arid soil of London, because they agree well with plentiful moisture in the soil. Chlorophyll, the beneficent agent in plants, is to vegetables what blood is to human beings, and no one who, standing near the noble grove of poplars where the band plays in the evenings in Hyde Park, could entertain any doubts about the health of trees bearing such deep-green masses of verdure, of which the rustling sound is like the murmur of a cascade. This pleasant noise, characteristic of aspens and all poplars, is the result of an interesting piece of leaf structure. The leaves of most flat-leaved trees have glands only on the under surface, the upper one being protected from sun-burn by a coat of varnish; but in the poplars the leaf-stem is suddenly flattened midway, whereby the leaf is caused to hang vertically, like that of the eucalyptus, escapes the direct rays of the sun, and is enabled to carry glands on both surfaces. It is this mechanism which produces the well-known tremor of the aspen, and no doubt it provides the whole family with protection against the mischief of smuts.

The upright Lombardy poplar is invaluable in the town landscape from the contrast it affords to the horizontal lines of streets; but there is one notable instance of its misplacement arising from ignorance of a peculiarity of this species. Of all deciduous trees, it is the only one which refuses to approach closely to another, or mingle its boughs with its neighbour. Some mysterious repellent quality enables it to maintain a clear space between individuals, however closely they may be planted. A very Lucrece among trees, it will rather die than be embraced. Hence the row of poplars which was intended to form a thick screen between Buckingham Palace and the roadway totally failed of its effect, and most of the trees have been felled.

Hot summers are all in favour of the Ailantus, which maintain dense, heavy foliage to the end. It is sometimes objected to this tree that it diffuses an unpleasant odour, but that is seldom perceptible in our climate. In habit the Ailantus, or Tree of Heaven, is prone to branch widely, and in London it seldom receives the timely attention necessary to keep it in shape. The largest Ailantus I can mention in London is one standing in the grounds of Stafford House, and is visible from the Mall.

But of all the trees which adorn our town, none is so conspicuously verdant in hot seasons as one of which not half enough use is made, the False Acacia (*Robinia pseudo - acacia*). Late in leafing, like the plane and ash, its beautiful foliage shines like malachite long after the elms and limes have become sere and unsightly. This tree cannot be spoken of too warmly for town planting ; as yet it is seldom to be seen. One of considerable size, standing at the corner of Sefton House in Belgrave Square, shows how the excessive drainage of the London area is precisely what suits it best.

What the parks are to the town, house walls might be to every street that is not given up to shops. Happily the Virginian creeper is already trained upon many house-fronts, and nothing can exceed its beauty in late summer and autumn. But as a cleanser of the atmosphere this luxuriant climber must yield to a wall-plant much seldomer seen, yet much richer in chlorophyll, equally patient of drought and heat, and not less beautiful. The fig is perfectly at home in the climate of London ; what matter though it put forth leaves only ? Leaves, and plenty of them, are what we most want, and if every householder who does not grow an Ampelopsis were to plant a fig-tree, it would be greatly to the advantage of himself and his neighbours. Our street architecture is not, generally speaking, so beautiful that we need hesitate to wrap it up in foliage; besides, there are neglected by-ways, such as the streets leading from Eaton Square to Eaton Place, where there is wealth of dead walls for which nobody seems to care. There is an unhappy fig-tree on the side of Herbert House, which only wants training to become a joy to the whole neighbourhood, such as is afforded by a large one on the corner house of Pont Street and Cadogan Place. The fig-tree, moreover, has this merit for our present purpose, that it produces the maximum of foliage with the minimum of root-room. The mulberry resists excessive heat, and is able to repel the attacks of acid in urban atmosphere. It is a fine tree for planting in London, whether as a standard or against a wall. Other excellent and beautiful wall-plants are the white jasmine and the blue Passion-flower (*Passiflora cœrulea*); of the last-named a good specimen may be seen in Chesham Place.

A word about humbler vegetation. The holly and aucuba have already been mentioned, but there is another evergreen which excels the holly in maintaining its verdure—namely, *Euonymus radicans*, not the variegated kinds but the plain-leaved species. The common privet has become a perfect weed in the squares; not another root of it should be planted, and a great deal of it should be cleared away to make room for the far more beautiful and equally robust kinds from Asia, which retain their leaves almost throughout the winter. There is an enormous variety of flowering-shrubs with which experiments should be made, avoiding those with clammy or viscous exudation; but it is to be feared that the practice is to go on planting the old kinds.[1]   Among the bamboos, *Bambusa metaké* thrives luxuriantly in sheltered places not overshadowed by trees, but its use as yet is confined to the parks under the management of the Office of Works.   Many other species of bamboo, introduced into Europe mainly by the diligence of M. Marliac, of Temple-sur-Lot, have proved perfectly hardy in the climate of Great Britain, and cannot be too highly praised for their grace and beauty.

To sum up.   The state of London plantations is very much better than might have been the case, considering the somewhat unkindly soil, the stringent drainage, intense heat, and impure atmosphere which have to be encountered; but there is much room and necessity for improvement in the choice of species, and their cultivation when chosen.   Year by year the town is eating outwards into the country, and no care is taken—it is nobody's business to take care—that trees should not be needlessly felled.   At the moment of writing a fine grove of oaks between Balham and Tooting Bec stands condemned to make way for bricks and mortar.   It is one of the chief ornaments of that sweet little oasis—Tooting Bec Common—yet nothing can be done, it seems, to preserve it.[2]   All the more reason to cherish the trees in town squares and parks, increase their number, and improve their condition.

---

[1] While I have been looking over the proof of this paper I have become aware of a lovely specimen of a good town shrub.   In Cheyne Walk, Chelsea, there may be seen a bush of *Althœa frutex* loaded with blossom in this month of August.

[2] The upper portion of this grove has already fallen.

GARDENS.

BY unravelling the mysteries of physical law, and compelling inanimate objects to unfold the secrets of their origin and development, science has contributed to the significance and even to the romance of natural scenery. A beautiful landscape speaks two languages to one who has learnt the elements of geology; wayside weeds are more than merely foreground garniture in the eyes of one instructed in botany; the bleak moor, the muddy estuary, the gusty hill-top, the forbidding morass— each has its store of interest for the instructed eye; there is hardly an acre of the earth's surface that refuses a harvest to knowledge.

But it must also be confessed that while with one hand science draws the veil aside from truth, with the other she ruthlessly casts down many pretty images of the false gods, before which crowds of worshippers have bent the knee. Over no kind of created things has there been thrown such a network of poetic imagery and sentiment as over flowers; so much so that the good old word "posy," now elbowed out of English speech by the foreign "bouquet," is but another form of "poesy," as if flowers were indeed but a visible form of verse. They appeal so directly to our sense of beauty that it is a common thing to apply intensive language to them. Even botanists, usually grave and staid as becomes men of science, yielding to enthusiasm, ransack the dictionary for names descriptive of the graces of different species, and unscientific folk see nothing but fitness in such superlatives as *elegantissima, formosissima, spectabilis, eximia,* and the like. But how dry and emotionless is the language used to describe some of the loveliest flowers! It is hard not to feel indignant when a graceful plant, like our native gladwyn, or wood iris, with delicate lavender blossoms and stars of bright orange berries, is ticketed with the ugly name *Iris fœtidissima,* the stinking flag, for no other reason than because its shining blades, when bruised, exhale the odour of cold beef.

Often as Perdita's exquisite catalogue has been repeated, it is difficult to resist quoting from it:—

<blockquote>
"O Proserpina
For the flowers now that, frighted, thou let'st fall
From Dis's waggon ! daffodils
That come before the swallow dares, and take
The winds of March with beauty ; violets, dim,
But sweeter than the lids of Juno's eyes
Or Cytherea's breath ; pale primroses,
That die unmarried, ere they can behold
Bright Phœbus in his strength, a malady
Most incident to maids ; bold oxlips, and
The crown-imperial, lilies of all kinds,
The flower-de-luce being one."
</blockquote>

Compare with this the sapless descriptions in botanical books. Bentham describes the daffodil as a "single, large, scentless yellow flower"; the charms of the violet are summarised coldly as "flowers nodding, of the bluish-violet colour named after them, or white, more or less scented"; while the primrose is dismissed with the comment that its "corolla is usually yellow or straw-coloured." So, when the same authority tells us that the blossoms of the sweet-briar are "pink, usually solitary," his language hardly conveys so vivid an impression of the flower as that contained in Tasso's glowing lines:—

> " Deh mira, egli cantò, spuntar la rosa
> Dal verde suo modesta e verginella,
> Che mezzo aperta ancora e mezzo ascosa,
> Quanto si mostra men, tanto è piu bella." [1]

But the poets are prone to push matters far further than this. Not content with truthful description, they have invested flowers with a fanciful symbolism, and often go so far as to enlist them in sympathy with human mood and passion. Tennyson saw far too deeply into the secrets of nature, and was too true an artist, to lend himself to this delusion. In the following famous lines, crammed as they are with sentiment as false as Perdita's was true, it is a morbid egoist, on the brink of insanity, whom the poet makes to speak :—

[1] " Mark ye (he sings) in modest maiden guise
> The red rose peeping from her leafy nest ;
> Half opening, now, half closed, the jewel lies,
> More bright her beauty seems the more represt."
> —Bayley's Translation.

> " The slender acacia would not shake
>   One long milk-bloom on the tree ;
> The white lake-blossom fell into the lake
>   As the pimpernel dozed on the lea ;
> But the rose was awake all night for your sake,
>   Knowing your promise to me ;
> The lilies and roses were all awake,
>   They sighed for the dawn and thee.
>
> .   .   .   .
>
> There has fallen a splendid tear
>   From the passion-flower at the gate,
> She is coming, my love, my dear ;
>   She is coming, my life, my fate ;
> The red rose cries, ' She is near, she is near ' ;
>   And the white rose weeps, ' She is late ' ;
> The larkspur listens, ' I hear, I hear ' ;
>   And the lily whispers, ' I wait.' "

Nothing is more clear than the utter indifference of Nature to human joy or sorrow : the daffodils are much concerned with the March winds, but with the sighs or smiles of men and women—not at all ; the roses, the larkspurs, and the lilies would have reflected precisely the same rays, poured the same incense, held their fair heads at the same angle, whether Maud kept tryst or broke her promise to come.   It is, in truth, not poetic insight but intense egoism that makes a man suppose that trees and flowers, seas and skies, are in sympathy with his feelings, and it is an impertinence even to pretend that they can be influenced by human vicissitude.   To do so is as much an error against right art as to import supernatural agency into romance, and is as far astray from the genuine aim of literature as astrology differs from astronomy.

But, on the other hand, one cannot help being delighted when scientific method and cold - blooded analysis break down, swept away before the imperious sway of beauty, and Linnæus bursts into tears on beholding for the first time an English common covered with gorse in bloom. That great marshal of the host of green things, whose clear-sighted genius first prevailed to rally and array the multitudinous forms examined and described by his predecessors into manageable genera and species, has left behind him, in addition to the imperishable monument of the Linnæan System, a touching proof of his softer feelings for the objects of his study. It was not with the gorgeous flora of the tropics, nor with the towering pines of Scandinavian forests, that he sought to link his name; but, choosing a fragile, trailing herb which rears its tiny pink bells not more than two or three inches above the moss and fallen fir-needles in northern woods, he gave it the name it still bears, *Linnæa borealis.* This lovely plant he made his badge; it forms the device on his bookplate, with the tender motto, *Tantus amor florum*—" So deep my love for flowers."

It is possible that the lovers of flowers in Linnæus's day may have thought him a tiresome pedant for arranging their favourites in artificial groups and genera, and regarded his system as an unnecessary interference with the beautiful art of gardening; but how much more seriously the latest results of botanical science threaten the sentimental significance of flowers! In childhood, in love, in war, in politics, in feasts and in mournings, in every kind of ceremony, parable and poetry, flowers have been the fittest emblems ever since the world began. To some they seem to have been created for the joy of man, to others

for the glory of God ; but now we are told to believe
that every use to which they have been put by human
beings has been an interference with their real purpose, and that every meaning that has been discerned
in them is utterly wide of their true function. Not to
fill man's heart with joy and gratitude for a beautiful
creation, nor yet to raise his spirit in adoration to the
Creator, were those lovely petals spread in myriad
forms and hues and all their alchemy of odour
devised, but solely to attract winged and creeping
things which, passing from corolla to corolla, should
carry the virtues of one plant to another, and secure
cross-fertilisation ! We are told of islands in the
South Pacific where, as yet, no winged insect has
ever come, and there the plants have no gay flowers
or attractive odours, and the pollen of one has to
wait till a favouring breeze wafts it to the expectant
stigma of another.

All this may seem to work sad havoc with our love
for flowers, which is, nevertheless, so universal that it
will take generations of materialism to uproot it.

Were proof wanted of how closely flowers are inter-
woven with the affections of civilised man, it would
only be necessary to cite the evidence of every house
in Europe which is worthy of being called a home,—
from that of the wealthy landowner, who spends many
thousands a year on his flower-beds and orchid-houses,
to the artisan's in a back street with its geranium-pots
in the window, or the Alpine shepherd's, with a box of
luxuriant carnations on the sill. Nay, strongest proof
of all, does not the British Parliament, that sifts every
pound voted each year in Committee of Supply with
ferocious scrutiny and suspicion of extravagance, allow

huge sums to be spent on the beautifying of London parks?

Seeing, then, that flower-gardens are sources of pleasure, and that much money is spent on them annually, it is worth the inquiry whether they are made to yield all the pleasure that might be had from them, and whether the money, as a rule, is well spent. It would be strange if this turned out to be the case, seeing that a very small proportion of those who own gardens care to learn anything about their culture, or know anything about flowers except their general effect.

In this country the art of gardening has been made to encounter a serious disadvantage arising from the way well-to-do-people have chosen to arrange their seasons; for, whereas Nature has provided that by far the larger number of plants shall put forth their blossoms in spring and early summer, that is precisely the season which "society" has perversely ordained shall be spent in town. Further, the hues of spring and summer flowers being much purer and brighter than those of late summer and autumn, gardeners have been obliged, in order to give satisfaction to their employers, to have recourse to plants from those regions where spring corresponds to our autumn. This complicates matters immensely: it is much easier to obtain good effects by enlisting the seasons on one's own side than when they are contrary, but it is a difficulty that has been very creditably overcome in big establishments. Unfortunately, in order to do so it was necessary to clear the ground of plants that had given pleasure to our grandmothers, and to their grandmothers before them: borders which, year by year, for generations, had glowed with the same jewellery of crocus, hepatica, narcissus, iris, lilies, and summer roses, had now to be cleared, and their contents, rich with all fond association, flung on the waste-heap, or, at best, banished to the kitchen-garden, to make way for glaring scarlet, blue, and yellow of geranium, lobelia, and calceolaria. I well remember, some twenty years ago, making prize of a barrow-load of roots of the white Madonna lily which had been thrown on the rubbish-heap of a villa garden in a small seaport town. They were planted in my borders, which they beautify to this day.

And the mischief did not stop with big fashionable gardens. People of far humbler means—even those who lived all or most of the year in their country homes—were induced to ape the prevailing mode, and chose, or were persuaded by their gardeners to be content with, brown barren beds for nine months in the year, provided a proper blaze could be prepared for the autumn. The scheme of gardening that could only be carried out successfully on a great scale was attempted in cottage and villa gardens, with deplorable results. Even where space and means were not wanting, the new materials were infinitely more hazardous than the old. To deal with plants chosen because they produce a profuse mass of strong colour requires a trained eye such as few gardeners can be expected to possess; the old - fashioned permanent borders might be trusted to throw up such a wealth of foliage and variety of form as to soften crude contrasts and disguise indiscreet juxtaposition; their general effect was a bank of various verdure, lit up by splashes and sparkles of bright or subdued colour: but the new system aimed at unmitigated breadths of intense hue, disposed in bands, concentric circles, or other uncompromising forms — in short, as unlike Nature and as like upholstery as might be. Often the effect was, and is still, excruciating; people sensitive to the beauty of Nature shunned the garden with its shadeless walks and fiery parterres, seeking in woodland paths that reposeful charm and those soothing perfumes which fashion had banished beyond the pale.

So universal was the submission to the new decree that the traditional English flower - garden almost ceased to exist, except about some quiet farmhouses in the South, and a few, very few, old Scottish mansions. The links in the long chain from the days of Queen Elizabeth and Shakespeare were severed. Spenser himself could not have described the modern garden as

> " Here and there with pleasant arbors pight,
> And shady seats, and sundry flow'ring bankes,
> To sit and rest the walker's wearie shankes ;"

and it would have been the very last place of resort for him of whom he wrote :—

> " To the gay gardens his unstaid desire
> Him wholly carried, to refresh his sprights ;
> There lavish Nature in her best attire
> Poures forth sweet odors and alluring sights ;
> And Art, with her contending, doth aspire
> To excell the naturall with made delights ;
> And all that faire or pleasant may be found,
> In riotous excesse doth there abound."

For everything that interfered with the general

view of the beds was cleared away, if timely inter-
cession were not at hand. Some years ago there
stood in the flower-garden of Bemersyde, near Dry-
burgh, four immense hollies clipped into dense domes
of green. One of these was said to be the largest
holly in Scotland, which was very likely true, for
of the two that remain, one is the largest I ever
beheld, either in Scotland or elsewhere. These four
stood in a square on the flat pleasaunce in front of
the fine old Border tower, till one evil day, it is said,
it occurred to the agent who managed the property
to lay out the ground in the fashionable style, and
because two of these fine trees infringed on the symmetry of the proposed parterre, he ordered them to be
cut down. O Priapus and Pomona! O Hamadryads
and Fauns! where were ye that day, that ye did not
hunt the wretched man into the deepest pool in the
Tweed, rather than such cruel havoc should be
wrought?

The result of this and other acts of violence was
an intolerable monotony. Go into one garden after
another, you would come on the same Mrs Pollock
geranium, the same ageratums, lobelias, and calceo-
larias named after various members of the plutocracy,
the identical cerastium and coloured beet. The only
variety was in the pattern in which they were
disposed.

For five-and-twenty or thirty years this tyranny
endured. Everybody conformed to it, but nobody
enjoyed the results very much, except the experts,
who vied with each other who could produce the most
fiery conflagration in autumn. People were dissatisfied, they did not know why, though the reason was

not difficult to divine, for form, scent, and refined colour had been exchanged for novelty of contrast and glare; association had been broken, and it was impossible to feel for bedding-out plants any of the affection inspired by the old favourites that held the same places in a border for more than a century, and faithfully told the changing seasons by their growth, blossom, and decay.

Gradually a reaction set in. Lord Beaconsfield, the anniversary of whose death has become so strangely associated with the rathe primrose, probably knew as much and as little about horticulture as the Emperor of Morocco, but he was exceedingly sensitive to popular feeling, even in small matters, and gave indication in 'Lothair' of what was coming. Corisande's garden (though it might have puzzled the author to define a "gilliflower") was described with some minuteness on a Shakespearean model. People were captivated with the idea suggested; it reminded them of what gardens had been when they were children, and presently an inquiry began for long-neglected herbaceous plants. Mr William Robinson became the energetic pioneer of the movement; his 'Alpine Flowers for English Gardens,' 'Hardy Plants and How to Grow Them,' 'The Wild Garden,' and other works, were written with admirable skill and taste, and showed complete practical knowledge. They met with so much success, and did so much to stimulate the revolt against "bedding-out," that he was encouraged to start a weekly journal, which continues, as it began, an effective advocacy of Perdita's flowers and their like, and a protest against the exclusive or general use of tender flowers. The true key-note is struck in the motto selected by Mr Robinson for his paper, 'The Garden':—

> "This is an art
> Which does mend nature, change it rather, but
> The art itself is nature."

The reform has been general; long-forgotten favourites have been hunted up from places where they had been suffered to linger, and already English gardens are throwing off that distressing similarity to one another which threatened to make their old name of "pleasaunce" a term of bitter irony. One feature they must always have in common, though it is capable of being disposed in a thousand different ways—namely, green turf. Thanks to our benignant skies, the "moist, bird-haunted English lawn" is never likely to suffer permanently from any passing freak of fashion, and with liberal breadths of closely shaven grass no piece of ground can be other than beautiful; as Bacon truly observed, "Nothing is more pleasant to the eye than green grass kept finely shorn."

There was one dominant feature in Elizabethan gardening which it were not well to see universally revived, and that is the art of the topiarist, by which almost every tree and shrub that would suffer the shears was clipped into fantastic similitude of men, birds, beasts, castles, and other figures. When this practice was as universal as bedding-out was a dozen years ago the effect must have been equally distressing. Nevertheless, such specimens of this treatment as have survived the lapse of centuries will, it is hoped, be jealously guarded, for, apart from their antiquarian interest, and the romantic association with which they are invested, they afford a grateful excitement to the eye accustomed to tamer and more uniform arrangement. Not many such remains; indeed, Lord Stanhope remarks, in his 'History of England,' that

Throughout the whole of England there remains, perhaps, scarcely more than one private garden presenting in all its parts an entire and true sample of the old designs; this is at the fine old seat of Levens, near Kendal. There, along a wide extent of terraced walks and walls, eagles of holly, and peacocks of yew still find, with each returning summer, their wings clipped and talons pared. There, a stately remnant of the old *promenoirs*—such as the Frenchmen taught our fathers, rather, I would say, to build than to plant—along which, in days of old, stalked the gentlemen with periwigs and swords, the ladies in hoops and furbelows, may still to this day be seen.

So great is the fascination of the garden at Levens, where flowers seem brighter and more luxuriant than in any nineteenth-century borders, by contrast with the formal, sombre yews and the sad grey walls of the old mansion - house, that it is strange that no attempt has already been made to revive the forgotten topiary art. Yet one shudders to think of the result should it ever become the fashion. Stripped of the glamour of eld, tortured shrubs and shorn trees are not objects in which the eye finds repose; the object should be to assist and control Nature, not to deform or travesty her. There is, however, one feature in the Elizabethan garden which should find a place in the Victorian more commonly than it does—namely, the close or pleached alley. It gives the seclusion which is of the essence of a garden, and how the artists of romance, from Boccaccio and Marguerite of Navarre onwards, love to loiter in these leafy corridors! So

Madelon, in the celebrated scene in the " Précieuses Ridicules," describes to the dumfoundered Gorgibus her notions of decorous courtship: " La déclaration se doit faire ordinairement dans une allée de quelque jardin, tandis que la compagnie s'est un peu éloignée."

It is no easy task to lay out or alter a garden. People with natural taste have not served apprenticeship to the craft; they have a general idea of the effect desired, but they don't know the means required to produce it: on the other hand, gardeners who have the skill and understand the materials rarely have had opportunities of cultivating taste. More than half the happy effects come by chance. Moreover, the newly awakened zeal for hardy plants is sometimes disappointing in its results. Spring flowers, most charming of all, are too often arranged to give a dotty effect: they blaze from the brown earth with no friendly foliage to lend breadth to the arrangement. In summer, the borders are apt to look rank and weedy, the weaker species struggling for existence with robust neighbours; and in autumn, unless wise preparation has been made, they are apt to be dull and flowerless. " Oh, I wish you had seen the garden a month ago; it *was* in beauty then, but the things have gone over now!" That is precisely where the gardener's art is wanted to assist Nature, and is quite capable of doing so with the wealth of material at his disposal. Perennial borders should never " go over," not even in winter, when they are generally given over to despair. There should always be *some* part of the garden, no matter what the season, where things are at their best. Yet there is a family of plants, too much neglected, the peculiar property of which is to

bridge the gulf between the embers of October and the
first sparkles of February.   This family is the Hellebore, of which the Christmas rose is a lovely and well-
known member.   The first to flower is *H. niger maxi-
mus,* which opens its great bells, of the colour of apple-
blossom, in the first days of November, and thenceforward—blow high, blow low, come sleet or snow or
frost or rain—will maintain great wreaths of bloom
till well on in January.   Then the other varieties of
H. niger, of which there are at least a dozen, take up
the running and keep things gay till the later kinds,
H. abchasicus, antiquorum, orientalis, and others produce their pink, purple, or white clusters.   By this
time we are well into the months of snowdrop, crocus,
winter aconite, and hepatica, and the dead months have
slipped away.   But on the Hellebore need not be thrown
all the work ; there is the fragrant coltsfoot (*Tussilago
fragrans*) blooming all the time, with a strong scent
exactly like heliotrope, and as hardy as its plebeian
relative of the roadsides ; the winter cherry (*Physalis
Alkekengi*), with the constitution of a burdock, hung
with quaint orange bladders from Michaelmas to
Christmas ; there are also certain shrubs, such as the
witch hazel (*Hamamelis arborea* and *virginica*), with
strange festoons of yellow and crimson stars on leafless
twigs ; the winter jasmine (*Jasminum nudiflorum*), a
very Mark Tapley among herbs, and, in mild districts,
the golden *Azara integrifolia* and the crimson *Rhodo-
dendron nobleanum,* all of which pour out in blossom
at that season the virtue stored in them by summer
suns.

People with well-stored conservatories and stoves
will think lightly of this garniture of winter beds,

liable any day to be buried overhead in snow; but without in the least undervaluing the luxury of glasshouses, one may be allowed to claim a special charm in the humble out-of-door flowers that reappear year after year in the same place, only asking to be let alone. Some of these lowly plants are of extraordinary longevity; it is impossible to guess the age of some clumps of iris, sweetwilliam, or scarlet lychnis, but there is no apparent reason why they should not outlive the oak, possessed as they are of perpetual power of renewing themselves.

One cannot be ungrateful for the skill which, by an elaborate system of forcing, supplies us with spring and summer flowers in mid-winter, and makes London flower-shops as attractive at Yuletide as at Whitsuntide. Still, there is a good deal of sense in Biron's speech in "Love's Labour's Lost":—

> "Why should I joy in any abortive mirth?
> At Christmas I no more desire a rose
> Than wish for snow in May's new-fangled mirth,
> But like of each thing that in season grows."

No doubt our enjoyment of spring and summer flowers would be keener if we were not accustomed to have lilies-of-the-valley at the New Year and carnations at Candlemas.

People with knowledge of and liking for hardy plants are apt to give the herbaceous garden too much the character of a botanical collection. They have not the resolution to exclude species of inferior beauty; but, with the wealth of all the ends of the earth to choose from, resolute discretion is necessary if the garden is to be one worthy of the name.

If a contrast were sought to the formal style of

gardening of the seventeenth century, so well exemplified in the beautiful pleasaunce at Levens above referred to, one more complete could not be found than in a garden of equal merit, though on a totally different plan, in Mr George Wilson's grounds at Oakwood, near Weybridge. The owner and maker of this paradise may best be described as a decorative botanist: deeply versed in all plant-lore, yet with a constant eye to what consists with beauty, he has enclosed several acres on the slope and crest of a hill, including a wood at the foot and a piece of water. Here he has assembled a vast collection of plants, carefully arranged, but with all trace of design studiously concealed. A lady lately visiting it expressed the effect in a single sentence. "I hardly know," she said, "what this place should be called; it is not a garden, it is a place where plants from all parts of the world grow wild."

Call this field of beauty what you will—garden or wilderness—and visit it at what season you may, you will be penetrated with its charm: whether in April, when the hillside is flashing with rivulets and pools of pure colour from squills, windflowers, daffodils, gentians, sweet alisons; or in early summer, when many kinds of iris unfold their gorgeous petals round the lake in floods of purple, blue, and gold; or in autumn, when the troops of gold-rayed lilies rise ghost-like in the copse, and African *tritomas* hold flaming torches along the paths, Mr Wilson has shown how royally English soil and climate will repay care and judgment with boundless wealth of blossom.

One great evil to be avoided in the design and contents of a garden is sameness. There is a phrase that constantly recurs in horticultural journals when some plant is being commended—" No garden should be without it." Unfortunately gardeners are too often content to grow the same flowers as their neighbours; are, indeed, dissatisfied unless they have the same species. Some years ago it struck somebody that the single dahlia was a more beautiful flower than the varieties hitherto approved, upon which great pains and much skill had been expended to get them as like ribbon rosettes and as little like natural flowers as possible. No sooner was the idea acted on than single dahlias became the rage, and now it is the rarest thing to go into any garden without seeing these plants, mostly of indifferent merit, sprawling over the borders. They were pleasing as a novel feature, but nobody gets much enjoyment out of them now; they perish with the first frost, and any scent they possess is disagreeable.

We have a hundred species to choose from now for every one that eighteenth-century nurserymen could supply. China, Japan, the Himalayas, Siberia, Australasia, North and South America have been ransacked; in every mountain range and island of the sea collectors have vied with each other in securing new plants, and each year many are added to the list of those which adapt themselves to our climate. It is about twenty-five years since the whorled primrose of Japan was introduced, and people willingly paid 30s. apiece for such a noble acquisition. Now it may be seen sowing itself in the borders with the freedom of an English " paigle." [1]

In Virgil's opinion, the ash was the most beautiful

---

[1] *Paigle* is the old English name for the cowslip.

woodland tree, but for gardens he commended the stone pine of the Mediterranean. How vastly greater is the variety of conifers from which we may choose, from the stately *Picea nobilis* of Colorado, to the fantastic *Salisburia*, the Gingko of Japan, less like a fir than a huge maidenhair fern. It is only necessary to remember that fifty years ago rhododendrons were hardly known, to realise how far we excel our grandfathers in wealth of material.

It is provoking to see people at the pains to cultivate and decorate their ground, yet often neglecting to bring out the special characteristics of their soil and climate. Zones of mean temperature run in these islands much more with degrees of longitude than of latitude. In Cornwall, Argyleshire, and Galway, shrubs and humbler plants flourish luxuriantly which would perish in a single winter in Oxfordshire or Surrey. Yet in the benign West one is just as apt to find the walls monopolised by plants adapted for the London climate as with the myrtles, lemon verbenas, Edwardsia, and other choice things that might both surprise and delight the visitor. Any one who has driven across the desolate upland lying between Clifden and Letterfrack, in Galway, will surely remember with pleasure the miles of hedges of crimson fuchsia with which Mr Mitchell Henry has had the taste to array the highroad near his place, Kylemore. Of course it is right to give individual preference for certain flowers ; there is no reason why, if the lord of the soil loves the various kinds of rose above other flowers, he should think himself bound to sacrifice them to camellias, in order to show the mildness of his climate : camellias he should have where they flourish (as every one will agree who has seen the fairy-like display they make in the open air at East Lytchett, in Dorsetshire), because they will distinguish his garden from ninety-nine hundredths of others; but he should also take the full of his climatic advantage in behalf of his favourite flower. Very few persons have ever seen the single white Macartney rose (*Rosa bracteata*), because, being somewhat tender, it will not reward culture in Mid-land or Eastern districts; but there is rare beauty in its thick ivory-like petals, clustered golden anthers, and glossy foliage. I well remember the impression it made on first seeing it on the wall of the boathouse at Port Eliot, in Cornwall — I rested not till I had procured it, though it was years before I found any nurseryman who kept it in stock. But the westward influence is not enough for some roses, such as the Banksian, which is patient of a very low winter temperature, provided it gets a more liberal summer sun than can be had north of the Trent. Even in the South it is sometimes so ignorantly and harshly dealt with by the pruner's knife, that its owner looks in vain for the profuse drift of snowy or sulphur-hued blossom that rewards the *laissez-faire* treatment of this rose.

This advantage the denizens of old English gardens possess over recent importations, that names hallowed by time and endeared by association have been bestowed upon them; for, Juliet's opinion notwithstanding, there *is* much in a name, and the rose would not have been such a favourite with the poets if it had been christened turnip. A distinct sensation of freshness, as of early summer mornings, is produced by simply repeating some of the old flower names, which

Mr Prior has arranged so handily in his ' Popular Names of British Plants.' The memory of childhood spent in the country is fondly stirred by the familiar names eglantine, lad's-love, fair-maids-of-France, goldilocks, lady's-smock, herb-paris (also called herb-truelove), gold-of-pleasure, &c. Many of them have a distinct significance ; Gerarde affirms that bachelor's-buttons (a double-white ranunculus) was so called from the similitude of the buds " to the jagged cloathe buttons, antiently worne in this kingdom " ; while another authority attributes the name to " a habit of country fellows to carry them in their pockets to divine their success with their sweethearts." Then the celandine owes its name to one of the most irrational traditions ever conceived, yet one that received the sanction of such hard heads as Aristotle's and Pliny's, and has been repeated unhesitatingly by countless writers on botany and natural history. The name is from the Greek χελιδών, a swallow,—" not," as Gerarde is at pains to warn his readers, " because it first springeth at the comeing in of the swallowes, or dieth when they go away, for, as we have saide, it may be founde all the yeare, but because some holde opinion, that with this herbe the dams restore sight to their young ones, when their eies be put out." The fleur-de-luce, generally written fleur-de-lis or lys, as if the last syllable had to do with a lily, is really *fleur-de-Louis*, and was the cognisance of royal France ever since it was chosen as his badge by Louis VII., " qui chargea l'écu de France de fleurs-de-lis sans nombre."

But of all flowers of the garden, none has had so many fanciful names bestowed upon it as the pansy, —*pensieri menuti*, idle thoughts, as the Italians call it.

"The Pansy next, which English maids
Call Heart's-ease—innocent translation—
As if each thought that springs and fades
Were but a source of jubilation."

The pretty name heart's-ease does not, indeed, belong by right to the pansy, but was applied to designate the wallflower, from its real or supposed virtue as a cordial, and the pansy itself has at various times and in different counties been known as Herb Trinity (from its three colours), Love-and-idle, Kiss-me-ere-I-rise, Jump - up - and - kiss - me, Three - faces - under-a-hood.

A place might surely be found oftener in the pleasure-ground for certain plants generally relegated to the herb-garden, such as rue, lavender, and rosemary. Their beauty, certainly, is of a lowly order, but there hangs about them such a mist of popular lore that they bring to mind a time before these thorny days of social science, county councils, and school boards— to return to which time, were the choice given us, it might be wise to hesitate, yet a time when our country was known among the nations as "Merrie England," when, if the poor were not less poor, the rich were not so rich, and no one vexed his soul by asking if life was worth living. The rue, Shakespeare's Herb of Grace, was supposed to flourish stronger if stolen from a neighbour's garden. Lavender, though strangely enough omitted by Bacon from his list of sweet-smelling plants, is endeared to us by a thousand proofs of the esteem our forefathers had for it; such as Izaak Walton's description of " an honest ale-house, where we shall find a cleanly room, lavender in the windows, and twenty ballads stuck against the wall, and my hostess, I may tell you, is both cleanly and handsome and civil." Rosemary—

> " Trim rosmarin that whilom crowned
> The daintiest garden of the proudest peer "—

also called Guardrobe from its use as a preservative of clothes, may now be looked for in vain in the gardens of most peers, though it deserves a better fate, were it only in memory of gentle Sir Thomas More. "As for rosmarine," he wrote, "I lett it run alle over my garden walls, not onlie because my bees love it, but because 'tis the herb sacred to remembrance, and therefore to friendship; whence a sprig of it hath a dumb language that maketh it the chosen emblem at our funeral wakes and in our buriall grounds." It may sometimes still be seen so used, being laid upon coffins, especially in the northern counties. But a more equivocal significance is also attributed to it, with which some may be inclined to connect its disappearance from modern borders; it is alleged that it only flourishes where the mistress rules, or at least has a fair share in ruling, the household.

Since the days of chaste Lucrece,

> " Their silent war of lilies and of roses,
> Which Tarquin viewed in her fair face's field,"

has gone on without intermission, though far from silently. Every one admits that lilies and roses excel all other flowers, but the controversy as to which is entitled to pre-eminence has never yet been, and never will be, settled. It is best avoided by having plenty of both, and truly no garden is worth a visit that is not well furnished with them. Alexander Montgomery had made up his mind about it when he penned the verse:—

> " I love the lily as the first of flowers
>   Whose stately stalk so straight up is and stay,[1]
> In whom th' lave [2] ay lowly louts and cowers,
>   As bound so brave a beauty to obey."

But another Scottish poet, Dunbar, had already, a hundred years before Montgomery, given equally emphatic verdict for the rose:—

> " Nor hold none other flower in sic dainty
>   As the fresh rose of colour red and white,
> For if thou dost, hurt is thine honesty,
>   Considering that no flower is so perfite,
>   So full of virtue, pleasaunce and delight,
> So full of blissful angelic beauty,
> Imperial birth, honour, and dignity."

On the whole, Queen Rose commands a wider allegiance than Queen Lily, in our own country at least, where she is not only the flower assigned by heralds as the emblem of England, but is associated with the bloody strife between the Houses of York and Lancaster—the Wars of the Roses—and the white rose is specially dear to Jacobites as being the badge of the ill-starred House of Stuart; while the lily was the chivalrous emblem of England's ancient rival—France.

The perfection and profusion of what are known as " hybrid perpetuals," combined with the desire for

---

[1] Stiff.   [2] The lave = the rest.

autumn blooms, have prevailed to throw into the background some lovely summer roses, such as still make paradise of cottage-gardens in June. Of such may be named the old double white (*Rosa alba*), the York and Lancaster, streaked with red and white; the Austrian copper, with single flowers of intense fiery orange, much rarer than the same species with sulphur-coloured petals; and the Celestial Blush, of matchless shell-pink, in exquisite harmony with its glaucous foliage.

Mr Ellacombe, in his pleasant volume, ' The Plant-Lore and Garden-Craft of Shakespeare,' quotes a bit of rose-lore gravely told in the ' Voiage and Travaile ' of Sir John Mandeville :—

At Betheleim is the Felde *Floridus*, that is to seyne, the *Feld florisched;* for als moche as a fayre mayden was blamed with wrong and sclaundered, for whiche cause sche was demed to the Dethe, and to be brent in that place, to the whiche she was ladd; and as the Fyre began to brent about hire, sche made hire preyers to oure Lord, that als wissely as sche was not gilty of that Synne, that He wolde helpe hire and make it to be knowen to alle men, of his mercyfulle grace. And when sche hadde thus seyd, sche entered into the Fuyr: and anon was the Fuyr quenched and oute; and the Brondes that weren bren-nynge becomen red Roseres, and the Brondes that weren not kyndled becomen white Roseres. And these weren the first Roseres and Roses, both white and rede, that evere ony man saughe.

Before passing from the rose, it may be permitted to allude to a term often used by Shakespeare but almost equally often misunderstood by his readers. The " canker " was the common name for the dog-rose, and is so intended in such passages as—

> " So put down Richard, that sweet lovely rose,
>   And plant this thorn, this canker Bolingbroke."

Or again, in the Sonnets :—

> " The canker-blooms have full as deep a dye
>   As the perfumed tincture of the rose."

But when Titania speaks of "killing cankers in the musk - rose buds," or the poet sings in the Sonnets that "loathsome canker lives in sweetest bud," the reference is to a parasitic worm.

Since the days when Montgomery championed the cause of the lily, the ranks of that fair flower in our own country have been strengthened by a vast reinforcement from foreign climes. The giant lily (*Lilium giganteum* or *cordifolium*) is as hardy as the hemlock, and soars to the height of 8 or 10 feet under favourable circumstances; the Isabella Lily (*L. testaceum*), of hybrid origin, almost equals it in stature, and is distinguished from all others by its delicate apricot hue; while of *Lilium auratum*, the gold-rayed lily of Japan, the most gorgeous plant that will endure our trying climate, it is worth recording that the variety *platyphyllum* is by far the finest and the most permanent, coming up year after year in the same spot, whereas the other varieties generally perish in the second or third season.

Gardeners love to prose about their pursuit: 'tis such a seductive hobby, and ambles along so pleasantly, that it were easy to strain the reader's patience; so only one other point in the decoration of grounds will be here alluded to. Statuary is seldom used in the decoration of gardens now, yet of all places where it can be seen to advantage it is there. It gives a feeling of repose which is an indispensable quality in garden scenery, and in return receives tranquil attention, which can seldom be bestowed on it in public places. With trees, flowers, fair statues, green-sward, and song of birds, what pleasant resting-places the pilgrims of life may make for themselves!

TROUTING TATTLE.

NOT long ago a traveller, sauntering through the demesne of a Scottish magnate, whereof the old-fashioned mansion has been lately replaced by an edifice of immense size and profuse ornament, came upon a gang of workmen employed by a London contractor in constructing an artificial rockwork and cascade. Something struck him as comical in the contrast between the puny operations of the landscape-gardener and the surrounding scenery: on one side lay the ocean; on the other, a range of the most fantastic peaks in the Western Isles of Scotland climbed the sky; between them, on this little angle of tormented soil, man was worrying himself with the problem how, by dint of leaden piping, cement, and broken stones, he should mimic the endless profusion of cliff and torrent, whence what Scotsmen call this "policy" or private park had been redeemed. The absurdity of the whole thing was enhanced by the difficulty of bringing a water-supply to that particular spot. The fluid which dripped from a thousand crags and thundered through a hundred linns within a few miles of the scene of operations was here provokingly deficient, and the visitor made some observation on this fact to a dapper little clerk of works who was superintending the operation.

"Yes," replied he, "it's true we have a very poor water-supply; but you'd be surprised, sir, what a wonderful effect our firm can produce with a one-inch pipe."

It is, indeed, the nature of water to lend itself to very easy magic. It is wonderful how soon the moisture oozing from a green, spongy place in the moor acquires the dignity of a water - course. It runs unnoticed as a mere gutter through the black peat, winding among clumps of rushes, and gurgling unseen under brown heather; imperceptibly it gathers volume, till suddenly you become aware of a miniature but complete waterfall, dashing itself over a ledge of opposing granite, and, falling into a basin excavated by its own movement, it assumes thereafter all the mystery of a brook, and exacts all the consideration attached to a permanent feature in the landscape.

This mystery has a fascination for human intelligence at every stage of civilisation. Let water but be so deep as to hide its bed from view, straightway fancy peoples it with marvellous beings. True that, in these days of school boards and daily papers, men move about the river-banks with never a thought of kelpies, and maidens may wade knee-deep in the fords without fear of froward river-gods; but let the angler smile never so wisely at these extinguished terrors, he cherishes his own credulous expectation of scaly prodigies. In every darkling pool, from behind

every sunken boulder where his fly may float, wherever
the water circles leisurely round a gnarled root, he
expects the heavy drag of a mighty fish, which, if his
tackle only hold good, will beat the record for many a
day. Were trout all of a uniform size, like partridges,
probably few would care to toil after them with rod
and line, not only at the mercy of the passing caprice
of fish, but the victim of every vicissitude of wind and
sun, seeing that a wisely worked net would fill his
creel in a tenth of the time and with a hundredth part
of the trouble. It is the charm of the unseen and
unknown that lures on the fisherman from pool to
stream, from stream to pool, and back to stream again,
—the chance that some day his fly will be seized by
a prodigious fish, the capture of which will not
only give him an indescribable thrill of triumph,
but cause his name to be revered by generations yet
unborn.

Several occasions have convinced me that this
mystery of the unseen is a chief element in the
fascination of angling. Midway between Guildford
and Dorking, at the foot of the chalk downs which
lie between these ancient towns, is the Pool of Sher-
borne—the Silent Pool, as it is called by the dwellers
in Albury. It is a deep basin, perhaps seventy or
eighty yards long and five-and-thirty broad, filled
with spring water of such crystalline transparency
that every blade of water-lobelia, every shaft of pond-
weed, shows as distinctly as the herbage on the banks.
At one end of the pool there is a pretty fishing-house,
so called, and the water is plentifully peopled with
trout of large size, which glide perpetually, like brown
phantoms, through the depths of pale aquamarine.

A fishing-house, indeed, but no one ever dreams of fishing here. Even to me, ever one of the most unresisting victims to the infatuation of angling, who spent two years of my 'teens within a mile of this pool, the temptation never presented itself of casting angle in these waters. Why? Because every fish could be seen, every movement watched, and there would have been no more excitement in catching them than in picking off poultry with a pea-rifle.

Here is a still more convincing case. A few years ago I was spending some of the autumn on Tweedside. The river was well stocked with the "grey school"; it had run low, however, and a vicious frost set in, which promised to put an end to fishing till after the next flood. I had arrived at mid-day at a certain pool on the Mertoun Water, where the river, after being pent between opposing rocks, spreads into a wide shallow expanse. The sun was very bright, illumining every yard of these broads, and the shadowy forms of a score of salmon could be detected lying in various parts of it. There was less of hope than of passive obedience in my compliance with the boatman's injunction to put a fly over them. It required a long line, for the fish were lying far out. Presently, as the fly swept over two of these fish, one turned and seemed to dart *away* from it. I thought that he had been scared; but, to my great surprise, the line tightened, and I was fast in the fish. Refraction had caused him to appear to be several feet farther off than his real position in the water, and when I thought he was fleeing from the lure, he was in truth pursuing it. Well, I hooked five of these fish, and landed three of them, with some satisfaction certainly, for the circumstances of water and weather were equally hostile; but the distinct impression left on my mind was this—that were salmon-fishing often conducted under conditions such as these, it would be robbed of half its charm.

Mystery is the spell that binds the fisher to his craft. Some minds are so constituted as never to feel its influence, and to such the marvel is that so many intelligent beings can be found to take so much trouble in a pursuit which offers such infrequent prizes. Others, again, devoted to angling for salmon and trout, cannot enter into the ardour with which those who enjoy opportunity and leisure for the nobler game can sometimes find diversion in the capture of any kind of fish that will take their lure. Yet such men, rare and extreme instances of infatuation, live and move and have their being. I have the privilege of friendship with one of them. He owns a rod on one of the best salmon-rivers in Scotland, and makes fruitful use of it; he has skimmed the cream of the waters of Norway, plies the dry fly with consummate skill among the wizard trout of Test and Itchen, the wet one with fatal effect on Scottish lochs and streams: yet no later than last summer he stirred my amazement by driving fifteen miles to fish for perch in a Lowland loch; and in the previous summer I saw him contentedly working an eight hours' day in the capture of inglorious roach. Nor is this, as some might suppose, the outcome of a vacant mind. It is the fancy of a cultivated gentleman of leisure, able and willing to discuss a

range of subjects far outside fishing and shooting
" shop." I put it down to the interaction of a quick
imagination and an active body.

It is to the imagination that fishing primarily appeals. It is the only sport wherein the pursued and
the pursuer inhabit different mediums, wherein terrestrial intelligence is pitted against subaqueous. Endless problems present themselves to the former. The
habits of salmon alone afford material for any amount
of speculation. What is the impulse, for instance,
which sends salmon out of the sea, where food abounds
and range is unlimited, to languish in river-pools
dwindling in the heat of summer? Why do they
ascend certain rivers in January and February, and in
others not a tail is wagged till September? A remarkable instance of this inscrutable caprice is afforded by
two rivers debouching within half-a-dozen miles of
each other in the north of Ireland—the Bush and the
Bann. The Bush is a sedgy, sullen, dark water, across
which, so to speak, you may kick your hat at almost
any part; into its canal-like channel salmon begin to
run in the first month of the year. The Bann, a fine,
sweeping flood, nourished from the clear depths of
Lough Neagh, attracts no fish till May. If it be
assumed that salmon leave the sea primarily for the
purpose of depositing their spawn, why do they leave
it six or seven months before a single pair of fish is
seen on the redds? Such conundrums might be multiplied indefinitely. It seems inexcusable to prose
about salmon when one has undertaken to talk about
trout, but, liberally viewed, the connection is not re-
mote. Originally salmon and trout, and all the other
species migratory and non-migratory, must have de-

scended from common parents.[1] The home of the salmon is in fresh water: he is tempted to the sea by the abundant diet to be found there; he returns home to escape from seals, porpoises, parasites, and other inconveniences, and to propagate his species. Nets and artificial flies are but things of yesterday, the inventions of mushroom men: when they have been plied for a few thousands of years, they may prevail in their turn to influence the traditional migration of the truly ancient family of *Salmonidæ*.

The mystery of trout-fishing is greatly enhanced by legendary lore. Every stream has its fables of enormous fish landed, or, more often, as happens in evil dreams, lost in the landing. How gently these stories stir the listener's hopes. Once, in the days when faith predominated over experience, my imagination was titillated by one of these fables. I was fishing the upper waters of a salmon-river in the west of Scotland, wherein was good store of moderate-sized trout. It is a wild, moorland district, where houses there are none, save widely scattered sheep-farms, each with its hopelessly belated patch of green corn. A solitary but affable native took an interest in my proceedings, and in reply to anxious inquiry, affirmed that there were undoubtedly very large trout in the stream if they would but consent to be caught. He proceeded to describe how a gentleman was one day fishing some distance higher up and hooked an immense trout, which made off down-stream in resistless fashion. It

---

[1] Some species of char resort regularly to the salt water in Scandinavia, and are caught at the mouths of the rivers; and, in our own country, if there is a big trout anywhere in a Scottish burn, it is in a pool at the mouth, wherein the tide flows twice a-day.

passed through one pool after another, the angler following over rocks and bushes, till, at last, three miles below where the fish had been hooked, they arrived at a wood, which put an end to further pursuit. This would have been the moment to put in practice old Izaak's prescription to Venator, who had just lost a good trout :—

Aye, marry, sir, that was a good fish indeed : if I had had the luck to have taken up that rod, then it's twenty to one he should not have broke my line by running to the rod's end as you suffered him. I would have held him within the bent of my rod (unless he had been fellow to the great Trout that is near an ell long, which was of such a length and depth that he had his picture drawn, and now is to be seen at mine host Rickabie's, at the George in Ware), and it may be, by giving that very great Trout the rod, that is, by casting it to him into the water, I might have caught him at the long-run ; for so I use always to do when I meet with an overgrown fish ; and you will learn to do so too hereafter ; for I tell you, scholar, fishing is an art, or, at least, it is an art to catch fish.

But no such resource was adopted by the angler. Dead beat, he came to a stand-still : not so the trout, which ran out all the line, broke it, and was seen no more.

"That must have been a salmon," I observed at the end of the story.

"Na, feth !" replied my acquaintance, " it was a troot, for I seen the spots on it as big as thae bramble-leaves. And that was the maist material troot that ever I saw in this water."

Needs it to be added that the glow of expectation kindled by this unscrupulous piece of fiction lasted throughout a long day's fishing, and was quenched

only by the falling shades of night. Not quenched—
only lulled; for as sure as I were to fish that stream
to-morrow, so the lapse of a score of years would not
have sufficed to deprive it of all its stimulus.

But of a sooth there is little use for fabulous lore to
enhance the seductive mystery veiling water and its
inhabitants. To what unimaginable antiquity must
recourse be had to account for the presence of trout in
some Scottish lakes and streams! The pedigree of the
fish that people certain rivulets mounts up to a time
anterior to the formation of some of the most salient
features in the landscape. Let one familiar Scottish
example be quoted out of thousands of others. Looking westward from Stirling Castle, the eye travels
over the level alluvium of the Carse, through which
the sluggish Forth meanders in countless loops and
curves. On the right are piled the Highland hills,
crest behind crest, and on the left runs a lower, but
continuous, ridge, part of the Lennox range known as
the Gargunnock and Campsie Fells. Much of the
northern side of this elevation is precipitous, falling
sheer, or almost sheer, several hundreds of feet towards the valley of the Forth. The moorland on the
summit forms the watershed between the systems of
the Forth and the Carron, whence the streams flowing
northward fall in lofty cascades over the precipices
of the fells. There are trout both above and below
these falls, those of the plain excelling in colour
and shape their dingy kinsmen of the moor, but undoubtedly descendants of a common ancestry. But
how did these moorland trout first get access to their
present haunts. They may pass down the falls alive
in times of flood, but no fish that ever was hatched

from roe could ascend them. Must one predicate a time anterior to the geological rift that reared this hill-crest, when these streams ran on a uniform incline from source to sea, and trout might traverse places which have for immense tracts of time been wholly impassable? If so, then how greatly increased must be our reverence for the grimy little troutlings which dart away as we step across their narrow homes, for even so must their distant progenitors have scuttled away when the earth quaked beneath the tread of the woolly elephant, or the jungle rustled at the passage of the *Machærodon*—the formidable sabre-toothed tiger. These humble representatives of the *Salmonidæ* are not merely links in the chain of animated nature: if our speculation is well-founded, their ancestors, identical in form and habits with themselves, must have been denizens of the Tertiary landscape. That this must be so, if the high antiquity of these isolated trout may be assumed, seems to be proved by the identity of the character acquired by trout collected from waters of different physical conditions, and submitted to uniform treatment in light, liberty, and food. The dusky little denizens of moorland dubs will, when transported to clear, deep water, with a liberal supply of stimulating food, expand into shapely, silvery fish, resembling sea-trout rather than their former selves, and scaling as many pounds as they could have weighed ounces in their native rivulet.

It is true that the trout of certain waters have, under the influence of abundant and excellent food, developed peculiarities of some permanence, and have on that account been erected into the dignity of separate species. The excellent fish of Loch Leven, the gillaroo of the Irish lakes, the great grey lake-trout, which looms in the angler's awed aspirations as *Salmo ferox*, have all had this distinction conferred on them; but scientific men are now generally agreed that the points of difference between them and *Salmo fario* of the brooks are not enough to constitute more than varieties of a single species. They will breed together, and their offspring are fertile—sure proof that they are not hybrids. But the local angler is loath to part with a classification which lends importance to his district and adds mystery to his craft. I myself possess a small lake not more than half a mile from end to end, which produces trout of very dissimilar appearance. Those at the lower end, where the bottom is dark and peaty, are dusky-skinned, yellow-flanked fellows, with few red spots, and tending to lankiness, though some of them are as symmetrical as could be desired. Those at the upper end, where the bottom is a fine mixture of boulders, gravel, and sand, are bright and clear, brilliantly spangled with dark spots, interspersed with sparks of vermilion. In size the dark trout average slightly larger, though two-pounders are by no means out of the common, even at the upper end. The natives will have it that these are two distinct species, and call the dark ones " bull-trout "; and indeed it would be difficult for any one not familiar with the remarkable variability of trout to recognise in one of the large-headed, sombre-hued male fish from the lower end of the lake an individual of the same species as a small-headed, gaily-attired female from the upper end. To the eye, there is at least as much difference between them as between a grey Norway rat and the old English black rat, which has wellnigh disappeared before its stronger rival. Nay, let the two fish be laid side by side, and the contrast will not seem less than between a grouse and a partridge. Yet there can be no doubt whatever that there is but one species of trout in this lake, of which the individuals assume different aspects according to their immediate environment and food.

Of course there is equally little doubt that these variations, and such as these, would ultimately prevail if isolation and special conditions were maintained long enough to establish distinct species, as they appear to have done in the case of char and other *Salmonidæ;* but long—immensely long—as the trout on the Gargunnock upland have been secluded from intercourse with those hundreds of feet nearer the sea-level, and greatly as temperature, soil, and food differ at the two levels, the upland and lowland fish, placed in a pond together and fed in the same way, would become indistinguishable from each other.

There are districts in Scotland where the movements of the earth's crust or its denudation would seem to have taken place before the streams contained any trout, or perhaps glacial action at a period of greater cold than the present extinguished all life in the upper waters. Certain it is that in some of the streams of Sutherland, trout abound below high falls, and are not found indigenous to the waters above. The tenant of some shootings in that county turned in a quantity of trout into the barren upper waters of one of these rivers. They grew and multiplied apace, and for some years afterwards the average size of these fish was very much larger than that of those in the lower waters, and their condition and appearance very much superior. This, no doubt, would continue to be the case until the normal process had been accomplished, and the fish had multiplied up to the limit of the food-supply. Any given area of water will sustain no more than a proportionate weight of fish. If the spawning accommodation is unlimited, this weight will be made up by swarms of small fish, as is the case in countless Highland lochs; in fact, it is almost inevitable that in a lake fed by abundant streams, and not haunted by pike, the trout will increase in numbers to such a pitch and simultaneously deteriorate in quality as to be useless for sporting purposes. The treatment of such lakes must be systematic in order to restore the right ratio of number to size. Private owners, as well as the angling associations which year by year show increasing inclination to rent and manage fisheries, may find some of the following suggestions of practical use. Hitherto human intelligence has scarcely been directed to the improvement of trout - fisheries; but in view of the annual rents now given for trout-fishing— as high in the south of England as from £50 to £100 for each rod — an incentive more powerful than sport is present to attract attention to their development.

Over - population is the evil from which many Scottish lakes suffer. If a lake contains, say, 5000 trout averaging 4 oz. in weight, it may be taken that it will sustain 1250 trout averaging 1 lb., or 625 averaging 2 lb. There is no doubt which would be the condition of its stock for which the angler would pay most freely.

Lakes which suffer from over-population may be classed comprehensively under two heads:—

1. Lakes fed by rivulets.

2. Lakes fed by rivers or large streams.

The first of these are most commonly of small size, though instances are not wanting of sheets of water, two or three miles long, supplied only by small brooks and springs. When a lake so formed lies in a hilly or moorland district, it is a simple matter to make the feeders inaccessible to trout bent on ascending them to spawn. Every such feeder may have a dam thrown across it, producing a fall not less than four feet high, up which no trout can pass. Spawning would then be possible only in the stream flowing out of the lake; and as it is the tendency of fry to *descend* from the beds where they are hatched, no undue number of young fish would enter the lake, and the effect of a reduction in their numbers would soon be visible in the weight and condition of trout taken in the lake. The right proportion of spawning-ground to lake area could only be ascertained after the experience of some seasons, but it could then be accurately regulated by opening and closing the inflowing streamlets.

So much for hill-lakes. In the management of low-ground lakes the conditions are complicated by consideration of drainage-levels : to dam the feeders might inundate a large quantity of valuable land. Recourse must then be had to gratings fitted in a frame and let into sides of mason - work. These gratings should be provided with horizontal bars— not, as is commonly done, with vertical ones: horizontal bars one inch apart will stop a smaller fish than vertical bars half an inch apart, and it is important to stop all fish large enough to spawn, because if all but small fish were stopped, the result would be perpetuation from the least desirable breeders. The gratings should be put in position about the beginning of September, and raised in the beginning of February, after the spawning season is over.

The second case—that of lakes fed by rivers or large streams—is a much more serious one to deal with. Such streams cannot, except in few instances and at great expense, be made impassable to the ascent of trout. The numbers in the lake must be reduced by systematic annual netting. As early in the season as ice and floods will permit, the water should be swept with a small-meshed net, and every trout under a fixed standard removed from the lake. The massacre or transportation will be immense, and somewhat heartrending at first, but season by season the proportion of undersized trout will become less; and in lakes of great size and depth, nature will provide the additional check of cannibalism. Overgrown trout will develop the characteristics which have gained for such individuals the title of a species, under the name of *Salmo ferox.* These fish lie in the dark depths of the lake during the daytime, moving up into the shallows at twilight to feed upon small fish of their own or any other species they may encounter.

Where does *Salmo fario* end and *Salmo ferox* begin? Of course there are those persons, neither unobservant nor unlearned in natural history, who maintain that they are totally distinct species. But there are times when such professors must find their acumen shrewdly tested. To wit—in the summer of

1890 an auspicious conjunction of the heavenly bodies led me to sojourn on the banks of one of the fairest, and not the smallest, of the lakes of the West Highlands, famed for good store of redoubtable *ferox*. For three long afternoons labouring rowers had pulled me where the water slumbered in awful gloom under towering cliffs, broke in billows on leagues of shingly beach, and anon spread shining in the sweep of sandy bays. Not a movement—not a check to the brace of phantom minnows revolving through the silent depths sixty yards astern. The flame of hope, erst so ardent, began to flicker parlously. In vain the stroke-oarsman gently fanned it with wondrous tales of how the minister (the Reverend Ebenezer Sticktilt, no other) "would be trailing the minnow past that point with the single rowan growing there, and it will have been taken by a fish to spang out the reel; the puir body was nearly frightened to fall out of the boat, so she was; but in the conclusion he was to get her, and she weighed like fifteen pounds whatever." Or again, how the English lord, when the boat had scarcely left the pier, and he had but a few yards of line out, " was for lighting his mushroom pipe, for he was the great smoker however," and at that instant a great fish took the bait, rushed off with it, and snapped the line like gossamer. Angus's *répertoire* of stirring incident and heartrending accident was certainly inexhaustible in variety, but it had lost its virtue; the third day was drawing to its close, and we were paddling slowly home in the shadow of darkling pines. The breeze had died away, the daylight had failed, so that lake and land melted imperceptibly into each other. All at once—*p-r-r-r-r-r*—

went the reel of the left-hand rod, the point of which
was dragged quivering under the water. The strain
was tremendous, but almost before the butt could be
seized, far astern a monster of the deep sprang aloft
and fell back on the surface with resounding splash.
At the same moment the great strain was relaxed;
still the weight of the line concealed from us what had
happened, till, reeling in apace, the sorrowful truth
became plain, that the solitary chance in three days'
fishing had come and gone—the fish was gone too.
He had been well hooked, but the treacherous metal
had bent in the mighty jaws; two of the triangles
were straightened out as if they had been pewter.
How that ponderous form haunted my dreams that
night: how often I was awakened by the great pull
on the line, and bitterly reflected how phantom minnows framed to deceive fish would sometimes betray
fishers.

I devoted next morning to the capture of some
troutlets in the stream, and, embarking at the pier
at three o'clock in the afternoon, fitted a brace of
these on some trustworthy tackle. If *ferox* were
not wholly apocryphal, I was determined to get on
terms with one of them. Just as we were pushing
off, my host's son, a small schoolboy, ran down and
begged to be allowed to join the party. Of course I
was delighted, and one of the two rods was given
over to his care. Whether the day was more pro-
pitious, or the natural baits were more attractive, who
shall say? probably the latter was the case: anyhow,
this was to be a very different afternoon to its predecessors. We landed five fish before dinner, the two
largest falling to the schoolboy's rod, greatly to his de-

light, and with mitigated reflex effect on myself. These fish weighed respectively 17½, 8, 5, 2½, and 2 lb. The moral of this long yarn is in this wise. Having been caught by trolling, these trout were all reckoned as *ferox*. Had the smaller ones been taken with the fly, it never would have occurred to any one to call them anything but common loch-trout. The biggest of the lot had all the features of his fellow-victims markedly exaggerated: his jaws were prodigious and fiercely armed, his eyes had a sinister, wolfish expression, his spots were multiplied and deeply dyed, his whole scheme of colouring was lurid and heavily toned. But between him and the modest two-pounder there was at least as much resemblance as between the venerable king whom Abishag warmed in her bosom and the ruddy stripling who smote the Philistine champion in the forehead.

It is not only in the profundity of Highland lochs that such leviathans are sheltered. Give the common brook-trout shelter secure enough and food galore, and he will develop the same traits as his northern brother. Below Romsey bridge on the Test is a pool darker and more turbulent than most reaches on that sparkling stream. High trees trail their lower branches over the flood; no fly-fisher may profane the serenity of that retreat—indeed, if he might prevail to do so, no notice would be taken of merely surface lures. Here there ever harbour mighty trout, nurtured on the town refuse discharged into the river at this spot, giants of their kind. Crafty dwellers on those shores know how a worm or prawn may be angled into the sacred depths, whereby each season some notable fish are brought to scale. I myself—

have I not seen with envious eye one such trout
taken there that pulled the index to within a couple
of hair's-breadths of a dozen pounds? With eye not
envious alone, but sorrowful; for to slay such a fish
with a pitiable prawn is surely like straining poison
into the cup of a monarch. Now that fish differed in
no respect appreciable to the eye save one from a
trout of like weight in a Highland or Irish lake. The
one point of difference was colour: the general tone
of the Test fish was many degrees lighter than that
of a *ferox*, but that is plainly to be accounted for by
the great depths frequented by the giants of the lake,
where the darkness must be almost complete.

It has been propounded above that if trout were of
uniform size anglers would be few, for angling would
be reft of its chief charm of uncertainty. So would
it be if fish were always equally disposed to bite. It
taxes our imagination finely to divine the cause of
the fasting and feasting moods of fish. We ourselves
may be grumpy in an east wind, but we do not become less greedy: for us neither fog nor frost prevail
to rob *cotelettes à la minute* or a juicy golden plover of
their attractions. But every fisherman knows how
sensitive is the appetite of trout to meteorological
influence; and how a change of temperature or hygro-
metric condition, imperceptible to his own grosser
faculties, may for good or ill affect the contents of
his creel.

Early in 1892 a singular and suggestive example
of this element in the angler's success presented itself.
I was spending a morning in the splendid marine
biological laboratory in the Villa Nazionale of Naples.

Dr Dörn, the accomplished manager thereof, conducted me round his chambers of beauty and marvel,
and then the feeding-hour arrived in the aquarium.
Turtles, cuttles, and fish of many kinds, all were
ready for their meal, till we came to a couple of tanks
inhabited by dog-fish — most voracious, one would
have said, of all.　To my surprise, Dr Dörn declared
it was no use offering them anything.　They were
lying at the bottom of the water, wreathed together,
as if for warmth, in groups of six to ten.　It was too
cold for them, said the attendant, and they would
refuse all food when they were in that state.　Now,
though it was the month of January, the temperature
was so mild that I had been sitting out in the gardens
before *déjeuner* that morning; but next day began a
memorable snowstorm which extended, it may be
remembered, over the whole of Europe, lasted for
some weeks, and finished up with the earthquake
that wrecked the island of Zante.　Some influence,
forerunner of this disturbance, told on the nerves of
these wolves of the sea ; and some such influence may
be held to account for many a weary hour of fruitless
flogging on stream or loch.

It is often charged against angling, that of all pastimes it is the most selfishly exclusive.　It is true
that there are moments when there is no room in the
angler's soul for any sentiment except envy, hatred,
malice, and all uncharitableness.　Of such moments
is the one when, full of tremulous impatience, you
are hurrying down to that pool on the river where
experience tells you lies your prime prospect of sport.
The water is right to the eighth of an inch in volume,
to the fraction of a shade of colour; the wind flows

softly from south-west, and the grey cloud rightly tempers the glare, but does not chill the grateful warmth of the sun. You have no glance to spare for snowy hawthorn-spray or flower-spangled meadow, no ear for treble of soaring lark or contralto of embowered blackbird: all your faculties are a-tingle to reach the stream and make use of every moment of this fecund fishing-day. If you do bestow a thought upon the warbling birds, it is that if you were one of them, *you* wouldn't fool away the time in singing, but would use your wings to carry you more swiftly to the river-bank. But when at last you come within view of the coveted shore, what is it that sends your towering hopes down in irremediable ruin?

"Obstupui, steteruntque comæ, et vox faucibus hæsit."

Your eye has detected a momentary arching gleam against the woody bank opposite your favourite spot —the light flashing from a varnished rod bent in the familiar curve, telling of a good fish fighting for life and liberty.

All is over! Your darling prospect is shattered: your footsteps have been forestalled,—you may devote the rest of the day to ornithology, or botany, or any other tomfoolery you like; the delights you promised yourself are for another, and you cannot muster enough altruism to resist wishing a long captivity and a lingering death to your unprincipled rival. This, indeed, conveys but a very imperfect idea of the savage tenor of your thoughts. So far, it must be conceded that angling promotes neither Christian charity nor philosophic equanimity.

But there are among the fraternity of the rod many

who would fain see enjoyment so exquisite and pastime so healthful provided for many more of our vast population than can share them as things are at present. There is plenty of open angling, indeed; but open angling, under existing arrangements, is synonymous with the minimum of sport, combined with the maximum of exertion, competition, early rising, and other engines of the evil one. There is in Scotland no close-time for trout. At all seasons the magnificent trouting waters of Tweed and Clyde and their tributaries are free to be ransacked with every imaginable bait — salmon-roe *nominally* excepted — with the result that from every flooded streamlet, as well as from the parent rivers, millions of gravid or exhausted fish are carried off, and some of the most famous waters have been effectively laid waste.

More than this, so poor are the only returns expected from open waters, that the incentive of stakes and betting must be had recourse to. Thus is the last barrier broken down between angling as a field-sport and as a gambling game, for the true test of the integrity of a field-sport is that no element of gain should enter into it. Racing men will gird at this ruling, but so it is: the turf, most ancient and honourable of field-sports, has become, under modern conditions, nothing but a gigantic game of chance. Even battue-shooting —already of dingy repute by reason of hot luncheons, overdone bags, and competitive slaughter—has not yet suffered the last degradation. When, if ever, it does so, the slender grade which elevates it above pigeon-shooting from traps will have been swept away; it

will cease to rank as a field-sport, for the mocking
gods look down with scornful eye on men slaying their
fellow-creatures for greed of pelf.

But trout-fishing, except for those who can acquire
or avail themselves of preserved waters, has already
sunk to the level of pitch-and-toss or *trent et quarante.*
The sport is so poor, owing to the depletion of the open
trout-waters, that they are given over to incessant fish-
ing-club competitions, and every fingerling that can
be gulled into swallowing fly or worm is added without ruth to make up weight.

It is in the power of our people to restore matters
to almost pristine excellence, and it is certainly in
their interest to do so. No one will stir unless the
demand somewhat inarticulately uttered of late for
legislation is formulated and pressed on the attention of county members—nay, of borough members
too—for trout-streams are grand playgrounds for
townsfolk.

The demand ought to take some such form as this.
Let Parliament confer powers on Scottish County
Councils to form a trout-fishery district, presided over
by a committee, whose duty it shall be to fix close-
times, regulate modes of fishing, and issue rod licences
at a moderate price. The revenue from such licences
would more than cover the expenses of printing, adver-
tising, &c.; the expenses of watching the waters and
prosecuting illegal fishers should of course be borne,
and would willingly be borne, by private owners and
fishing associations. It would then be worth the while
of owners and lessees of waters, or for the body of
licensed anglers, to undertake the replenishment of

depleted streams and the management of fish-hatcheries.   Under these circumstances, less would be heard of the inveterate jealousy of anglers, fair fishing would be brought within reach of thousands who do not think it worth trying under existing conditions, and a health-giving recreation would be secured to that class of the community for whose amusement it is essential to good government that provision be made.

SALMON-FLIES.

THERE is no subject, perhaps, on which more harmless nonsense has been talked and written than
that of salmon-flies. I call it harmless, believing as
I do that it is absolutely immaterial to the angler's
success what colour predominates in the lure presented
to a salmon. The important matter is—first, to exhibit a fly of such size as will be neither so small as
to escape notice altogether, nor, when noticed, be too
insignificant to awaken the curiosity, appetite, or anger
—whichever of these be the motive that prompts a
salmon to seize the fly—nor too large to arouse alarm
or suspicion; and, second, that it shall be exhibited in
such a way as to distinguish it among the innumerable
objects that float down a stream. And if it is harmless in the angler's interest that he should be persuaded
to multiply his patterns, it is undoubtedly in the
interest of the tackle-makers. It would be impossible
to estimate the gain which would be lost to that esti-
mable class of men were the superstition to be exploded
that certain flies are indispensable in certain rivers;

x

that flies with bodies of silver tinsel are good for frosty weather, and those with black bodies for sunny days. It is not likely that any observations of mine will tend to the detriment of trade by leading anglers to the cold conclusion which watchful experience has long since led me to adopt; otherwise I might pause before giving expression to it: so long as fish are fickle (and what charm would be left in salmon-angling if they ceased to be so?), so long will fishers believe in the infallibility of particular flies; and so long will boatmen and gillies attribute ill-success to neglect of prescribed combinations of feather, fur, and foil. Nevertheless, in the interest of truth it is worth while examining the evidence on which rests one of the most deeply rooted and widespread delusions to which an intelligent body of men ever yielded assent.

This may be done most conveniently by propounding a list of questions, and analysing the answers which knowledge of the habits of salmon enable us to supply:—

1. Does the salmon seize the fly for food?
2. What is the natural food of the salmon?
3. Does the salmon possess the sense of colour?

Does the salmon seize the fly for food? At first sight this may seem a foolish question. When a child puts something into his mouth, the odds are that he means to swallow it, and the fact that a salmon takes an artificial fly into his mouth may seem conclusive of his intention of swallowing it under the belief that it is edible. But if a small bird or a butterfly enter a room where there is a child, that child will probably go for that bird or that butterfly, and try to catch it, though with no intention of eating it. The child is moved by curiosity, modified by mischief. And if, while I am writing these lines, a large blue-bottle were to buzz round my ears, I would certainly go for that blue-bottle, though with no desire to swallow it: my motive would be justice modified by irritation. I have this advantage over a 20-lb. salmon, as the child has over the 5-lb. grilse, that having hands to handle with, neither of us is likely to be found with the blue-bottle, the bird, or the butterfly in his mouth. But the salmon and the grilse have no hands: their sole prehensile organ is the mouth; and it seems rash to assume that the motive of either in taking the fly into its mouth is neither curiosity nor irritation, but carnal appetite. When a glittering Wilkinson dances up and down and round and round the watery chamber of a lively grilse, is it idle to imagine that curiosity has something to do with his seizing it? and, if that be the impulse, who can say that it is more or less likely to be roused by a Poynder or a Jock Scott? Not even among French novelists, who sometimes invest Englishmen with unsuspected attributes, has there been found any one to explain the passion of fox-hunting as inspired by hunger.

In the arms of the city of Glasgow there is represented a salmon with a ring in its mouth, commemorating a legend hardly more exacting on our credulity, methinks, than the marvellous powers which according to most fishermen, enable salmon to discriminate between a Black Doctor and a Black Dose, or between a Dusty Miller and a Silver Grey. The Queen of Strathclyde, so runs the story, gave a ring

which she had received from her husband to a certain
soldier who was her favoured lover. One day the
soldier lost this ring in the Clyde. After a while, the
King, having reason to suspect his consort's fidelity,
asked her why she never wore the ring, and being dissatisfied with her excuse, insisted on the jewel being
displayed on an approaching *fête*-day. The Queen, in
extremity of terror, sought out St Kentigern, better
known as St Mungo, the patron saint of Glasgow.
He, sympathising with the penitent, directed her to
have a certain pool in the river drawn, and to cut open
the first salmon that should be caught. His instructions were carried out to the letter; the salmon was
found to contain the lost ring, which was duly worn
on the appointed day, and her Majesty's rickety reputation thereby saved.

Suppose a lusty five-and-twenty-pound kipper to
have escaped the perils of the estuary in August, and
sailed up a roaring summer flood in all his panoply of
silver mail to some cool, deep, twilight pool in the
middle reaches. For a while he is charmed with his
new quarters: there are no seals or porpoises to annoy
him; there are comfortable rocks to lie alongside; the
water flows pleasantly along his scaly sides; for exercise he can move up into the strong water at the head
of the pool, and when the sun is strong he can drop
luxuriously back into the stiller, darker depths. Best
of all, those tiresome tide-lice, which all through the
summer have tickled and stung him to distraction,
have all sickened in the fresh water and dropped off.
He has a few agreeable companions too,—not too many,
for he is sociable rather than gregarious in his tastes;
just two or three of his own sex, and some lovely hen-

fish, with whom he looks forward to disporting himself on the shallows when the nights begin to get frosty. Oh! it is splendid: life is really worth living under such conditions, and inspired by this reflection our friend rushes to the surface, and by a jerk of his powerful spine and broad grey tail sends himself clear out of the water, and falls back with a resounding splash.

On the third day after his arrival an unpleasant little incident takes place. The flood has subsided, though the current is still full; the sunlight shines through the amber-coloured fluid with a mellow lustre such as falls into a cathedral aisle through old *grisaille* windows. The attention of *Salmo salar* is suddenly arrested by a small dark object moving through the water above him in a series of easy jerks. While he is speculating on its nature — it is gone: by some mysterious agency it has left the field of vision altogether.

"Pity, now!" mutters our friend, blowing a string of bubbles out of his gills. "I'd like to have had a nearer look at that thing—never saw anything like it before—perhaps it was good to eat."

He is still speculating on its nature when—

"Hullo! there it is again. By Neptune! I must have it!" and, suiting the action to the thought, he spreads his broad fins, sets his great bulk in motion, and glides like a shadow after the intruder. A nearer view does not explain the mystery; he does not relish being puzzled, so with a sudden forward dash seizes the thing in his mouth. At the same moment a sharp pang shoots through his tongue; he feels his head held fast for a moment: he opens his mouth, shakes his head, and manages to expel the foreign object. His curiosity has not been satisfied; but now there is mingled with it some suspicion of a trick, and sinking slowly back to his resting-place, he spends the rest of the morning in meditation beside a sheltering rock.

After this, matters do not mend with our friend. The water runs low, and the sun's rays are at times unpleasantly hot. He makes up his mind to push farther up the stream, but there is not enough water now to make the exertion an easy one, so he is fain to make the best of his present abode. But his philosophy is interfered with by the fate which throws him in love with a buxom hen-fish whose lair is a few yards above his own. She receives his advances coldly, moving off as often as he approaches her. Vexing, that! and it is beginning to tell upon his health, too. His silver armour is getting tarnished; ruddy blotches appear on his gills; he does not move with the same alacrity as of yore; and spends most of the day dozing, alternately dreaming of his love and blinking at her through the tepid fluid.

There comes, however, an improvement in the weather. The sun is overcast, rain begins to fall, and within twenty-four hours all is astir in the pool. The water is murky and runs strong; logs and branches, corn-sheaves, haycocks, turnips, and other agricultural spoils, float down the Lammas flood; the fish have to lie at anchor in such shelter as they can find, but there will be brave times after this. The spate runs its course, and begins to subside. So soon as the water is clear enough, our acquaintance looks out for his lady-love. There is a hateful fellow, a few pounds heavier than himself, with his eye on the same object, and our salmon has to be wary, for weight will tell, you know, in every encounter. He resolves to watch their movements at a respectful distance. Evidently the lady is preparing for a journey. She is restless, and moves up and down the pool, waiting the moment when the stream shall be in good travelling trim. At last she is off; like a Whitehead torpedo she cleaves the rushing torrent at the head of the pool, and meanders through the broad ford above it, closely followed by the big rival of our fish, who keeps them well in sight. At last his chance comes. They have been swimming for some hours, and our hero's fins and back are beginning to ache, when they arrive in a deep basin, half-filled with churning foam. A heavy fall comes in at the top, at which the undaunted lady, after a quarter of an hour's rest, makes a gallant spring. It is too strong for her, and she rolls back end over end into the cloud of blinding bubbles. Again and again at intervals of a few minutes she renews the attempt, and fails, till at last—luck in odd numbers—she wins her point at the seventh leap, and all her admirers see is a flourish of her dark tail as she glides into the channel above. Her biggest follower, meanwhile, has tried his luck two or three times in vain; his weight is against him, and he has dropped down into quieter water to rest himself. Our salmon feels that his chance has come. He has been lying quiet all this time, gathering strength, and now he dashes upwards with all his force, and — blessed fortune ! — succeeds at the first trial. There is a still deep pool a hundred yards farther on, and there—oh, happy day !—he finds himself once more in the presence of his beloved, *without* the presence of his hated rival.

Who shall describe the bliss of that September night? Who but can imagine the solace of companionship in the silent hours beneath the moon? Be it mine to tell what befell on the morrow. The day was some hours old, and the fond couple were reposing after the labour of yesterday's journey. The fair one, now that her bigger courtier was left behind, showed herself far less coy than heretofore, and it was almost as good as arranged that our friend and she should be partners on the "redds" later in the autumn. He lay in pleasant contemplation of the future, gently fanning the water with his pectoral fins in sweet security. All at once he became rigid as a rock.

"May I be eternally gaffed!" he exclaimed, as loud as he could (for be assured that fishes have voices if we could only hear them as clearly as they hear ours), "if there is not that confounded animal that pricked my tongue. Odds fins and scales! but he shall pay for this intrusion."

With these words he rose quickly from the depths and swooped after the insect, which, with the same jerky floating motion he remembered so well, was travelling a few inches below the surface. A moment more and the strong jaws closed on the prey, and a sweep of his tail swung him round for the descent. Ah! but he is fast this time. In vain for some moments he lashes the water into foam, his rage fast giving place to terror. Then he manages to get down a few feet, but a strange power is upon him. He feels no pain, but he cannot go as he would; he rushes up-stream, the weight upon him getting ever more resistless; he flings himself aloft into the air, but it is still there when he falls back into the water. Five minutes more and his strength is giving way; he rolls on his side, recovers himself for another rush, and rolls more helplessly than before. *Quid multa?* The end is at hand, and presently he is drawn from the water, receives the *coup de grâce*, and the lady of his affections is free to receive the attentions of another admirer.

Now, even if this be nothing better than a purely imaginative description of events in one of our salmon-streams, it is after all on imagination aided by observation that terrestrial creatures must rely in prying into subaqueous secrets. It is, at all events, more likely to lead us aright than the dogmatic assertion of professional fishermen or the anxious hypotheses of anglers. While it may be admitted that salmon sometimes take the fly for food, it seems not unlikely that just as often they seize or strike at it from curiosity or irritation.

This leads naturally to the second question propounded—*What is the natural food of the salmon?* whereby we are landed in face of a problem of even greater complexity than the other; for it is a well-known fact that although the stomachs of other fishes when captured are often found to be stuffed with dainties, that of the salmon, whether caught in the sea or in rivers, is almost invariably empty. I remember the delight of an English clerical friend who, one September day, caught nineteen pike in a lake on my property. The largest of them scaled 15 lb., and observing a considerable convexity in its paunch, I directed this fish to be cut open. Among the contents was a smaller pike, which, in a semi-digested state, weighed 2 lb., thus reducing the weight of the pick of the basket to 13 lb. No such betrayal of the salmon's secrets is ever vouchsafed.[1] He has been supposed to have the power of ejecting the contents of his stomach as soon as he finds himself in difficulties. Yet is the salmon a predatory fish, and it must require no meagre supply of food to maintain his rapid growth, and to enable him to carry up from the sea such a mass of exquisitely flavoured and richly composed muscular and fatty tissue. In all likelihood salmon are sustained in the sea by a great variety of animal diet—small fish, crustaceans, medusæ, and other forms of marine life; but the case is altered as soon as they pass up from the estuary. Some rivers, it is true—such as the Tweed, the Severn, and the Hampshire Avon—swarm with trout, minnows, or coarse fish, and upon these and a plentiful supply of insect life it might be supposed that salmon might subsist; but they frequent other rivers also, wherein there is not more than enough food to sustain a few starveling trout. Entering such streams in the spring or early summer months, when they are flooded with melting snow, the salmon find themselves, when the waters subside, penned within deep rocky pools which must be the reverse of productive larders.

And if this be the case now in our populous land, when nine-tenths of the salmon are stopped by nets

---

[1] In the 'Field' newspaper for December 2, 1893, is a letter from a correspondent describing the capture of American salmon containing small herrings in a semi-digested state.

in the tideway — nine - tenths, moreover, of a stock sorely diminished by many years of excessive netting —how must it have been when the fish ascended the rivers in countless thousands, as they do at this day on some parts of the western American seaboard? Obviously it is impossible that the rivers could have supplied more than an insignificant portion of food for each fish. That it is not in search of food that salmon leave the tide has been lately demonstrated almost to a certainty during the researches of a German *savant* into the habits of Rhine salmon. He has shown that the fish enters the river with his stomach in a highly serviceable condition—an elastic capacious sac. The effect of fresh water is to make this sac shrivel; the sides of it thicken and become corrugated, till at last it shrinks to the thickness of a man's finger, and is incapable of admitting any food at all. The clear conclusion is that although salmon will occasionally feed in fresh water, they suffer from no ardent appetite, and are fitted to endure months of total abstinence, supported by the good store of fatty and nitrogenous matter laid up in their tissues during their submarine surfeit. They only leave the sea when they are glutted with nourishment, and what they find in the rivers must be classed under the head of extras. Descending kelts, however, are ravenous enough, and must suffer horrible pangs while waiting for a flood to carry them to the sea : it is easy to imagine their orgies when they get there.

But even if it be granted that salmon in a river are habitually on the outlook for prey, the third question —*whether they possess the sense of colour*—is one that bears shrewdly on the prevailing notion that success in angling depends on the nice adjustment of hues in the composition of what we fondly call flies. Fish, especially those of the salmon kind, are notoriously quick-sighted, which contributes almost as much to the angler's success as to his discomfiture, for it is surprising how small a fly will sometimes be detected and taken by a fish in rough and rapid water. But no structural contrivance for detecting the different colour-rays in a beam of light, such as is well known to exist in the human eye, has yet been recognised in the eyes of fish. In the human eye there is a delicate membrane formed of an arrangement of minute rods and cones, groups of which vibrate in response to various colours, and transmit the impression of violet, red, green, and their compounds to the sensorium. When these fibres are imperfect or absent, the result is partial or total colour-blindness, the most common form of which is insensibility to red, from the rods and cones appropriate to red rays refusing to act or not being present. I chanced one evening to be standing with a friend, whom I knew to be partially colour-blind, beside a bed of brilliant scarlet geraniums. He assured me that he could not distinguish the slightest difference in hue between the leaves and the flowers. It so happened that the wife of this gentleman possessed a delicate skin and lovely complexion of milk and roses, to which her husband's defective eyesight must have made him quite insensible. This was the more unlucky, because the lady's features were not of classic mould, and her bloom can have had for him no higher charm than a good photograph. This, then, it seems not unlikely, may be the kind of sight possessed by a salmon, intensely keen for form and gradations of light and shade, but incapable of distinguishing colours, or, at all events, sensible only of some colours. There is the greater reason to believe this probable, that it does not seem as if the sense of colour would be of much use to salmon either as a guide to food or a warning against enemies. In obtaining food the sense of smell, and in avoiding danger the perception of size, would be effective adjuncts to keen monochromatic vision. At all events, it comes to this, that although there is no certainty that salmon can distinguish one colour from another, yet we take infinite pains and incur considerable expense in obtaining brilliant and costly feathers, and delicately dyed silks and wools, in order to suit the caprice of a hypothetical taste. We anglers willingly give half a guinea for the skin of a blue chatterer, or twice that sum for that of an Indian crow, whereas there is good reason to believe that precisely similar results might be attained by the use of the feathers of a blackbird or a common rook.

There is one test of the colour sense of fish which may be suggested, though it is hardly likely that any will prove so disinterested in the cause of science as to put it in practice. Let some floating May-flies be dyed a bright scarlet, — they will reflect about the same amount of light as the ordinary yellowish-grey imitations,—and let some devoted searcher for truth use one in a southern stream what time the May-fly is on, and the big trout are sucking down the floating insects by scores. If it were found that the highly educated, nervous trout of an English chalk - stream showed themselves as ready to accept scarlet, pink, sky-blue, or yellow imitations as the ordinary grey or green drakes, one might surely argue thence that fish have no discriminating sense of colour, and the whole theory and practice of fly-fishing would be subverted. But who is there so self-sacrificing as to give up to the experiment one of those brief and magic hours when the May-flies are floating down in mimic fleets, and every fin is astir? For it is at such moments only that the really big trout are tempted to surface-feeding during daylight, and the angler may be pardoned if he declines to risk his fortune by doubtful experiments.

Let me turn aside to dwell on the pleasant remembrance of the capture of a real socdologer. It took place on Whit - Monday of 1893, that memorable summer when, for weeks and months together, our land was flooded with divine sunshine. There is a certain fair demesne on the lower reaches of the Test, where the river runs deeper and flows more smoothly than in the trout-water above Romsey. The owner of this demesne is no craftsman of the gentle mystery, hence it comes that the foliage, of which there is wealth, is disposed to serve the purposes of fair landscape rather than of angling. There are many roods of stream where the great trout feed securely, for never a line may the angler cast over them, angle he ever so wisely. Yet this is water which to fish is a high privilege, for here the trout run heavier than in the shallower streams higher up. All Whitsunday the fly had been coming down in myriads; every pool and stream had been astir with greedy trout. Whit-Monday was intensely hot; the water was crystal clear after the long drought, and the brazen sun beat fiercely upon it from a cloudless sky. It was near mid-day before I could go a-fishing, and hope of success in such broiling weather was not very great. A young lady who had never before wielded a landing-net was my only companion; but, as was shown in the end, all misgiving as to her efficiency was unfounded.

I selected a pool where the river makes a right-angled turn; lofty beeches trail their branches in the stream on the left bank, and on the right the water circles sluggishly past a bed of reeds, and eddies under a precipitous earthy bank some four feet high. The May-fly had begun to come down; the grayling were rising at the tail of the pool; but in mid-current, higher up, two or three trout were showing themselves. It was so bright and hot, and the water was so clear, I had not the pluck to put on a May-fly, but mounted a modest sedge, and despatched it on a special embassy to where a good fish of 2 or 3 lb. had shown himself. But just as the fly touched the water, before it had begun to float down to the spot—lo! a mighty shadow-like form is seen moving to the surface three or four yards higher up, and, making an incredibly small dimple on the surface, a splendid fish sucks in a passing fly. Instantly I recovered my line, let out a few more yards, and, without venturing to move from my position, threw the sedge a few feet above this greater fish. It was a moment of intense suspense: the fly had fallen well, and was travelling true. When it reached the right place that shadowy form reappeared, touched the lure with closed lips—a cold salute—and sank once more out of sight. Chilled with despair — for surely such a fish would not give a second chance

—I threw my line on the grass, and watched, in the faint hope of seeing him again. Nor had I long to wait; for presently he rose once more, as unconcernedly as if no such things as steel hooks and silkworm gut, not to mention split-cane rods and sweetly running reels, had to be reckoned with. Once more the little sedge winged its flight, this time to surer purpose, for the great trout came at it open-mouthed, and, as soon as he felt the steel, rushed straight and swift down-stream to where I was kneeling, — an embarrassing strategy, to which Test trout are peculiarly prone. The water was deep, and fairly clear of weeds; but there was an ugly row of half-rotten piles protecting the hither bank, towards which the fish kept boring in an ominous way. However, on the whole he played in most gentlemanly sort, and gave less trouble than a $2\frac{1}{2}$-pounder I had landed near the same place on the Saturday before. So shall you sometimes find a many-acred peer easier to get on with than a fussy irritable squire of far smaller importance. But now came the critical time: the bank was steep, the water was deep, the trout was big, the net was small, the tackle was fine, the lady was a novice, and the angler trembled with anxiety. Four times was a portion of that trout raised in the net from out the water, and four times he wallowed out and wobbled into mid-stream. The fifth time, by some incalculable chance, he was enclosed, and my clever ally dragged him up the bank, and flung him safely into the deep meadow-grass.

He weighed just over 6 lb. — a shapely fish, in prime condition — and by half a pound beat the record of fish taken with the fly in that water.

True, there was one caught in 1892 weighing 11½ lb.; but that—*infandum dictu*—was taken with the prawn.

How incorrigibly prone fishermen are to prate of their own feats! Here am I, having undertaken to treat of salmon-flies, babbling through a couple of pages over the capture of a brook-trout.

To sum up the conclusion to which this desultory speculation has brought us, there seem to be three opinions of the power of discerning colour possessed by salmon. First, that they can distinguish the rays of the prism as clearly as we do—a belief which, although prevalent among, and generally acted on by, fishermen, rests on very slender evidence; second, that they may have the perception of certain coloured rays, though insensible to others; and, third, that they are totally colour-blind. But a further consideration should be kept in view — namely, that whereas artificial flies are displayed on or near the surface of the water, and salmon lie near the bottom, the lure passes between the fish and the light, in silhouette against the sky—the very worst arrangement for exhibiting gradations of tint in an opaque object. To human eyes, notwithstanding their complex and sensitive provision for the reception of colour-rays, every fly presented in this way would show very dark, almost black, against a bright background, save where some coloured sparkles shone through transparent material. Take such a fly, for example, as the Blue Doctor—a well-known killer in every stream where it has been tried, and deservedly a favourite; pass it at moderate speed overhead against the sky at a distance of four or five feet, the usual depth of water over a salmon in a cast. Can you detect the delicate tint of the body of pale-blue floss, or the laps of brilliant scarlet worsted on the head and butt? Or can you distinguish the fibres of bustard, turkey, dyed swan, and guinea - fowl feathers composing the wing? Not at all: all that is visible is a small dark object crossing the bright space behind. At that distance even those flies which are relied on for the glitter of tinsel seem no gayer than a Black Dose or a Sir Richard. Only white feathers can be distinguished under these conditions, and these as a rule are more sparingly used than any others in "busking" a salmon-fly. It would seem, indeed, as if all the taste and trouble engaged in the attempt to suit the caprice of salmon by the nice adjustment of tints were futile, and that one who persistently used a single pattern of different sizes would have as good a chance of success as another equipped with all the myriad æsthetic productions known by the most seductive names. It is true that by such philosophic asceticism salmon-angling would be robbed of some of its charm. Most people love to be mystified, and for them the problem of imitating something unknown to men, but irresistible to salmon, has a great attraction. Moreover, it is impossible to disprove the grounds of their belief in the efficacy of certain patterns. On a certain day there happens to be a good stock of fish in the water in a rising mood. The angler begins with, say, a Jock Scott or a Greenwell, and the fish take it so readily that he has no inclination to change it throughout the day. He has excellent sport, and very likely it is duly chronicled in the local and sporting prints :—

Mr Liverpill had a splendid day on the Noodlecombe water, landing no fewer than thirteen salmon, weighing 234 lb., besides running and losing three others. All Mr Liverpill's fish were taken with the same fly, a medium-sized Jock Scott, which he had no occasion to change all day. We have had the privilege of inspecting the fly, which, as may be supposed, shows considerable signs of wear. It is remarkable how so great a weight of fish could be brought to bank on a single slender steel.

Immediately Jock Scott rises into prime favour; the tackle-makers are set to work to tie them night and day to fulfil the orders of customers, to whom it never occurs that Mr Liverpill's Jock Scott was a very different object when, chewed, tattered, and soiled, the last fish took it in the evening, to what it was when it first flew across the stream in spick-and-span livery of sable and gold floss. It was the same *hook* with which every fish was landed; but, practically, the *fly* had been changed. The unromantic probability is that, had Mr Liverpill put on a different fly after landing each fish, he would have enjoyed just as good sport, making allowance, of course, for the loss of precious time involved in changing.

The reputation of a fly may be made in another way. The river may be just as full of fish as on Mr Liverpill's famous day; they may be rolling and rising all over the pools, yet they will not be persuaded to take anything. Vainly is the aid invoked of the Doctors—black, blue, and silver—of the Butcher, the Policeman, and Tommy Atkins; equally futile are the allurements of Kate, the Lassie, and Silver Grey, all of which are plied over and among the rising fish; till at last perhaps a Highlander or an Usk Grub has been mounted, and the fish simultaneously pass into a taking mood. Pull after pull follows in the failing light, and thenceforward the successful fly has a place among the river gods.

I may illustrate this kind of chance by a bit of recent experience. One morning in the autumn of 1892 I began fishing Cromweil, a cast on the Tweed opposite Old Melrose. I mounted a small gold-bodied fly of my own devising, and landed two heavy fish. On arriving at the bottom of the Gateheugh cast lower down, the limit of my beat for that day, I went to see how a friend had fared who was fishing Bemersyde pool, a far more productive bit of water than mine. There was a good stock of fish, and I should not have been surprised had he landed half-a-dozen. To my astonishment, I found he had fished the pool once over without a single pull. Jokingly I told him he was not using the right sort of fly, and handed him that with which I had just landed two fish. I left him attaching it to his line; but I had not proceeded far before he gave a view-halloo, and, turning, I saw he was fast in a fish. He landed it, and another immediately after, and lost a third. These were the only fish he had to do with all day. There never, surely, was a clearer case of the merit of one fly over another, yet am I so sceptical as to believe it was a pure fluke, and that had he kept on the Silver Grey he was using when I came to him, he would have got these fish just the same. To some people this will seem rank iconoclasm; others, I am vain enough to hope, will recognise it as ordinary ratiocination.

Suggestive names have much to do with the reputation of certain flies. One such is the Sun-fly, with a body of jet black mohair and a wing entirely composed

of the lustrous crest-plumes of the golden pheasant.
It is held to be murderous in the glare of unwelcome
sun, and so it has often proved itself, but it is equally
effective—*probatum est*—in gloom and rain. The
Lassie, again, is beloved of fishermen in the lower
reaches of the Tweed, and takes her name from a
liberal tuft of russet hair from the head of some un-
selfish maiden. The orthodox Lassie should display
a lock of golden red; but lately, looking through the
lures of the presiding genius of one of the Dubs, I
noticed several of these large flies, three or four inches
long, dressed with a woman's brown hair.

"You're still fond of the Lassie," I observed.

"Oh ay," was the reply; "ye see they're far easier
gotten at than the big birds."

Few negatives admit of proof, and it would be most
difficult to shake the belief so firmly rooted that when
a salmon has risen at one fly and missed it, it is
prudent to change it before trying him again. I was
fishing some years ago in a small river in the west of
Scotland within a few yards of high-tide mark. The
sun was very bright, but it was *behind* the fish, for the
stream runs south, and the fish, of course, lie with
their heads up-stream towards the north—a circumstance of no light moment to the angler in sunny
weather. A salmon dashed up at the fly in a strong
stream at the neck of the pool and missed it. I changed
the fly and tried him again, with the same result. Six
times that fish rose and missed the fly, and each time
I put up a different one, till at the seventh offer he
was hooked and landed. It is quite impossible to
prove that the change of fly had nothing to do with
ultimate success; but my firm belief is that this lively

fish would have come just as readily seven times at the same fly, as he did once at each of seven different ones. He had meant all along to have the moving object, but the strong stream had made it travel too fast for him.

Some local fishermen are great tyrants in the matter of flies, and show displeasure with strangers unless they obey implicitly every direction which they may receive. For knowledge of the haunts of fish, the depth of water, the best size of fly, the local man is invaluable—almost indispensable where fish are scarce; but in the matter of different kinds of fly, he who has angled in many rivers, using his own flies with equal success in all, is the more likely of the two men to have formed a right estimate of the motives which cause a salmon to come to the fly. It is provoking, when fish are not rising well, to be continually admonished to change fly after fly, when one is conscious that advice is founded on *a priori* hypothesis that fish prefer one colour to another, if one could but hit on it. It is well to indulge your attendant's fancy within reasonable limits, for he is as anxious for your success as you are yourself; but you are strongly tempted at times to remind him that, after all, you are spending all this time flogging the water primarily for your own amusement and not for his.

Sometimes your fisherman will look through your box, and, rejecting everything in it as unsuitable for his river, produce his own flies, which he recommends you to prefer. Now, if you were a believer in the power of discernment with which salmon are credited, your inclination surely would be to insist on showing to the fish in this river flies as unlike as possible to

those most commonly used by local anglers: for the
unfamiliar patterns would be less likely to arouse
suspicion than those which, season after season and
day after day, have been travelling over the pools.
But experience and common-sense have made you
sceptical of the superiority of one fly over another, and
you would be as willing to use your fisherman's flies as
any others, but for two considerations, one practical,
the other sentimental. The first is, that you have no
knowledge of the temper of strange hooks. There are
few moments, even in this woe-beset world, of keener
anguish than that when the strain of a heavy fish is
suddenly relaxed, and you feel that something has
given way. You wind your line in mournfully—let
your words be few, for they are sure to be impious—
the fly is still there, but as soon as it is in your hand
the truth is apparent,—the steel has snapped behind
the barb. Ah! that *was* a fish; 30 lb. if he was a
pennyweight, for you caught sight of the gleam of his
broad flank just before the direful moment. Sharp as
is the tooth of ingratitude, grievous as is the chill of
shattered fortune and the anguish of love betrayed,
these are pangs which time touches mercifully into
painless scars; but ever as the years roll on will you
mourn more deeply over that irreparable moment, ever
will the potential weight of that salmon mount up, and
your grandson will hearken with dilated eyes to the
story of how you lost the 50-pounder. "True as steel"
runs the saying, but nothing is more treacherous than
badly tempered steel; and I will pay Messrs Hutch-
ison of Kendal the well-deserved tribute of saying that
it is many years since I have lost a salmon from a broken
barb, and I never use hooks except of their make.

The other and purely sentimental consideration is that, if you are a true fisherman, you feel more gratification in landing fish with your own flies than with those of other people. An angler's rod becomes to him *fetish*, his flies *gri-gri*, and if the last are his own handiwork, so much the more pride will he take in their performance. Among my most cherished idols is a salmon-fly—a double-hooked Childers—which I tied wellnigh a quarter of a century ago. With this fly I began fishing in the Hargroves on the North Tyne one September morning. A fish rolled up at the fly, was held for a moment, and the gut snapped. The salmon was free. Next day there was a small flood and no fishing; but on the third day the river was again in trim. My companion began fishing half a mile or so above where I had met with mishap. When we met for luncheon, he showed me a fly which he had found fixed in the breast of the first fish he had landed. It was my lost Childers. I put it on, and killed two salmon with it that same afternoon.

There is a well-known salmon fly used on the Tweed called the Jonah, dressed with a silver body, blue hackle, and peacock herl wing. Its name was conferred when it was recovered after being three days and three nights in a fish's mouth.

Let a moment's digression be allowed to observe what a comfortable reflection it is that fish suffer little pain from the hook. A couple of years ago a friend of mine, fishing in the same loch where the clergyman above mentioned took his pleasure, hooked a pike which made good its escape by carrying off a triangle hook. A few minutes later he landed the same fish, and found his lost hook fastened in such fashion across the gullet that no food could ever again have passed down that way. A still more remarkable instance was described to me by a Tweedside fisherman. His son, a small boy, was fishing with worm in the Bemersyde water, and lost two flights of Stewart tackle by the gut breaking. Next day his father, fishing with fly on the opposite side of the same pool, landed a bull-trout with *both* the Stewart flights hanging in its mouth.

Talking of the Tweed—and what fisher is not fain to babble about that beloved stream ?—there is no river which better illustrates how flies are invented to please fishers rather than fish. Stoddart, writing fifty years ago, gave prescriptions for the flies most in favour then, and they were uniformly of sober grey or brown cast. The mottled scapulars of the mallard and the tail-feathers of the dun .turkey (now hardly to be obtained) were those most highly prized—nay, so timid of too much display was this excellent angler, that he warned his readers against the gaudy patterns used in Irish rivers, and, in describing the furniture of a certain fly, he directed that it should be lapped with *tarnished* silver tinsel. How different are the lures most in vogue now on the Tweed ! the Durham Ranger, gorgeous in orange, scarlet, and blue, and (present prime favourite) the Wilkinson, with its body of burnished silver and crimson gorget. Yet I am as firmly convinced as one can be of anything not capable of logical demonstration, that were a good fisherman to use nothing but Stoddart's old dingy patterns, he would kill just as many fish as he would with all the artillery in Forrest's and Wright's arsenals.

In the old days, when travelling was slow and

costly, it was natural that the dwellers on a river should imagine that their own stream and the fish therein had peculiarities compared with others, and that the flies used in the Shannon and Blackwater were unsuited for the Tay or the Dee. These lines are written during a daylight journey from London to Edinburgh—a matter of little more than eight hours. In that short space of time many famous streams are crossed—the Trent, the Wear, the Tyne, and the Tweed. Is it rational to hold the creed that fish of the same species frequenting these rivers should be so divergent in their tastes and habits as to prefer in one river a plain fly, in another a gaudy one? For, be it remembered, these flies are prepared in imitation of no animals frequenting these rivers. It is a purely arbitrary dogma that prescribes bright flies in the Tweed and dull flies in the Annan, rivers rising on the same hill and nourished by the same clouds. When, many years ago, I fished the North Tyne for the first time, they assured me that the salmon would not look at anything but sober-tinted flies—their favourite being the Chipchase Captor, winged with grey supplied by the farmyard drake. But in those days I dressed my own hooks, and scandalised the natives by the audacity of some of the designs. It so turned out that I enjoyed first-rate sport, and thereafter was allowed perfect liberty in the exhibition of any lures. At the present day brightly hued Tweed flies are all the fashion on Tyneside.

As has been above said, fishing in many rivers produces a philosophic indifference to the kind of fly used. Salmon are, like all wild animals, exceedingly conservative. Year after year, from time immemorial, they have sought the same estuaries, ascended the same streams, haunted the same pools, and the angler knows from faithful tradition exactly the boulder from behind which he is most likely to receive the indescribable thrill communicated by the strong pull of a good fish. Is it likely that animals so unchanging in their habits should within half a century have so completely altered their tastes as to be more easily attracted now by bright flies, and less liable to be tempted by dull ones, than they were in Stoddart's day? The thing is incredible: let every man attach to his line what he fancies most himself, for there is no greater significance in fashion of flies than in that of ladies' bonnets. We ourselves are as susceptible of lasting injury from the ridiculous little structures of feather and gauze perched on the fluffy fringes that prevail in this our day as our fathers were from the coal - scuttle shapes that enclosed the banded and bandolined glories of the early Victorian nymphs.

Long, long ago I received the present of my first fly-book, within which was pasted a leaf of "Advice to young Anglers." It was sound counsel, whereof observance has been fraught with infinite good, and it ended somewhat in this way: "Do not lose much time in changing your flies. Remember that the fisher whose flies are longest in the water will generally take home the heaviest bag."

This essay has run in such discursive fashion that it will not suffer if an old story be dragged in here. A Scottish gentleman was leaving a well-known and hospitable house on Tweedside where a fishing-party was assembled. Just as he was starting, an English guest came to the door and called out—

"I say, will you order a fly to be sent out for me at once from Kelso?"

"All right," said the other, with his thoughts full of salmon,—"from Forrest's, I suppose;" and drove off. Later in the day arrived an express from the celebrated tackle-vendor, with a splendid assortment of Rangers, Doctors, and other killers.

It had not occurred to the bearer of the message, being a north countryman, that in England *flies* roll upon four wheels.

Vox clamantis in deserto. This prophet has no vials to pour on the heads of those who differ from him. There is, after all, no evil in this fetish worship, but a great deal of innocent amusement. Bright flies catch salmon quite as readily as grey ones, and the discussion only affects those who concern themselves with the discovery of physical truth. Perhaps ere long we shall have learnt to fish by night with an electric fly, illumined by a current supplied from accumulators stored in the hollow butt of the rod. It is natural in speculating on the visual powers of fish to be led to the consideration of their powers of hearing, and it is passing strange how few fishermen ever reflect upon this. Can fish hear? is a question which as many anglers will answer in the negative as in the affirmative. Now I am able to adduce two instances in personal experience which convinced me long ago that fish not only hear, but hear very distinctly. The first of these concerned marine fish.

At Logan, near the Mull of Galloway, there is a most interesting tidal fish-pond. A rent in the cliffs facing the Irish Channel admits the salt water through a narrow fissure, protected by a grating, into a circular rock basin some thirty feet in diameter and twenty feet deep. The cliffs rise high all round; stone steps descend on one side to a ledge levelled into a pathway at the water-edge. No sooner does the visitor's footfall resound on the stair than the green water, hitherto motionless and apparently lifeless, becomes peopled with large brown fish rising from the depths, gliding and dashing about in a great state of excitement. These are cod, lythe, and saithe, which, caught on lines in the sea, have been transferred to this pond to be fattened for the table. They are fed daily by the keeper, and experience has taught them to connect the sound of footsteps with their meal-times. Formerly, a clapper used to be rung to summon them, but this was no more than a trick of the stage; the footfall on the stones is quite enough to waken them to activity. Most of the cod, being deep-water fish, became totally blind in captivity from excess of light; but they become so tame and accustomed to their keeper as not only to feed out of his hand, but some of them allow themselves to be lifted out of the water. One may witness the strange sight of a huge cod, more than an ell long, dandled on the knee like a baby, his mouth stuffed with mussels and limpets, after which he is returned to the water with a mighty splash. On the table these fish, thus tended and fed, prove much better than fish brought straight from the open sea.

The other instance concerned the hearing of freshwater-fish, and was not less suggestive to the angler. I was sitting painting by the side of a large loch one still day in October. The shallow water at the margin was full of small fry of some sort, probably young perch. About two o'clock in the afternoon, a shooting-party made their appearance on a hillside distant about three-quarters of a mile. Their shots were infrequent; I could see the flash and smoke, and several seconds later the sound of the discharge came through the quiet air. At each report the fry in the shallows darted off into the deep water, then drew gradually back towards the edge, to be startled again to flight by the next shot. This occurred seven or eight times in the course of half an hour, and there could be no doubt whatever that, whether these fish heard the reports as clearly as I did, or less clearly, they heard them so distinctly as to be alarmed.

Now, how many anglers ever bestow a thought upon precautions against alarming fish by sounds? You may hear one, who is scrupulously careful not to show himself to the fish, clattering along the shingle on his way to the cast. Or perhaps when you are working your fly skilfully over a glassy run where a pull may be expected at any moment, a friend comes to the opposite bank and roars an inquiry across the river what luck you have had. You are obliged to roar back a reply. Again, how often it happens that your boatman, standing waist deep by the gunwale, will knock out the ashes from his pipe with a prolonged tap-tap-tap, which must echo a significant warning to every denizen of the quiet pool you are fishing. Sound will not travel so far through the grosser medium of water as it does through the atmosphere; still, the ears of fish, being constructed to receive sensation from the vibration of water, are probably capable of far more distinct impressions than human tympana would be under similar circumstances.

Here is the conclusion of the whole matter. It

greatly profiteth the angler to adapt his art to the faculties known to be possessed by the objects of his pursuit. Among these may certainly be reckoned acute vision, sensitive hearing, and the power of discriminating odours. To the last named, little attention has been devoted, although the preference shown by salmon and trout to real minnows over artificial ones is certainly suggestive of its importance. If, in addition to these, we choose to credit fish with a nice taste in colour, the worst that can be said is, that the complexity of the art is increased without aught being detracted from its charm.

INDEX.